AN INSIDER'S GUIDE TO
PRAYING
FOR
THE
WORLD

AN INSIDER'S GUIDE TO
PRAYING
FOR THE WORLD

- COUNTRY-BY-COUNTRY PRAYER GUIDE
- INSPIRING FAITH STORIES
- ON-THE-GROUND INSIGHTS
- UP-TO-DATE MAPS

BRIAN C. STILLER

BETHANYHOUSE
a division of Baker Publishing Group
Minneapolis, Minnesota

© 2016 by Brian C. Stiller

Published by Bethany House Publishers
11400 Hampshire Avenue South
Bloomington, Minnesota 55438
www.bethanyhouse.com

Bethany House Publishers is a division of
Baker Publishing Group, Grand Rapids, Michigan

Printed in the United States of America

ISBN 978-0-7642-1727-2

Library of Congress Control Number: 2015950823

Some names and identifying details have been changed to protect the privacy of those involved.

Maps by FreeVectorMaps.com (http://freevectormaps.com)

Cover Design by Gearbox, Chris Gilbert

Author is represented by Mark Sweeney & Assoc.

16 17 18 19 20 21 22   7 6 5 4 3 2 1

To Max and Gaylene Munday—
for they hold in their hearts the world
and see it through eyes of faith

CONTENTS

Introduction 9
How to Use This Book for
Prayer 11

1. Somalia 15
   *Sometimes One Needs a
   Warlord*
2. South Africa 20
   Prayer and National Building
3. Cambodia 25
   Surviving the Killing Fields
4. Sri Lanka 29
   Pearl of the Indian Ocean
5. Caring for the
   Vulnerable 34
   *Sometimes It Takes a Broken
   Heart to Heal Another*
6. Mozambique 40
   Finding Answers on an ATV
7. Albania 45
   *When Blood Is the Only
   Solution*
8. Romania 50
   A Prime Minister Steps In
9. China 54
   *Homeless and Forgotten in a
   Crowd*

10. Syria 58
    A Battlefield of Many Nations
11. Ethiopia 62
    A Door Closes, a Door Opens
12. Haiti 67
    Pearl of the Antilles
13. India 73
    Over a Billion, and Growing
14. Japan 79
    Punching Above Their Weight
15. Prison Ministry 83
    *A Beautiful Moment in an
    Awful Place*
16. Egypt 88
    *A First-Century Miracle in
    Twenty-First-Century Garb*
17. Rwanda 93
    The Devil Never Travels Solo
18. Rwanda—Bishop
    John 99
    *Guiding a Nation in Finding
    Salvation*
19. South Korea 104
    *The Second Largest Missionary-
    Sending Country*
20. Honduras 109
    Hope Matters

Contents

21. Colombia   114
    The Way Forward
22. Nicaragua   119
    Before and After
23. Indonesia   124
    A Jaw-Dropper
24. Vietnam   129
    A Place of Surprises
25. Vietnam—Evangelist
    Nick   133
    Serendipity Redefined
26. Kazakhstan   138
    *Landlocked but Finding
    Freedom of Faith*
27. Thailand   143
    *The Power of Indigenous
    Leadership*
28. Laos   148
    Standing on Holy Ground
29. Lebanon   152
    *A Country Squeezed by
    Neighbors*
30. The World Prayer
    Movement   157
    *It Is Happening Around the
    Globe*
31. Turkey   163
    *Where Christian Faith Was
    Almost Snuffed Out*
32. Ukraine   169
    Which Road Ahead?
33. Persecution and
    Martyrdom   175
    The Price of Believing
34. Venezuela   181
    A Country on the Edge
35. The Pope   187
    It Matters That He Is Wise
36. Malaysia   191
    *"Allah" Outlawed for
    Christians*
37. Kenya   196
    A Canary in a Mine Shaft

38. Muslims   200
    *Why Rage Over Burning a
    Qur'an?*
39. South Sudan   205
    Turning Swords Into Plowshares
40. Greece   210
    *Few Countries Are More
    "Christian" Than Greece*
41. Burma/Myanmar   215
    *As Wise as Serpents and
    Innocent as Doves*
42. Nepal   220
    *A View From the Top of the
    World*
43. Bangladesh   224
    *A Young Country With Ancient
    Needs*
44. Palestine   229
    *Political Complexity Is Not Its
    Only Story*
45. The Czech Republic   234
    In the Heart of Secular Europe
46. The Philippines   239
    Missions Take Many Forms
47. Lithuania   243
    *Resisting the Skeptical,
    Believing the Impossible*
48. Finding New Places of Spirit
    Empowerment   248
    A Surprising Saga
49. Poland   253
    *Where the Church Held a
    Country Together*
50. Russia   258
    Search for Identity
51. Prison Ministries   263
    *In the Darkness, Light Shines
    Its Best*
52. Mexican Prisons   269
    *Not What I Expected on the
    Inside*

Acknowledgments   275
Prayer Journal   277

8

INTRODUCTION

An Insider's Guide to Praying for the World is a journey to see what God is doing in people and places around the world. When I first began as Global Ambassador for the World Evangelical Alliance, I landed in lawless Somalia. I shouldn't have been there, but after leaving, I wrote a report to our then Secretary General, Geoff Tunnicliffe, that found its way into many email boxes. That was the first story of what became dozens of dispatches.

My literary agent, Mark Sweeney (he had published my first book in 1983), saw these dispatches as a way to encourage people to pray. His rationale was this: In our Western countries, so much captures and holds our attention that we rarely think of, let alone pray for, other countries. Thus began this joyful adventure.

I can thank Janet Sweeney for helping me see that critical to each chapter is the travel that you and I are making together. I just happen to be the one on the ground in these many countries—seeing, hearing, and feeling the dynamics of human life in a myriad of circumstances. But this is a journey that we take together. As your eyes and ears, I listen to and observe the work of the gospel as it upends societies, transforms people, and calls the most unlikely into service. In seeing and listening, our hearts then are turned to our Father, and in our conversation of prayer, we intercede on behalf of peoples and nations, ministries and vocations, doing what the Lord himself asked us to do: "Pray to the Lord of the harvest."

Most chapters are focused on an entire country. But as I prayed for the world, certain peoples, missions, and needs surfaced that fit within our global praying. You'll note a chapter that covers the beginnings of World Vision—a window that provides a glimpse of ministries that care for children and communities. When I traveled with Ron Nikkel to prisons, I was reminded of Jesus' prayer and our inclination to forget those in prison. You'll also see a couple of countries that I just couldn't keep to one chapter. Demographic information was drawn from a variety of sources, including Operation World, a marvelous resource on each country. The statistics presented here are not meant to be comprehensive, and in many cases they are estimates, which explains why a country's religion percentages, for example, may not add up to 100 percent.

I encourage you not to rush through this book. Feel the texture of ideas, listen to the heartbeats of those God is using, and observe the societal struggles of so many different countries. Verses from the Bible will help to root you in the place or people we've just visited. Then, as we read the prayers together, allow the intensity of our requests to be felt. The Lord wants, and indeed invites, us to ask of him, so let's ask boldly. Let's put the needs before him with what the older Bible translations call "importunity," meaning "insistent solicitation and entreaty."

I want to thank Carole Streeter for her editing and consultant skills in drafting this book. Lily, my wife, joined me on many of these travels, and together we witnessed God at work.

Now, as we walk together, may our hearts be filled with feeling, seeing, and being. As we see what the Spirit of God is doing in people and places, let's join them in prayer. Andy McGuire, of Bethany House Publishers, asked what I would like to see from this book. It is this: that as you read, it would cultivate in you stronger habits of praying for countries other than your own, becoming acquainted with ministries and people you hadn't known, and then being generous in support and care for those who walk the roads of ministry in these many lands.

HOW TO USE THIS BOOK FOR PRAYER

Each of us has our own daily patterns, habits, and inclinations. Prayer is a personal and often private discipline that we configure in ways that fit our personality, schedule, and interests.

Some of us pray on our own, within a marriage setting, with a friend, or as happens increasingly, in a prayer or study group. As you take up *An Insider's Guide to Praying for the World*, here are some suggestions on how you might use it.

As you scan a chapter, you will see how it is laid out. First, it really matters that we locate the country. Some of them will be new to you, and their locations are often obscure. Next is a brief background to the country, since each nation has its own realities that impact life and spiritual well-being.

The dispatches, written after I visited each country, come from the backpack of my travels, exchanges, interviews, and observations. From this, a Bible portion is chosen to put our prayers in the wider context of God's message. From each topic and country, I've identified several items for prayer as a way to focus on a person or a need.

I had wondered about writing the prayers, but I came to realize that this was something you and I will be doing together. As I wrote each prayer, I would feel another person saying the prayer with me. The language used is quite ordinary. It's for us to read with understanding and passion, speaking to our Father, who listens with joy when he hears his children trust him with their inner desires and requests.

Praying on Your Own—Some Suggestions

1. Review the country, getting in mind its location and something about its character and dynamic. In most chapters you are located in a country, so it matters that you focus there.

2. I encourage you to underline in the dispatches. It's your copy, so you can make notes on the pages for future reference. Read it carefully, noting people, places, issues, and events. Feel free to use the Prayer Journal pages in the back of the book or your own notebook.

3. Before moving on to the Bible passage, ask, "What surfaced in the dispatch? What do I want to think about further?"

4. Bible verses. After several readings, ask, "What dots can I connect between the dispatch and these verses from the Bible?"

5. Items for prayer are written to help you be specific in your prayers. You will note other items in the reading of the dispatch, so add those to this list.

6. Prayer: This is what you and I do together. But after this prayer, go on with "And Lord, in addition, I pray . . ." Expand your prayer to include others you know and care about, and items that will surface as you read a chapter, a Bible verse, or even as you pray.

Praying in a Group—Some Suggestions

1. Once you've read the demographics, take a moment with the group to talk about the land and its people. But keep this to

no more than a few minutes. It is here that time can be lost, and you want to focus on prayer.

2. Assign different paragraphs of the dispatch to those in the group. You can give each person a number, and he or she can read that section. Again, it's your copy, so underline for future reference.

3. Before moving on to the Bible verses, ask the group what surfaced for them.

4. Read the Bible verses. Since the readings are short, have them read twice by different people. After reading, ask what dots they might connect between the dispatch and the verses.

5. Note that the items for prayer are to help you make your prayers specific. Invite the group to also mention other items for prayer that they will want to include when the group does its go-around of praying.

6. Prayer. You may want to ask each member of the group to pray and then conclude with the written prayer. Or you might begin with the written prayer and then continue with your members praying. As you expand your prayer time, give opportunity to add those people and issues that caught the attention of your members earlier. But here is what is most important: Pray for those people and places linked to the country you are praying for, allowing the Spirit to catch you up in intercessory prayer.

Blessings to you as we join hands in prayer across the globe.

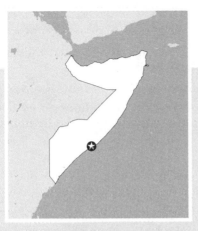

1

SOMALIA

Sometimes One Needs a Warlord

Somalia has gone through tragic periods of devastating wars and terror. Today, lawlessness grips the country. Piracy on the high seas extorts huge sums. Al Shabab, a militant group affiliated with Al Qaeda, exercises considerable control in central and south Somalia.

Drought hit hard in 2011, and famine followed. It has been said that while drought is an ecological disaster, famine is a politically induced disaster. Christian aid groups were forced out and exploited by Al Shabab.

The Africa Union Army controls much of Somalia's capital, Mogadishu. Yet Somalia continues as an unruled land, even as the world community attempts to help them establish a working government.

Location: an African country bordering the Indian Ocean, northeast of Kenya and southeast of Ethiopia
Population: 10 million
Religion: Muslim 99%

Dispatch

I really should not have traveled to Somalia, a war-torn country run by pirates and warring tribes. I had been appointed as Global Ambassador for the World Evangelical Alliance at the same time a massive famine broke out in northeast Africa, affecting up to 11 million people.

In this country, driven by harsh religion (93 percent of its girls are circumcised) and its men and family clans at war, women and children are left on their own in refugee camps, where they fight for food and search for places to lie down. The walls of their shacks are thin, hardly able to keep out the blowing sand. When their children pick up dysentery or a contagious infection or disease, these mothers plead for help.

I had gone to east Africa, encouraged by a promise that I would be flown by a relief agency to the Dadaab camps. When I arrived, my travel plans fell through. In Nairobi, I was briefed on the violence in the Mogadishu area and the vast numbers fleeing violence, drought, and famine. The morning news reported that Al Shabab, a terrorist group that controlled much of Somalia, had been pushed out of Mogadishu. We decided to try to visit the city. Aiah Foday-Khabenje, the African head of the Evangelical Alliance of Africa, and I got visas along with troubling warnings. We still set out into a country that was out of control.

Mogadishu

After we arrived in Mogadishu and were waiting in the terminal to get through immigration, a French photojournalist asked why we were there. I fumbled with an answer. Then he asked who was looking after us. I replied we had not figured that out yet. In rough language he said, "You're an idiot. I work in dangerous places, but this is the most dangerous city in the world. Don't leave the airport."

Finally, after interrogation, an immigration officer said we couldn't leave the terminal without protection. In time we were introduced to Amir. As we walked out of the terminal, a parked truck with five soldiers with AK-47 guns awaited us. Here was twenty-four-hour protection. Amir, a warlord with his own hundred-man army, owned a highly secured hotel in the center of the city.

He escorted us to his souped-up truck. We drove streets lined with bombed-out buildings and shattered marketplaces—devastation in all directions—and worked our way through a maze of concrete roadblocks into the backyard of his hotel.

Soon we were heading to a camp on the edge of the city, where I saw women arriving with children. They were loaded with all they could carry. With no men in sight, the women scrounged to find a small patch of ground where they could assemble a hut, built with anything they could find. Thousands upon thousands of these huts dotted the camps.

Walking through one camp, I saw a woman crying, her head covered, sobbing into her hands. Our aide-de-camp, in hushed tones, said, "Sir, she has lost two children, and an hour ago she lost her third."

"From what?" I asked.

"Hunger."

Later in the afternoon, back at the hotel, we wandered out to an open area protected by walls and steel gates. Men were sitting around playing cards, chatting, and waiting. It was Ramadan, and no food could be eaten until sundown. Many senior government officials and ministers lived in the hotel, where they were safe. It was also close to their parliament building. My warlord friend introduced me to several officials.

"This is Brian, the crazy Canadian."

"Why are you here?" a cabinet minister asked, looking up from his card game. "I thought Canadians were cowards. . . . You only come to Kenya, not Mogadishu. You are the first Canadian I've seen in years. Thank you for coming. But why are you here?" It was time to tell him the real reason.

"I'm a Christian, and while I know you have a terrible reputation worldwide of pirating and killings, I'm here to tell you that God loves Somalia and he loves Somalians."

I've preached many sermons about God's love, but in that moment a breeze seemed to blow through the courtyard. Men of different faiths and cultures, we were connected by a few simple words. The atmosphere changed. We were now brothers.

When entering the airport for our flight back to Nairobi, I noticed a young Somali working the metal detector and wearing a T-shirt with the English statement "This Is True." I asked him if he knew what his shirt read. In clear English, he responded, "Yes, I do know." I pushed him further and asked about the "John 3:16" reference also on the shirt. Not only did he quote the verse, he briefly shared his testimony. Here in the face of unrelenting

Christian opposition, this young man was not fazed by his vulnerability. His faith was strong, and it was public.

As we waited for our return flight, the immigration officer who had earlier arranged our security came to say good-bye. I found myself wrapped in his muscular arms, not once but three times. What our broken verbal languages didn't communicate, body language made up for. On my writing pad he wrote his name and phone number, asking me to contact him on my next visit.

Somalia is a country of such enormous needs that one almost wonders where to begin to pray. What never ceases to surprise me is that in the darkest of places, the Spirit is at work. Countries plagued by oppression, war, brutality, or famine, while seemingly hopeless to us, do not turn away the face of our Lord. God's economy relies on our faithfulness. Investment of prayer activates the Spirit to be in places where we can't go.

Today's Reading

Love and faithfulness meet together; righteousness and peace kiss each other. . . . The LORD will indeed give what is good, and our land will yield its harvest. Righteousness goes before him and prepares the way for his steps.

Psalm 85:10–13

Items for Prayer

- Pray for women and children caught between hostilities, and their need to survive.
- We need our global community to see that amidst desperate challenges come opportunities to demonstrate true Christ-like compassion. Pray for Christian aid organizations, that they will be given safe and open opportunities to minister to Somalis, bringing medical, educational, nutritional, and spiritual life.
- Pray for strength among Somalia's very few Christians, that they will be protected with wisdom, grace, and courage in their service.

- During this time of intense need, pray also for Somalis attempting to rebuild a functioning government.
- And let us not forget the many Somalis living in other countries. Pray for them as they deal with the horrors and hurts of their past.

PRAYER

Father, in this country of Somalia, where sorrow and tragedy seem the lot of so many, I pray there will be rain for harvest, peace to bring an end to the unceasing inter-clan warfare, and opportunity for the development of a stable government. Regardless of religion, these are people whom you love and for whom you gave your life. May young men and women be found who will learn of this love and with joy give witness to others of their faith, even as this young man in the airport was willing to give his. Bring your special blessing to Somalia. Amen.

2

SOUTH AFRICA

Prayer and National Building

South Africa became infamous for imposing apartheid in the twentieth century, a political and legal means of keeping distance between the races.

Christianized by both the Dutch and the British, its legacy of apartheid created in Africa a nation with both a Christian witness and a violent set of laws. Nelson Mandela, famous for his African National Congress (ANC) leadership and later imprisonment, became the means whereby laws were repealed and democratic free elections held. He was elected in 1994 and died in 2013.

Location: southern region of Africa, on the Indian and Atlantic oceans, bordered by Namibia, Botswana, Zimbabwe, Mozambique, and Swaziland

Population: 53 million—80% of black ancestry

Religion: Christian 75% (Evangelical/Protestant 45%, Roman Catholic 6%, Anglican 3%); Muslim 2%; Hindu 1%

Dispatch

I stood in the prison cell where Nelson Mandela spent eighteen of his twenty-seven years imprisoned. As the photo shows, it looks like any other cell, but it is a hallowed place for many, and noteworthy because of the man it imprisoned. Walking around Robben Island, just off the South African coast near Cape Town, I imagined Mandela's feelings in his many conversations with colleagues in the ANC: a sense of futility mingled with hope.

The transition away from white minority power is a story like none other. A political system called apartheid had evolved through the early years of the twentieth century and come to full bloom in the 1960s. As South African laws became more repressive and absurd, Mandela led an underground resistance and was eventually convicted by the white courts, as were many of his ANC associates. As the resistance grew to rebellion, the government finally realized the laws needed changing, and they eventually consulted Mandela while he was in prison. They promised he would be released and that general elections would be held.

In 1990, the world watched and wondered as Mandela left prison and boarded a ferry to Cape Town. His peaceful presence, his measured words, his respect for his captors, and his carefully considered convictions showed that he was a leader of a different stripe. His mature wisdom and gracious manner suggested how he might someday govern.

This is the story we all saw. But behind it is another story less reported. After decades of harsh rule under apartheid, the oppressed majority could have easily pursued retribution. And yet their antagonism was focused primarily on their own people, as the black community was divided. Mandela led the ANC, while Mangosuthu Buthelezi, chief of the large Zulu tribe in South Africa, led the Independence Freedom Party (IFP). The two sides were at each other's throats, with killings on a regular basis.

South Africa was ruled by people steeped in doctrines of the Dutch Reformed Church mixed with their own need to survive as a minority. There were similarities to early settlers in the United States who perpetuated the practice of slavery while defending it biblically. But there were other spiritual influences in South Africa, including Andrew Murray, a minister who died in 1917 but left a rich heritage of Christian thinking in his more than two hundred books. He is still read and appreciated around the world for his writings on prayer.

Fear of Bloodshed

Christian leaders in South Africa saw conflict likely to happen, so they mobilized in prayer for a peaceful resolution. At the same time, the leaders of the ANC and the IFP knew violence had to

21

stop, so they invited Henry Kissinger from the United States and Lord Peter Carrington from Britain to assist in mediation. Adding to the foment was Buthelezi's threat to forbid Zulus to vote in the coming election. This meant that when Mandela was elected—a foregone conclusion—Buthelezi could then declare that the election was illegitimate, since a major tribe didn't participate in the vote. This would, in effect, make Mandela a president without a mandate. This accusation could rally the troops to further conflict at the very time the white laws of apartheid were crumbling. What was seen as a wonderful transition was turning into a nightmare.

Michael Cassidy, South African leader of African Enterprise, saw the futility of high-level mediation without relying on God's intervention. He reached out to Washington Okumu, a Christian professor from Kenya called "the gentle giant," to join in negotiations.

On April 14, 1994, thirteen days before the election, Kissinger and Carrington boarded planes and headed home, with Kissinger predicting a million people would die in what he saw as a coming civil war.

TIME TO PRAY

Michael Cassidy went into action and rented a stadium in Durban and started prayer meetings all over South Africa. While prayer meetings were going on, Washington Okumu worked all night with the IFP to find a way to avoid the conflict. With an agreement in hand, he sped to the airport in Johannesburg to get Chief Buthelezi's endorsement, but arrived too late. Buthelezi's plane had already left. But a few minutes into the flight, his pilot said they had an instrument problem and had to return to Johannesburg, and Okumu got his meeting with Buthelezi.

On April 17, twenty-five thousand people turned out for prayer at the Durban stadium, matched by smaller prayer groups around the country. In the VIP lounge, Okumu and Buthelezi had final discussions on a settlement with President de Klerk, hammering out a plan while thousands were praying for a peaceful settlement.

Ten days later elections were held. The chief allowed his Zulu people to vote. Mandela was elected, and not one person died from tribal conflict. The Durban *Daily News*, under the headline "How God Stepped in to Save South Africa," quoted Chief Buthelezi: "It was [as] though God had prevented me from leaving [Johannesburg], and I was there like Jonah, brought back. . . . My forced return was a godsend."

The convergence of leadership, skill, and a will to pray brought change to a nation racked by decades of cruelty. Into that world, at a time of enormous potential for good, came a threat so severe that the country could have been torn apart. Michael Cassidy provided Christian leadership. Washington Okumu, a scholar and of Christian faith, lent his considerable skill in negotiating. Thousands upon thousands reached out in prayer for their nation, believing that the Spirit would intervene in ways no one could predict. And God had his man, Nelson Mandela, to lead the people through the coming days.

Today's Reading

LORD, you have assigned me my portion and my cup; you make my lot secure. The boundary lines have fallen for me in pleasant places; surely I have a delightful inheritance. . . . Therefore my heart is glad and my tongue rejoices; my body also will rest secure, because you will not abandon me to the realm of the dead, nor will you let your faithful one see decay. You make known to me the path of life; you will fill me with joy in your presence, with eternal pleasure at your right hand.

Psalm 16:5–6, 9–11

Items for Prayer

- The effects of evil laws are not easily or quickly erased. Pray for the well-being of this nation, for its Christian witness, as believers turn to love justice and do mercy.
- South Africa is vital to all of Africa—politically, economically, and spiritually. Pray for its leadership in all arenas, that the witness of Christ will powerfully fill the land and inspire a rising generation to put its trust in the risen Lord.

- Issues continue to reverberate across its land: racial conflict, the scourge of HIV/AIDS, violence, unemployment, a wide gap between the rich and poor. Pray for a national revival of hope and peace so that they will find new ways of living together in this marvelous country of great human skills, beautiful vistas, and natural resources.

PRAYER

Gracious Lord, King of life and ruler of all people, we lift South Africa in prayer, a people and land of remarkable beauty and energy, yet a land laden with failures and hurts. You, our God, our transforming presence, can bring new life—your new birth—to its people. May this be a bread-basket of spiritual and economic blessings served across the continent of Africa. This prayer we offer because you are the only one to whom we can turn. Amen.

3

CAMBODIA

Surviving
the Killing Fields

"The killing fields" of **Cambodia** ring as foreboding as "the ovens" of Auschwitz. In 1975, Pol Pot (name derived from "political potential"), with his Khmer Rouge, carried out genocide, killing more than two million Cambodians. The educated and the city-dwellers were "reeducated," forced into the countryside to work as manual laborers. Pol Pot was ousted by Vietnam, and the United Nations governed from 1992–1993. In 1997, a coup gave power to Prime Minister Hun Sen and the Cambodian People's Party.

Located: in Southeast Asia, bordered by Thailand, Laos, Vietnam, and the Gulf of Thailand
Population: 14.8 million
Religion: Buddhist 95%; Christian 3%

Dispatch

We drove two hours north of the Cambodian city of Siem Reap. The first hour was uneventful, but then it was back roads, mudholes, and wandering cattle. Sokreaksa Himm ("Reaksa") pointed out the field where his family of seven had spent their first night in 1975. The newly rising Communist party was deconstructing society—"reeducating" anyone with an education or position, and gang-marching them out of cities to work on farms—and Reaksa's family had been targeted because his father was a teacher.

We reached Kokpreach, the village where Reaksa's family was forced into manual labor. He pointed out the school he had built recently from profits of his first book, *The Tears of My Soul*. We drove slowly down the only road, watched by curious eyes looking out from houses built on stilts to escape the monsoon floods.

It was here that Reaksa, at age thirteen, had watched villagers hack to death his father and brothers and later his mother. He escaped by lying under dead bodies in a pit where the killers had dumped their victims. After everyone had left, he fled to the jungle and lived alone until he was taken in by a village family.

Years later he reached a refugee camp across the border in Thailand. From there he was sent to Canada, where World Vision cared for him and their staff led him to faith in Christ. He then studied at Tyndale University College, preparing for ministry. It was there that we first met.

After the Rain

Plaguing his young mind were not only memories of how his family was killed but also forgiveness, an idea he learned in his newly found Christian faith. His early journey of survival was now into its next phase. In his second book, *After the Heavy Rain*, he explains:

> I could tell that something was wrong with me, and underneath the façade I suddenly realized that I needed to forgive totally. Forgiveness is not easy, but if I allowed the big ball of fire to keep burning inside my heart, my life would not be worth living. . . . When I could not forgive, I was actually burying myself into the grave of bitterness, anger, and hatred.

Determined, Reaksa returned to Kokpreach and found the man who had killed his father and mother. As a symbol of forgiveness, Reaksa tied a Cambodian scarf around the man's neck as well as his own. Then he gave him a Cambodian Bible and read from Luke 23:34: "Father, forgive them for they know not what they do" (ESV).

We drove to the end of the village, turned around, parked, and walked to a house where a woman was sitting. A man in his early sixties came over to us and smiled. "These are my adoptive parents," Reaksa told me. After his family had been slaughtered, it was this family that offered him protection and a home.

Because I had heard other Cambodian Christian leaders describe their survival of the killing fields, I wanted to visit with Reaksa the place where his life had been turned into a nightmare. I also wanted to understand how faith enables a boy to become a man. For Reaksa, it had been crucial to shed the guilt for having survived and yet deal with the anger toward his family's killers.

How does one forgive? This was put under a microscope back in Phnom Penh, the capital of Cambodia, as I sat with pastors and learned that two of them had been soldiers in the Khmer Rouge army. Here, years later, they were forgiven by their colleagues, some of whom had lost family in the massacres. Further, these men, who had been part of Pol Pot's killing machine, had learned to accept forgiveness.

Monsoons are an annual event in Cambodia, and the rice fields depend on them. One follows the other, and as Reaksa notes in *After the Heavy Rain*, grace gives courage and strength to move from terrible moments of fear and killing into new ways of seeing oneself and others.

Today's Reading

He has broken my strength in midcourse; he has shortened my days. "O my God," I say, "take me not away in the midst of my days—you whose years endure throughout all generations!" Of old you laid the foundation of the earth, and the heavens are the work of your hands. They will perish, but you will remain; they will all wear out like a garment. You will change them like a robe, and they will pass away, but you are the same, and your years have no end. The children of your servants shall dwell secure; their offspring shall be established before you.

Psalm 102:23–28 ESV

Items for Prayer

- Many of today's pastors in Cambodia were children during the genocide. Out of their loss and sorrow they've learned to forgive. Pray for their continuing capacity to offer to their people transforming grace and freedom in Christ.

- While there is official religious freedom, pastors face pressures in organizing a young church. Pray for the younger leaders in their pastoral and leadership roles.
- Corruption continues to pervade the culture. Pray for the church in its witness. Mission Kampuchea 2021 is a vision by national leaders to plant churches in all of their cities and towns.

PRAYER

Father of love and care, this blood-soaked land of Cambodia, made so by evil men, needs the gentle and forgiving life of your Son. May those burdened by living through those terrible years feel the lifting of those memories and come to know your undergirding strength for their lives. We praise you for the life and witness of Reaksa and others who survived to tell the story of your love to their own people. In this country where your name is so unknown, we pray for this initiative of Mission Kampuchea 2021 to plant churches throughout the land, places where the story of your love will be made known and where people will be nurtured in the life-giving message of your coming. Amen.

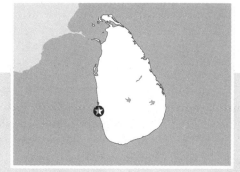

4

SRI LANKA

Pearl of the Indian Ocean

Sri Lanka, home to many ethnic groups, religions, and languages, consists primarily of two major peoples: the Sinhalese, also called Sinhala (76%), and the Tamil. Each group has its own language. The Sinhalese tend to be Buddhist, and the Tamil are mostly Hindu. Buddhism is the national religion.

Often referred to as the Pearl of the Indian Ocean, Sri Lanka (formerly called Ceylon) is politically organized as a republic with a presidential system. Colonized by the Portuguese, Dutch, and British, it became independent in 1948. Civil war raged between the Sinhalese and the Tamil from 1983 to 2009.

Location: an island off the south coast of India
Population: 21 million
Religion: Buddhist 70%; Hindu 13%; Christian 9%

Dispatch

Sri Lanka, a Garden-of-Eden country, is a teardrop-shaped island just a few miles off the south coast of India and is celebrated for its tea. Its Buddhist government is unsympathetic to those of Evangelical/Protestant faith, and condones persecution of religious minorities.

It is one of two Buddhist countries (the other being Myanmar/Burma) where the calming influence of the Dalai Lama, Buddhist leader from Tibet, is absent. Instead, the land is ruled by religious fundamentalism.

In today's devotional prayer we will see Sri Lanka through four windows.

Leadership

My visits to Sri Lanka began in 1978, when I spoke at a Youth for Christ staff conference, alongside longtime friend Ajith Fernando. Known by some as the John Stott of Asia, Ajith is a pastor, leader, and theologian who models indigenous leadership. Sri Lanka is a place from which many hundreds of thousands have emigrated in recent years. Ajith and his wife, Nelun, and their family chose to stay. In conversations with him over the decades, he never failed to tell me of his love and burden for his own people. His many talents made him an obvious recruiting target for world organizations and centers of training, but he never lost his focus. For Ajith, practicing theology meant living among his own people, working out the challenge of evangelizing youth, and training staff to serve.

Ajith's many books have been bestsellers. His presentations at Urbana and other international conferences have given him a world stage. Yet he stays and lives among people devastated by war. His witness continues through his writing and speaking, and is made visible through his staff and within the complex ethnic struggles of the Tamil and Sinhalese. Few model servant leadership as does he with theological discipline and skill, and motivation to inspire a new generation of leaders.

Witness

It is not easy to live out one's Christian faith in Sri Lanka, especially as an Evangelical/Protestant. In a recent visit, I was to have been part of the sixtieth anniversary of the National Christian Evangelical Alliance of Sri Lanka, but the gathering was postponed because of persecution and harassment. Celebration seemed inappropriate, given the price being paid by pastors and people for their faith.

Evangelicals, lacking sufficient public recognition by the Buddhist government, face all sorts of problems: buying property, accessing permits, obtaining visas, and accessing education for their children in government-sponsored schools.

Persecution

I had been invited to speak about persecution of Christian leaders in Sri Lanka. *What do I have to say?* I wondered. *I've never been persecuted.* However, the Bible has something to say in the parable of the unjust judge and the widow (Luke 18). Luke begins with, "Then Jesus told his disciples a parable to show them that they should always pray and not give up." He concludes the parable with no sympathy, but speaks of his coming: "When the Son of Man comes, will he find faith on the earth?" In effect, Jesus says, "If this unjust judge will eventually cave in and give justice to the widow because of her relentless persistence, how much more will your heavenly Father be fair and gracious in his response?"

When suffering unjustly, don't give up. Keep pressing for justice.

Ministry

My wife, Lily, and I drove into the countryside to meet a pastor who faced persecution in planting a church. Reverend Ayesha, a graduate of the Assemblies of God College, had seen in a vision the exact location where she felt led to start a church.

As she did so, Buddhist priests began their harassment. No one would rent a place for Bible studies or worship services, so the church met in the open. When it rained, they used plastic sheets for cover. But intimidation continued. One day, surrounded by men of the village, they were told that if they continued, they would end up in the hospital.

One night it happened. While meeting from late in the evening until early morning, studying and praying, a gang broke in. They took four women, including the pastor, and beat them and attempted to rape them. Finally, the women were forced to kneel and were pressed to shout, "My lord is Buddha." Ayesha refused. They beat her so badly that she was hospitalized for weeks. After some time, charges were brought against the assailants, and villagers were required to pay a fine of 100,000 rupees, about $800 U.S.

The church eventually bought land for a building. But one night villagers tore down the concrete pillars and leveled the partially constructed church. So they began on another piece of property and completed a place of worship. Their church is often stoned, windows are broken, and Christians are intimidated. When they seek protection, the police are reluctant to provide any help.

Ayesha's children aren't allowed to attend public school, and even private schools in the area won't register them, so they drive forty-five kilometers to attend a school outside of their area.

These friends know much more than we do about the cost of serving Christ. Our offerings are simple in contrast to their faithfulness and courage. We believe that their humility in service is core to their powerful witness.

Today's Reading

In a certain town there was a judge who neither feared God nor cared what people thought. And there was a widow in that town who kept coming to him with the plea, "Grant me justice against my adversary." For some time he refused. But finally he said to himself, "Even though I don't fear God or care what people think, yet because this widow keeps bothering me, I will see that she gets justice, so that she won't eventually come and attack me!" And the Lord said, "Listen to what the unjust judge says. And will not God bring about justice for his chosen ones, who cry out to him day and night? Will he keep putting them off? I tell you, he will see that they get justice, and quickly. However, when the Son of Man comes, will he find faith on the earth?"

Luke 18:2–8

Items for Prayer

- Even the United Nations has come out strongly on the matter of religious freedom in Sri Lanka. Pray for a political solution so that people of all faiths will not be overrun by religious nationalism, but will have opportunities to worship in security and with freedom.
- The ministry of Youth for Christ has had unusual impact among the youth of both ethnic communities. Pray for its leadership and funding, and for creative and bold initiatives

to open the hearts and minds of young people to the life of Jesus.

- Postwar stress continues, with Christians from both communities attempting to bring reconciliation and hope. Pray for those working for peace where religious domination intimidates.
- Pastoral training continues to be a pressing need—preparing a younger generation to lead the church in witness of the gospel to society, especially in public engagement. Pray for these young men and women as they prepare themselves to lead in the coming years.

PRAYER

Father, we know you grieve over harsh and brutal war that kills and destroys many. Within the lingering hatred and unresolved issues in Sri Lanka, we pray for the witness of your people to the wider society. May there be boldness in the lives and ministry of Christians, showing that in Christ there is meaning to life and true peace. For young men and women seeking to instill hope and understanding, may they too know your wisdom and abiding peace in all that they do. Finally, we pray that government leaders will respond to requests for fair policies. May they provide protection and freedom, allowing Sri Lankans to worship as they choose. Amen.

5

CARING FOR THE VULNERABLE

Sometimes It Takes a Broken Heart to Heal Another

In the 1880s, the Salvation Army provided both a biblical rationale and a model of caring for the poor. After WWII, evangelicals started organizing more efforts, built on an understanding that Christ not only calls us to be concerned about the poor, but also to do something about it.

For today's prayer, we look at the rise of one of the largest ministries of caring for the poor in the world—World Vision. I knew its founder personally and have seen its impact in countless countries. In this dispatch, I want us to see how the Spirit takes hold of people and brings about means by which the hands of Jesus are extended.

The founding of World Vision in 1950 set in motion one of the most amazing stories of care, built on the idea of supporting a child each month. Today, globally, World Vision has thousands of staff members and supports 4.3 million children.

There are many other ministries whose prime focus is to help those in poverty and distress, but also address underlying food, educational, and justice issues. These include Compassion International, Tear Fund, World Relief, Food for the Hungry, Samaritan's Purse, the Mennonite Central Committee, and church denominations that have relief and development ministries.

Dispatch

Walking down the stairs from my hotel room in Nairobi, Kenya, I heard worship songs similar to what I've heard the world over. I peeked around the corner and found a group of adults switching back and forth from praying to singing. So I snuck in the back, sat down, and listened.

I learned the gathering was a regional World Vision staff meeting. Before any business, their hearts were focused on personal nurturing of the spirit and on the reasons for their calling. I wasn't surprised. This global movement, which challenges people to care for the poor, came about through an obedient heart.

Across the developing world, signs of social stress, economic poverty, and physical disability assault the spirit—so much so that unless you build certain immunity to its constant bombardment, emotional stress will overtake you. Ah, but there's the rub. An impenetrable layer covers the soul, shutting out the message. Surely the lesson of the Good Samaritan, in the words of Jesus, is ample warning for us religious types who might "pass by on the other side."

Not so for World Vision founder Bob Pierce. I first met him in Saskatoon, Canada, at a Youth for Christ (YFC) rally. I was only eight or nine, but I was struck by his passion for children in need. He showed a powerful film, which soon was overshadowed by his stories about children. This remarkable man was a catalyst in helping people see missions with a wider vision, including the lifting of people from social and physical distress.

How It Began

YFC began in 1946, led by Billy Graham and colleagues holding evangelistic rallies, and quickly became a national movement. Headliners were dynamic preachers, including Billy Graham and Bob Pierce. Years later, Bob told me that he left North America because Billy was so popular and he didn't have that many preaching opportunities. He went to China, where thousands came out to hear this enthusiastic American.

But Bob's life was about to change. A Dutch missionary, Tena Hoelkedoer, put into his arms a battered and bloodied girl named White Jade. She had committed her life to Christ, and the family feeling dishonored, beat her up and threw her out. Moved by the story, Pierce told the missionary the obvious: "I can't care for her." Still, he reached into his pocket for what he had—his last five American dollars, with the promise that every month he'd send money for her care. That's how child sponsorship started.

Pierce increasingly saw the world with new eyes: poverty and hunger everywhere. China soon closed as the Kuomintang under Chiang Kai-shek fell in 1949, and Mao Tse-tung and his Red Army pressed out any missionaries. So Pierce went south to Korea, a country breaking from within, and from his YFC base he formed World Vision.

Decades later, donations are serviced by mega organizations that manage billions of dollars. And given world needs, without World Vision and her many counterparts, we'd have no means of helping half a world away. These organizations matter—their heartbeat is set by the life of Jesus. While the United Nations and many secular organizations do marvelous work, there is a distinct ethos that shapes the life and work of Christian missions in matters of poverty, need, and catastrophe.

Why It Matters

The worship service I stumbled upon in Nairobi, and others like it, is essential to World Vision's identity and calling. It's not that other organizations can't deliver services to the poor, or that we must not funnel our funds through those who make no claim to the gospel. However, there is a connection between our reason for giving and those who carry out the mission. Bob's utmost prayer was, "Let my heart be broken by the things that break the heart of God." Giving is not to be perfunctory. Neither is it to meet a quota or percentage. "Just giving" is dangerous—sending the check, transmitting funds electronically. Both are cold and removed. When we give through a ministry organization, however, it creates a link from our account to the hands of those ministering and to the lives of those God so loves.

There is a second matter. In the early half of the twentieth century, Evangelicals (especially in North America) often divided the gospel between evangelism and social service, with emphasis on the "soul" side of the equation. I well remember our small church; we were poor but we felt rich. We were taught to give to both preaching the gospel and lifting those in physical need. The Salvation Army had already wed the two ministries of preaching salvation and helping the needy. But it took a major breakthrough from people like Pierce to kick-start giving and to set up large, well-run Christian agencies.

Our giving today helps to sustain and encourage these and other new start-ups, means by which Christ's love is extended. In an environment of religious cynicism and a culture of secular intimidation, the developing of Christian agencies dedicated to disaster relief, emergency help, education, medical care, agricultural development, justice issues, and social nurture matters a whole lot.

Why is that? The natural slide of any organization is to leave its initial calling, ending up as a do-gooder, which in itself can mean doing an awful lot of good. But it does so without a continuing dependence on the provision, empowerment, and transforming presence of Christ. Holding these ministries within the bonds of Christian faith is renewing. But there is something else: It matters that we continue to grow a public-square presence of Christian initiatives, seeding our society with the leaven of Christian personnel, language, ideas, and leadership. The more we are silent about who we are, the less we speak out about what drives us and who provides support, the more we become like governmental aid. And when we do, a gospel presence is camouflaged and witness muted.

It Is Not Easy

This is tough work. In countries where Christians are hard to identify, agencies have to find others to do the work, and sometimes they are criticized for this. Raising funds is expensive, and most are careful about keeping within proscribed percentages. Ensuring that funds are well used takes careful oversight, all within shifting fences of donor attitudes, expectations, and concerns. In my global travels, I've been profoundly moved by men and women who daily slug out ministry, most unreported, but faithful to witness in the name of Jesus.

Let generosity rule. Pray and give. Agencies can be trusted. We need them. They allow us to do what we could not do without them. By lending our resources, our lives and witness are extended into places where those who act on our behalf can go.

Praying Pierce's prayer is dangerous: *Let my heart be broken by the things that break the heart of God.* So frame your own: a prayer calling away from self, the immediate family, obvious needs, and preoccupation over national interests. See others. Pray for the hundreds of thousands engaged in giving a cup of water, freely given in the name that is above all names.

Today's Reading

Let the morning bring me word of your unfailing love, for I have put my trust in you. Show me the way I should go, for to you I entrust my life. . . . Teach me to do your will, for you are my God; may your good Spirit lead me on level ground.

Psalm 143:8–10

Items for Prayer

- Globalization links us closely with so many, yet it can lead to being blasé about astounding needs. Try praying Bob Pierce's prayer: "Let my heart be broken by the things that break the heart of God." Allow your heart to be made fallow for the seed of his love to reproduce a compassionate and prayerful response.

- Pray for World Vision and other ministries as they choose where their limited resources can be best used to meet hunger and other needs, and help break the cycle of poverty.

- Ministries proactive in relief and development are at their best when led by able and committed Christian personnel. Pray for the development of resourceful young people to fill the ranks of these ministries over the years ahead.

Prayer

Loving Savior, you who came in poverty, reminding us by your Word and daily presence to love those whose needs press against your loving heart, help us feel your broken heart. Break down apathy and self-interest that too often control our days, so that we may see through your eyes those around us who are in need. Show us how we can help others in our own world and what we can do to assist ministries equipped to act in larger areas. We pray for these ministries. Keep them faithful to you and your message of life. Help their leadership and personnel in the challenging task of working in so many difficult places. For those who receive this help, may their lives be changed by your saving presence and their hearts lifted toward you in praise for your healing of their lands. In your name we confess our need and give thanks for your loving generosity and goodness. Amen.

6

MOZAMBIQUE

Finding Answers on an ATV

Colonized by Portugal in the fifteenth century, **Mozambique** won its independence in 1972. This was followed by a disastrous civil war from 1977 to 1992. Its Marxist government made every attempt to destroy the Christian presence and witness. The ending of the civil war was in part brokered by friends at Sant'Egidio, a Christian community located in Rome whose combined focus on prayer and Bible study includes working for peace.

Mozambique is resource-rich with a fast-growing offshore gas industry. Currently, it scores among the lowest of countries on the gross domestic product (GDP) scale. Its population with a Christian majority grew rapidly after the cessation of its civil war.

Location: southeast Africa, bordered by the Indian Ocean on the east, south of Tanzania and Malawi, east of Zambia and Zimbabwe, north of South Africa

Population: 25 million

Religion: Christian 47% (Evangelical/Protestant 12%, Roman Catholic 21%); ethno-religionist 32%; Muslim 18%

Dispatch

An hour out of Maputo, the capital of Mozambique, our truck pulled off the highway onto a seemingly impassible trail. Pastor Abreu, riding his all-terrain vehicle (ATV), led us through a maze of huts, open fields, and bleating goats into a courtyard. We climbed out and came face-to-face with a broad and infectious smile as the pastor welcomed us with loving warmth into his place of calling.

Speaking a mixture of Portuguese, English, and local dialect, he introduced us to women working on treadle sewing machines, making clothes and other items for sale. They cared for twenty-one village children who had been orphaned by AIDS, and the church was looking for ways to help both orphans and widows.

The resourceful pastor had five acres. Because the villagers didn't earn sufficient funds to pay his salary, he not only did his own farming, but he had developed it into a village industry. He proudly showed me his granary of drying corn. But there was a problem.

We walked to another small building and saw the problem: a broken pump and generator. This past year they had only one crop in a country in which two can easily be harvested. Without the machinery operating, during the dry season they couldn't pump water needed for irrigation.

Outside, I climbed onto his ATV and motioned for him. He understood I wanted to see his land. I'm a farm boy at heart, and talking about land and seeing it are two different things. So off we drove, bumping across hills, slashing through bush, bouncing across a precarious bridge.

Then he stopped, got off, and motioned for me to follow. We walked through a stand of mango, banana, and papaya trees, and fields of sweet potatoes and maize (corn). Here, a few hundred meters from the river, was the potential of two crops.

"Pastor," I asked, trying to make myself understood through words and motions, "why don't you get it fixed?" He looked down at the ground. I learned the village simply didn't have the $800 to order parts from South Africa.

Then I knew why I was there. So I held up two fingers, asking if they could raise $200. He thought for a moment and nodded his head. "When you raise yours, I'll find the balance of $600," I told him. We shook hands, and back with our translators, I made sure we clearly understood each other.

A few villagers had gathered in the church and we sang, and then he asked me to bring a short message. After we had prayed, we sat outside, talking about what mattered to him. Pastor Abreu's larger vision surprised me. Located in this rural area, farming and shepherding his flock, he also cared about his country and the witness of Christ to his people. In 1992, he had helped birth the Evangelical Alliance, serving as its treasurer. But in 2003 it died. I needed some history to understand his concerns.

Of its twenty-five million citizens, 12 percent are evangelicals. Congregations and missions are scattered about from slums to upscale communities, in villages and the countryside. Thousands of churches and local ministries have sprung up spontaneously. Converted people have a passion for their neighbors, and out of their hearts begin a church plant or, as we saw in the slums of Maputo, nursery care and centers for the afflicted.

That's the upside. The downside is a fragmentation of people whose faith in Christ and love for the Scriptures has no common center—no sense that they are joined with tens of thousands of other like-minded people of faith. In such fragmentation, there is little opportunity for a synergy of resources or the raising up of a common identity.

The World Evangelical Alliance (WEA), the second largest of world Christian communities (Roman Catholics 1.2 billion; WEA 600 million; World Council of Churches, including Orthodox, 550 million) has 129 countries in which national bodies (called alliances or fellowships) have opportunities to create an identity of fellowship, common activity, and voice.

Needing a Common Voice

I wondered why the Mozambique Evangelical Alliance had collapsed. The answer was all too familiar. Massive floods some years earlier had triggered interest around the world. Mission and relief and development agencies rallied, and Christians worldwide gave millions. The alliance in Mozambique became the clearinghouse of funds. But they didn't have in place the infrastructures needed to handle processing and reporting. When the floods dried up and accounting was called for, international funders lost interest. Not having built a sufficient organization for the long term, it had no choice but to close its doors.

Here is my point for prayer and action: Evangelicals believe God leads individuals and groups to start churches and missions—an approach that is often valuable and productive. But when they stand alone, there is little accountability or fellowship. That's why an alliance or fellowship can matter, providing joint identity, a common voice, and cooperative fellowship and initiative.

Mozambique needs prayer and support as Christians build a national alliance. In time this country will flourish. Today, the evangelical community tends to be poor, and the alliance needs help to sustain it during renewal. Disasters will occur again. When they come, a national alliance, properly staffed and trained, will lead its people in managing resources. To make this a reality, Mozambique needs help to create and sustain this network.

My pastor/farmer got his irrigation equipment fixed, and his people are on their way to doubling their annual crops. What Pastor Abreu really cherishes, however, is a renewal of that nationwide fellowship he helped to start years ago.

Today's Reading

Then I thought, "To this I will appeal: the years when the Most High stretched out his right hand. I will remember the deeds of the LORD; yes, I will remember your miracles of long ago. I will consider all your works and meditate on all your mighty deeds." Your ways, God, are holy. What god is so great as our God? You are the God who performs miracles; you display your power among the peoples. With your mighty arm you redeemed your people. . . .

Psalm 77:10–15

Items for Prayer

- Given Mozambique's economic difficulties and need for business, pray for Christian entrepreneurs as they work to create enterprises for employment and for the agencies that serve in poverty relief, education, and medical care.
- There is an enormous need for training pastoral and missional leaders. Most have little to no educational preparation for the task. Pray for the few schools, mostly concentrated in the south, for financial support, and that the Spirit will call able and committed men and women to prepare themselves to serve the church.

- It is important to note that of the countries in the southern region of Africa, Mozambique has the most unreached people. Pray that nationals and those from other countries will see Mozambique as a place to invest their lives, building the church in this country of great potential.

PRAYER

Dear Father, Lord of creation, I lift up the people of Mozambique in faith, believing that this country, currently so impoverished, might become strong and able to bless others from its newly found strength and resource. I pray for the church, your bride. It is here that your life and truth finds ready soil.

I remember Pastor Abreu, his many pastor colleagues, and their vision for a national alliance. By your Spirit, cause a bond of unity to bring together church leaders in friendship and cooperation. May this bond be nurtured into productive growth. Send your Spirit to call able people to offer their lives in service, and may there be resources to equip and enable these ministering servants. Amen.

7

ALBANIA

When Blood
Is the Only Solution

Albania was as closed to the gospel as a country could be. A Communist government took control in 1944, and under Enver Hoxha it was declared to be an atheistic country, denying religious freedom and imposing a severe ban on any expression, information, or texts of faith. After the Soviet empire fell, Albania removed its anti-faith policies, allowing an increased expression of faith.

Located: in southeastern Europe, with the Adriatic Sea to the west and Ionian Sea to the south; bordered by Montenegro, Kosovo, Macedonia, and Greece

Population: 3 million

Religion: Muslim 62%; Christian 30%

Dispatch

In the 1990s, the Balkan wars brought notoriety to Albania and the surrounding region, but for many, its land and borders are still confusing. Often it takes traveling through a country before its geography comes into focus and conflicting issues begin to make sense.

Albania, tucked into southeast Europe, across the Adriatic Sea from Italy and strung along a mountainous coastline, is mostly unknown and unremarkable, except for its post–WWII declaration to be atheistic. Brutal and demanding, it was more than Communist in economic and social policy. Dictator Enver Hoxha prided himself on following Stalin, but he went further, declaring that anything religious would be outlawed. Churches, mosques, and synagogues were demolished or turned into everything from barns to factories, making neighboring Communist dictator Josef Tito of

Yugoslavia seem like a saint. Few countries, notably North Korea, were in Albania's league of total religious exclusion.

Declaring belief in any illegal religion creates within the culture a pragmatic utilitarian ethos and leaves a browbeaten people whose values rest uneasily on the quicksand of obliged loyalty to the state.

Elona and the Kanun

I sat with Elona, a widow, in downtown Tirana's Stephen Center Café, run by Christian entrepreneurs, and listened to a story for which I had no warning. It was blood-chilling and bizarre, yet magisterial in its biblical vision.

Albania was occupied by the Turkish Ottoman Empire from 1385 to 1912, and its Muslim dominance chased Christians from urban areas into the mountains. This was especially true in the north around the city of Shkodra.

Families fleeing the Turks over time coalesced into tribes around family names and identity. An ancient set of oral laws dating from the fifteenth century, but probably having evolved from the Bronze Age, were codified in the 1800s in written form called the Kanun. These laws covered all aspects of life and applied to both Christians and Muslims. During the Communist reign, the Kanun was abolished, but in the 1990s, ironically with the fall of Enver Hoxha, people distrusted the police, especially in north Albania, and reestablished the Kanun as their rule.

Embedded in these ancient tribal laws are rules regarding blood revenge—how a family deals with the murder of one of its members. As ancient as Cain and Abel, if a member of your family was killed, then it was your duty to ensure that a person of the offending family was also killed. That obligation would continue for four generations until the offense was repaid.

It was into one of those families that Elona wed. Coming from the south, where such a practice was unknown, her life would soon be trapped by the ancient custom of blood feuding. The family of her husband, who was pastor of an evangelical church, was caught in a blood feud in Shkodra. One of his uncles had killed a young man, and now twenty-four families were seen as linked to that uncle.

The men of each family feared for their lives, and thus wouldn't leave their homes, not for work, not for anything, unless camouflaged or hidden in the trunk of a car. Financially strapped, the wives would have to earn the family income while the males often descended into alcoholism. Domestic abuse typically followed.

Fleeing for Safety

Elona's husband, Dritan, never left their house for four years, yet they continued to co-pastor their congregation. Finally, they fled to England, but after two months, Dritan said he no longer would hide from the sin of his community. He would return, pastor the church, and trust God for his safety.

For thirteen months, he openly cared for his congregation, even inviting the offended family (as the Kanun custom allowed) to meet and to try to find a means of reconciliation other than bloodshed. However, they refused to meet, and he knew that his life was in danger, even though the Kanun forbids killing a priest.

One day, as he was leaving his church, he was struck by seven bullets and he died, the first pastor or priest to die from blood revenge. Elona was asked by a television reporter for her response. "I forgive," she said. Then, when asked if she was going to press charges, she replied, "Revenge is for God alone, but for us, perfect revenge is forgiveness."

While the impact on the family and the church was enormous, what was surprising was the freedom triggered by Dritan's death. The twenty-four men under the blood curse were no longer captives within their homes. The offended family had exacted its price.

As the blood of sheep lifted the curse of sin for the wandering Israelites, pointing forward to the sacrifice of Jesus for our sins, freeing us into eternity, so Dritan knew his death would lift the curse from his extended family. He was willing to pay the price.

Elona, meanwhile, continues to pastor the congregation while completing a PhD in psychology.

Today's Reading

Lord, you alone are my portion and my cup; you make my lot secure. The boundary lines have fallen for me in pleasant places; surely I have a delightful inheritance. I will praise the Lord, who counsels me; even at night my heart instructs me. I keep my eyes always on the Lord. With him at my right hand, I will not be shaken.

Psalm 16:5–8

Items for Prayer

- Praise for the impact of many who have had a part in giving witness of Christ after the doors of Albania were opened. Their stories of effective outreach provide evidence of God at work.
- Pray for the leadership of the Albania Evangelical Alliance as they seek to bring churches, fellowships, and agencies together in a spirit of unity and witness.
- Pastors and Christian leaders live under the stress of gaining sufficient support to care for their families, all the while serving as pastors and leaders in their missions and churches. They so need our support and prayers.
- Pray for training missions and schools providing teaching for the people of God.

Prayer

Father, we can see how your Spirit was at work in Albania, even during the dark years of repression when public worship was excised from the country. Today, while there are a growing number of churches, we pray for villages and towns where there is no witness, and for ethnic minorities who don't even have the Bible in their own tongue. We give thanks for Elona and her faithfulness, and her ongoing ministry among her people. Lord, make us willing to give our lives for the freedom and belief of others. And on behalf of hundreds of thousands of Albanians living in nearby Kosovo and other countries, we ask for a strong witness of faith among them, that they would be fervent and convincing in their testimony of Jesus Christ our Lord. Amen.

8

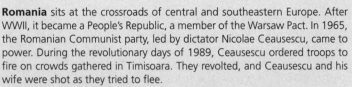

ROMANIA

A Prime Minister Steps In

Romania sits at the crossroads of central and southeastern Europe. After WWII, it became a People's Republic, a member of the Warsaw Pact. In 1965, the Romanian Communist party, led by dictator Nicolae Ceausescu, came to power. During the revolutionary days of 1989, Ceausescu ordered troops to fire on crowds gathered in Timisoara. They revolted, and Ceausescu and his wife were shot as they tried to flee.

While Romania is officially a secular state, the Orthodox Church is dominant. A recent law makes it difficult for other denominations or charities to register.

Location: Southeastern Europe, on the western shore of the Black Sea and bordering Hungary, Serbia, Ukraine, Moldova, and Bulgaria

Population: 21 million

Religion: Christian 97% (Orthodox 87%; Evangelical 7%; Roman Catholic 5%)

Dispatch

It wasn't unexpected, so when the secret police, the Securitate, arrived asking for Paul Negrut, he knew his time had come. Some of his Christian friends had been swept up in Ceausescu's nets earlier, so Paul knew for him it would be just a matter of time.

It was the 1980s, and the harsh heel of Communist dictator Nicolae Ceausescu was coming down hard on the people of Romania. In power since 1965, he had modeled his regime after Stalin, even creating the infamous Securitate. Ceausescu's control, surveillance, and dominance were considered the most repressive in Europe.

Since Paul served as a pastor, he expected the police would be calling. And they did. He was sent to a concentration camp rather than a prison so that officials could avoid the annoyance of filling out documents.

Previously a clinical psychologist, Paul had spent six years working in the local hospital, but he found that his real love was to pastor. In time he left the hospital and became minister of a Baptist church in Oradea.

What he didn't know then was that scores of people, some close colleagues and friends, were linked into the surveillance network of the Securitate, looking for reasons to draw him into their net of control. The only reason given for sending him to the camp was that he was considered a fanatic.

A Surprising Question

After six months, a senior official of the concentration camp showed up and abruptly asked Paul, "Who do you have higher up?" Unclear what the question meant, Paul responded, "I have God." The official retorted, "Don't give me any of that. Who do you have on your side in Bucharest?" Again, Paul simply said, "God."

"Well, get your things. You are leaving." As Paul walked from the camp to the waiting car, he kept looking over his shoulder, convinced this was a hoax and they would change their minds and take him back. But no one did. He arrived home and into the arms of his beloved wife. But the "why?" was left unanswered. As often happens, behind such a story, the work of prayer continues.

Several months earlier, a Canadian working in Romania had heard of Paul's arrest and went to Paul's apartment and asked his wife for a photo of him. Composing a letter to Canadian Prime Minister Brian Mulroney, he described the stifling oppression and lack of religious freedom, never sure if his letter would actually reach the prime minister's desk.

Canada, producer of the Candu nuclear reactor being built in Romania in the 1980s, was linked to the country's economic life. This required many professionals to move back and forth between Canada and Romania.

Bilateral talks necessitated that President Ceausescu visit Canada. On one occasion, after official niceties, the prime minister sat down with the Romanian president for a private conversation. After asking him about the state of religious liberties in Romania, and getting the usual song and dance of the freedom his nation enjoyed, the prime minister had a surprise.

Reaching into his briefing file, he pulled out a picture of Paul Negrut and asked, "Then why is this Baptist minister in prison?" Buffaloed by this unexpected confrontation, within hours Ceausescu sent a curt message to Bucharest: "Get Negrut out."

Freedom

In 1989, the wall of repressive communism tumbled and the country found itself in a liberated eastern European world. The Soviet world was reduced to Russia, and Yugoslavia came unraveled. The failed experiment in Albania of building walls to harbor atheism manifested its shallow and bankrupt ideology. And Romania, a people and nation pushed and pulled over the centuries by Ottoman Turks, Hapsburg Hungarians, and more recently by communism, was now released from the political constraints of its past.

In Romania today, the Orthodox Church is dominant. Evangelical Protestants have emerged as a small but vital voice of faith and political fairness. Often marginalized as a religious minority, they have chosen to go public in their concern for social issues rather than retreat into narrow sectarianism and personal protection.

The story of Paul Negrut continues. He completed a PhD, and today he is president of Emanuel University in Oradea. Besides his role as president, he challenges people worldwide to engage in the issues of life, never taking for granted one's freedom.

It took the unheralded and critical initiative of one who heard of a need, and the simple yet precisely timed question of a prime minister to sponsor freedom. Let's be ever ready to listen to the promptings of the Spirit to do what we can do.

TODAY'S READING

LORD, our Lord, how majestic is your name in all the earth! You have set your glory in the heavens. Through the praise of children and infants you have established a stronghold against your enemies, to silence the foe and the avenger. When I consider your heavens, the work of your fingers, the moon and the stars, which you have set in place, what is mankind that you are mindful of them, human beings that you care for them? You have made them a little lower than the angels and crowned them with glory and honor. You made them rulers over the works of your hands. . . . LORD, our Lord, how majestic is your name in all the earth!

Psalm 8

ITEMS FOR PRAYER

- Romania is pivotal for gospel witness in Eastern Europe. Pray for boldness among its young people in venturing out, making known Christ and his power to change lives and society.
- Years of atheism have nurtured a moral emptiness. Pray for pastors and Christian leaders, for Christian colleges and universities, as they train a new generation in ethical living and moral conviction.
- Cooperation and trust in each other is a challenge when for years mistrust has ruled. Pray for the leadership of the Evangelical Alliance and other fellowships, for a bonding in Christ and a willingness to work together in faith.

PRAYER

Father, we know that your Spirit is at work everywhere, speaking and prodding, calling your people to act, to move forward, to do what they can. Take their obedience and multiply their efforts with your sovereign timing. As with Paul, there are so many imprisoned in other places. Activate your people to be courageous and bold and faithful in praying, even when it seems your witness has been submerged beneath political and religious oppression. May our prayers be done in faith, believing you are always at work. In your strong name and for your glory we offer this prayer. Amen.

9

CHINA

Homeless and Forgotten in a Crowd

China is a place of dynamic Christian growth. In the early twentieth century, following years of foreign mission work, the Chinese church became more independent, developing its own leadership. The 1908 Manchurian revival defined the emergence and developments of a uniquely native evangelical tradition. In spite of the wars and revolutions of the 1930s and 1940s, Chinese evangelicals launched a wide range of ministry and mission.

After Mao Tse-tung and his Communist regime took control in 1949, church-state relations became a decisive factor in the life of Protestant churches. During the Cultural Revolution, many congregations became part of "the underground church." Today, the government attempts to monitor the church by way of the Three-Self Patriotic Movement and China Christian Council, the official means by which churches are registered. So-called house churches, formerly known as underground churches, are not registered.

Location: Asia

Population: 1.3 billion

Religion: nonreligious 45%; Chinese traditional 28%; Buddhist 12%; Christian 8% (estimates range between 30 and 140 million)

Dispatch

It was to this ancient yet modern country that Robert Glover came. The former professional British football (soccer) player was now specializing in social work. And here he was, being asked by the Chinese government to help solve one of their most pressing problems: over a million orphans left on streets or languishing in countless orphanages. This is the story of how 250,000 Chinese orphans have been placed in Chinese homes.

Long before Robert had thoughts of China, a visiting speaker at his home church in the United Kingdom told him, "Robert, you will be father to children like the stars in the sky." Thinking it rather hyperbolic, he continued in his social work.

In 1996, he was invited to study the problem of orphans in China, and while there he was given tickets to the Chinese Special Olympics. That day, seated next to a member of the Chinese Politburo, he was asked, "Robert, why do you so care for children?" He replied, "What I do for children, I do for the Father. God intended that family be the place in which children are nurtured. When you warehouse children, they die." The Politburo member said, "Meet me at eight tomorrow morning. There is someone I want you to meet."

The next morning, Robert met staff of international organizations working with children. He listened as they talked about the government's failings. When asked what he would do, he replied, "Quite simply, you integrate them into Chinese families and train those families how to care for traumatized children who have been left destitute." The minister asked, "Would you help us?"

Back in England, the British Foreign Office called Robert and told him that in bilateral discussions, the Chinese had asked for help. The Foreign Office said, "Robert, if you will go, we will fund it."

Selling everything, Robert with his wife, Elizabeth, and their six children moved to China. They began working in Shanghai, constructing a radically different model of caring for orphans, based on what he had refined in England. He named the organization Care for Children.

Doors were opened, red tape was cut through, and over time, Care for Children has helped 250,000 orphans get family-based care instead of institutional care. Sixty percent of the children have had disabilities and 84 percent have been girls. So far, they have worked with three hundred orphanages and four thousand workers in post-placement care for each child and the receiving family. Orphanages have become centers to serve the families and their needs.

Families of any or no religion are invited to adopt. One day Robert was asked by the government to initiate his model in an area where, he was warned, there were no Christians. Thirty couples wanting to adopt showed up for the orientation. The government official tried a little humor: "You know, this man Robert is a Christian." No one laughed. So he tried it again. Again no laughter. Finally a woman put up her hand and said, "Yes, but I'm a Christian." The person next to her did the same. They went around the room and everyone there confessed to Christian faith.

On the way home, the official asked, "Why would Christians want to do this?" Robert took out his Bible and showed the man where Jesus said it was our calling to care for the little ones.

The work of Care for Children has been noticed by government-sponsored media. One story featured a little girl who had been placed with a family after doctors determined she was dying of a hole in her heart but was too weak for an operation. Three years later she was the picture of health. It was then decided that she was strong enough for surgery. But when the specialist examined her, he announced with tears spilling down his cheeks, "But there is no hole there anymore." Journalists called her "The Miracle Baby, Healed by the Love of a Mother."

More recently, Robert was flown in by helicopter to the summer palace of the King of Thailand and asked to set up his nongovernmental organization (NGO) in that country.

Working with senior government officials, free to use prayer and Bible studies in their programs, armed with skills developed in social work, and toughened by years on the football field, Robert Glover took on an intractable problem of those thought to be least important. His vision and practical solutions brought hope to a society recently rooted in atheism. Doors were opened. By this witness of the gospel, many are experiencing social transformation, and families are nurturing once-forgotten children.

TODAY'S READING

He said to them, "Let the little children come to me, and do not hinder them, for the kingdom of God belongs to such as these.

Truly I tell you, anyone who will not receive the kingdom of God like a little child will never enter it." And he took the children in his arms, placed his hands on them and blessed them.

Mark 10:14–16

ITEMS FOR PRAYER

- This work is not over. There are so many children in China and elsewhere in need of family care. Pray for Christians giving love and service to children left orphaned in China, many of them girls.
- The importance of children being raised in caring families is not something only for China. Many countries are in need of training and placement of orphaned children. Pray for a multiplication of this ministry in Asia as well as in Africa, where disease has left tens of thousands orphaned.
- While Robert's story is unique, linking with government in providing solutions is not. Pray that Christians everywhere will be resolute in looking for opportunities to bring answers to public issues faced by government and its citizens.

PRAYER

Dear Father, may my heart be touched with the needs of children in China and Thailand. I pray that your Spirit will raise up mothers and fathers who will take children into their homes, giving loving support so they may grow into maturity and faith. As the church in China grows, may your hand be upon its leaders. Keep them faithful to your Word, loving, and at peace among themselves, Christ-led witnesses to their government, community, and people. Help us to be as little children to receive the kingdom of God. And may the power of that witness overcome forces that would attempt to intimidate, showing instead the gentle and resilient love that Jesus offers to all. Amen.

10

SYRIA

A Battlefield of Many Nations

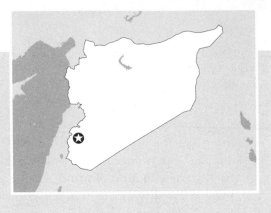

Syria gained its independence from France in 1946, and is home to diverse ethnic and religious groups. Its capital, Damascus, is considered one of the oldest continuously inhabited cities in the world.

When Hafez al-Assad took control in 1970, he gave senior positions to members of his religious Alawite sect (12% of the population), which dates back to AD 1000. (In a curious way, Christians were generally protected in Syria, as they were under Saddam Hussein in Iraq, as long as they said nothing against the regimes.) When Hafez al-Assad died in 2000, there were 3,000 public statues of his son, Bashar al-Assad, who took control. In 2011, civil war began. Millions of Syrians are now either refugees or displaced.

Location: the eastern shore of the Mediterranean, bordered on the north by Turkey, the east by Iraq, and the south by Jordan, Israel, and Lebanon

Population: Before the recent war it was 22 million.

Religion: Muslim 90% (Alawite, Muslim/Sunni, Druze); Christian 6% (Roman Catholic 3%, Orthodox 3%, Protestant/Evangelical 0.5%)

Dispatch

Syria is undergoing enormous destruction and change, making prayer vital for the country and those in refugee camps on its borders with Jordan and Lebanon. Millions are trying to keep their families alive and countless others have fled the country. In such conditions, war and its untold suffering takes on a different look as we see it through the eyes of those attempting to flee death.

Just inside Jordan, on the southern border of Syria, I was welcomed into a tent by a family who wanted me to hear of their

58

hopes. We shared a plate of dates and passed around a bottle of water. "Could I take your picture?" I asked. Eagerly crowding around, they smiled.

Syria continues to play out its story of death and violence as jets scream in swooping destruction, tanks from both the government and rebel sides exchange blasts, and soldiers go nose to nose in this all-out civil war. Newer groups, such as ISIS, carry out horrific acts of killing. All around there are bloody bodies and the wails of ambulances. This day I wanted a face-to-face conversation with those who had escaped.

Relieved to be out of harm's way, they ached for family and friends left behind and for the more than 300,000 who have died. Now safe with their children, they have a clean tent and boxes piled in the corner with rations, clothes, and the rudimentary tools of daily living. They are dry and out of the wind, yet in a tent with no insulation, and it is zero degrees Celsius—freezing.

In Syria—multilayered with centuries of cultures, bruised and battered by war—tribes live cheek to jowl, jostling for respect and power. So what are we to make of it all, and where is the presence of Christ in such mayhem?

How It All Began

This latest Syrian civil war began in earnest when a thirteen-year-old boy from Daraa, a town near the Jordan border, scribbled anti-government graffiti. Thirty days later his body was returned to his parents: knees and neck broken and genitals severed. Syrians, living since 1962 under Emergency Law and the unbridled powers of police, were unwilling to let this horror of mutilation be ignored.

Christians have sat atop this Syrian "volcano" for years. Not unlike other Middle Eastern countries, Christians are casualties with ongoing pressure from the majority religion to force them from their ancient homes. Syria previously had some 1.4 million Christians. A Syrian Maronite priest told me that even though he knew of the atrocities of the secret police, Christians had freedom to pastor, worship, and move about. Two Syrian Baptist pastors told me very different stories. One said only the president could bring stability; the other decried his violence. Now the brokenness of Syria is made worse by lawlessness, which only adds to the terror and despair.

The longer I stayed, the more Syrian families gathered around from their shacks, interested in answering my questions of how they were getting along, what they needed, and their views of the homeland.

When I asked if I could pray for them, their faces lit up. I told them I was a Christian and would pray in the name of Jesus. I said that Jesus is noted in the Qur'an, and that he too was a refugee, fleeing with his parents to protect their lives.

At one camp, as I closed the prayer, I asked the leaders of the camp to step into the center for a special blessing. After the prayer, Ibrahim, a dentist from Damascus, invited us into his shack for tea, a common sign of hospitality. As we talked, he asked about Jesus. The Christian young men from the ministry Heart for Lebanon who had driven me to the refugee camp gently took the conversation as far as was appropriate, and then promised they'd be back in a few days with a Bible for Ibrahim.

While the metaphor "Arab Spring" first seemed to promise new life, late winter blizzards have reversed the expected thaw. If there was ever a time to pray for Syria, it is now.

Today's Reading

Who is like the LORD our God, the One who sits enthroned on high, who stoops down to look on the heavens and the earth? He raises the poor from the dust and lifts the needy from the ash heap; he seats them with princes, with the princes of his people. He settles the childless woman in her home as a happy mother of children.

Psalm 113:5–9

Items for Prayer

• Syria has been in meltdown for some time. Today as we pray, think about what has recently been reported. Especially remember those who live in refugee villages and those who have fled to other countries and are displaced. Parents are often unable to give their children education and the benefits they so desire for them.

- Pray for the leadership of Syria that there would be a settlement of the deeply divided factions in government and the military.
- As we look into the future, pray for leadership to rise—godly, able, and fair—bringing stability and a measure of peace to this nation and region.
- Christians throughout the Middle East are forced to vacate, leaving so many cities without a gospel witness. Pray that Christians would be spared from the vile and ruthless treatment served by radically violent groups, and that there would be a return of Christians to their land to provide an ongoing presence of Christ's church in Syria.

PRAYER

Gracious Father, our brothers and sisters in Syria and its surrounding refugee camps wonder why they have been forsaken. Our prayer for those who have been forced to flee is that they will locate food and shelter and that their hearts will find peace and joy in you. We pray for Heart for Lebanon and other ministries serving refugees in this region, for their spiritual sustenance and material needs. We lift to you the leadership of Lebanon and other strategic countries in the area. Holy Spirit, give them wisdom to find ways to ameliorate human tragedy and to be courageous in finding solutions. Amen.

11
ETHIOPIA

A Door Closes,
a Door Opens

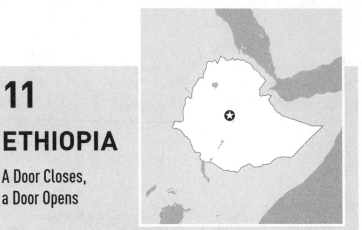

An ancient civilization, **Ethiopia** is Africa's second most populated country and is famous for originating the coffee bean. It has been ruled by a monarchy for most of its history. It is home to some eighty different ethnic groupings. Prior to 1980, there were a number of Ethiopian Jews, known as the Beta Israel; many of them now live in Israel.

In 1930, Haile Selassie became emperor, layering on himself titles such as "King of Kings" and "Conquering Lion of the Tribe of Judah." In 1972, a Soviet-backed Communist force known as the Derg established a one-party state. A half million people were killed during its purge, with a million dying from famine. In 1991, the ruling force was overturned.

Location: Northeastern Africa, in what is called the Horn of Africa. It is bordered by Sudan, South Sudan, Somalia, Kenya, and Eritrea.

Population: 92 million

Religion: 65% Christian (Orthodox 43%, Evangelical 23%); Muslim 34%

Dispatch

Traveling the ancient land of Ethiopia, you encounter many tribes and languages, landscapes, and faiths. Ethiopia bridges the Middle East and Asia to the African continent. Mystical, colorful, ancient, a habitat of early human existence, it's a land that has been ruled by both the ruthless and the benevolent.

It is the place where the earliest of church plants occurred. In the early fourth century, Christianity became Ethiopia's state religion. Citizens embraced faith in a way that did not depend on personal conversion or choice. Until 1974, when Emperor Haile Selassie was forced out of power after thirty-four years, the Ethiopian

Orthodox Church was the center of national Christian identity, education, and culture. From then until 1991, Marxist socialism ruled. Even during the oppressive Communist rule, an explosion of Christian conversions changed the face of this country. Here, as in other places, a story critical to the advance of the Christian story happened when the Spirit took a problem and turned it into an opportunity.

A Door Closed

A young Ethiopian, Hika, born in 1856, lost his father when just a lad. An Oromo ex-slave from Wellega, he was renamed Onesimus Nesib. Raiding tribesmen stole him from his mother, and after being traded four times, he ended up in Massawa on the Red Sea at a boys' school run by the Swedish Evangelical Mission. He eventually was converted and early expressed his desire to evangelize his Oromo people, the largest tribe in Ethiopia.

In a series of bizarre twists and turns, Nesib studied theology in Sweden and sought to return to Ethiopia, determined to minister to his people. Four times he tried to enter his homeland, but was turned back. In one of his periods of uncertainty, he began to translate psalms and write hymns and books in the Oromo language. He translated Christian literature, including John Bunyan's *Man's Heart* and Luther's *Catechism*.

It took Nesib thirteen years to complete the first translation of the Bible into Oromifa. For the next seventy-five years, that was the primary Bible for use, and his translation was foundational for the spread of the gospel throughout the country. Disappointed as he had been by the refused entries, those delays became golden moments. His translation not only made known the gospel to those who had never heard, but was essential in building churches for recent converts.

Then a Door Opens

The Spirit used a freed slave, turned into a fine theologian, to become a founding pioneer of the Ethiopian Evangelical Church, called

Mekane Yesus (Jesus' Dwelling Place), the country's second largest denomination. The first is the Ethiopian Kale Heywot (Word of Life) Church planted by SIM, an international mission organization.

When I met His Holiness Abuna Mathias, Patriarch of the Ethiopian Orthodox Church, I was reminded that Evangelicals too often think the church began with Luther or the founder of their particular denomination. It is misleading to see the church only within our own recent or immediate experience. If we concentrate too much on contemporary issues, we can miss the rich history that tells us how the Spirit has been building the church continuously for two millennia.

Representing forty million Ethiopians, Mathias's church is directly linked to an early New Testament witness: Philip. Led by the Spirit, he left the revival fires of Samaria to speak to an Ethiopian government treasurer of Queen Candace, who had been attending Passover in Jerusalem. Hearing the Scriptures explained to him by Philip, the official believed and was baptized before returning home to Ethiopia (Acts 8:26–40). In the year 301, the Ethiopian Axumite Empire was the second empire to adopt Christianity as its state religion, after Armenia. This community of faith has stood for Christ and has learned to live peaceably for hundreds of years with their Muslim neighbors.

As often occurs, during the harsh repression of the Communist regime, the gospel found access into the hearts of Ethiopians. The astounding growth of the church in recent years can be attributed to three factors, starting with the sovereign activity of the Holy Spirit. After the fall of Communism, people who for the first time experienced the personal work of the Spirit were energized by this newly found knowledge and presence and were contagious in their faith. Second, the effect of thirty-five ethnic groups having the Bible in their own language was almost instant. Hearing the Bible in one's own tongue turns words into life-giving music. Finally, healing and exorcisms demonstrated faith beyond words. As one said, "When a person goes home from a prayer meeting either changed as a person or healed from a disease, the next week their family and friends attend as well. It just can't be stopped."

A Crossroad

Geographically, Ethiopia is a crossroad between Asia and the rest of Africa. It is also at a figurative crossroad. Eastern traditions connect with the African world by location and history. There is also a remarkable affiliation with the Hebrew ethos mixed with the Christian story. These traditions provide a place where the Islamic message does not have ready access as in other northern Africa countries.

For Ethiopia to survive the communist debacle was no small feat. Rising from its devastating famine, the country today seeks commercial productivity to ensure national well-being. However, the surging tide of Islamic fundamentalism, which has turned their neighbor Somalia into a lawless land, is within shouting distance.

The Ethiopian church has two major components: the Orthodox and the Evangelicals—one ancient, the other recent—both with a sincere interest in finding ways they can work together.

I pray that those who call themselves by the Christ of Nazareth will combine their witness to strengthen the Christian story. And further, that this faith will be dynamic, finding places and means of cooperation so that the ongoing history of the gospel narrative will bring peace and national strength to this place of antiquity and remarkable possibilities.

TODAY'S READING

Ascribe to the LORD, all you families of nations, ascribe to the LORD glory and strength. Ascribe to the LORD the glory due his name; bring an offering and come into his courts. Worship the LORD in the splendor of his holiness; tremble before him, all the earth. Say among the nations, "The LORD reigns.". . . Let the heavens rejoice, let the earth be glad; let the sea resound, and all that is in it. Let the fields be jubilant, and everything in them. . . . He will judge the world in righteousness and the peoples in his faithfulness.

Psalm 96:7–13

ITEMS FOR PRAYER

- A country of this size and with centuries of Christian presence has the potential to influence others in Africa. Pray for

Christian leaders as they advance the gospel in their land and to other peoples and nations around them.

- With such a large Christian population—both Orthodox and Evangelical—pray the gospel will influence the work of Ethiopia's public leaders, and that spiritual vitality will characterize its people and land.
- Because it is located like an island in a sea of Islam, pray for a strong witness of Christ, both within Ethiopia and to its neighbors.
- The Ethiopian Orthodox Church has much influence within the country and among its people. Pray for a spiritual renewal among its leaders and congregations.

PRAYER

Gracious Lord and Savior, it was to this land that the earliest of gospel witness came via a senior government official. And to these people you have continued to bring, generation after generation, an ongoing presence of your love and your gospel. Out of their heartache from oppression, set aflame the passion of knowing you within all elements of the church. May the transforming story of Jesus be birthed in the lives of seeking Ethiopians. And, Lord, we offer a special prayer that the various groups and different expressions of Christian faith will find a meeting place of unity in you. Lord Jesus, revive the church in Ethiopia. Amen.

12
HAITI
Pearl of the Antilles

Haiti is 94% African. The island nation was settled by the French in the early 1700s. Thousands of African slaves were forced to work the sugarcane fields. Eventually, slaves overthrew their European masters. Today, the country struggles with poverty, corruption, and violence. Much of its social service is carried by mission agencies, both Catholic and Protestant. The UN has a strong presence both in peacekeeping and in reconstruction after earthquakes and storms. Among Haiti's many challenges is a form of modern-day slavery called *restevak*. Some 10% of its children—typically orphans or children from rural areas—are taken in by families, yet treated as slaves.

Location: the Caribbean, sharing an island with the Dominican Republic
Population: 10 million
Religion: Christian 95% (Roman Catholic 70%, Evangelical 20%); ethno-religionist 3%

Dispatch

I first set foot in Haiti in the 1970s while making films. Today, I find her much the same, yet so different. Tent cities planted after an earthquake in 2010 are almost gone, and yet on the outskirts of Port-au-Prince an unnamed shanty city, housing hundreds of thousands, has grown up—a squatter community with no sanitation, no water, and no schools. Even so, the people's will to remake, reconstruct, and renew is boundless.

One quickly falls in love with Haiti—its noisy "tap-tap" buses, vibrant colors—but not its potholed roads. Like parts of Africa, so much of this land and its people rise in tragic moments with hope, resolute determination, and faith.

I was drawn to its younger Christian leaders who are moving this Pearl of the Antilles from the underwater of its past to the surface, manifesting a spirit to remake this island country.

Education and Medicine

The story that matters for our focus in prayer is the determination of churches and Christian missions to make real what Jesus came to do. Out of its thousands of churches, many have their own schools: Ninety percent are run by Christian and Nongovernment Organizations (NGOs). Professionals may complain of the inequality of standards, but without these church schools, millions of children would grow up with no education.

Alongside education are the medical ministries, Christian clinics, and hospitals funded by missions and churches, doing what government cannot. Seventy percent of Haitians have no access to health care. To add to this loss, 30 percent of medical professionals have left for Canada or the United States. In this world of topsy-turvy political maneuvering, it's the Christian presence in education and health ministries that embeds ballast in a ship so vulnerable to cultural and physical storms.

A Land of Wide Gaps

This Caribbean country displays such extremes, from pervasive poverty to stores with almost anything one could want; from literacy rates of 55 percent to the well educated; from curious and troubling religious practices to the inspirational and rigorous.

Haiti is breathtaking in beauty, yet troubling in squalor. Less than a two-hour flight from southern Florida, this country with African roots defies adequate description. To understand Haiti, it must be felt.

Its long history includes a most astonishing military feat. In 1803, its ragtag army kicked out Napoleon's military, making it the first army of its kind to successfully defeat a Colonial power.

Of course, Haiti's recent history of brutal dictatorship—from "Papa" Doc Duvalier to "Baby" Doc—stigmatized this Caribbean country; and even today, while ruled by an elected government, its ability to operate as a democracy is fragile.

In 2010, a cataclysmic earthquake ripped open its earth, toppling buildings and resulting in the death of a quarter million people. Then as Haiti was lifting itself up by its bootstraps, two years later, Hurricane Isaac blew its monstrous wind and deluge of rain, destroying much that had been rebuilt.

Few countries are more religious than Haiti. Christianity arrived in 1630, first by Catholic missionaries, and then Protestant missionaries in 1807. Embedded in its heritage is voodooism—a reworked African understanding of the world of spirits of good and evil—which permeates the country. The Roman Catholic Church is criticized for syncretism, the wedding of Christian faith and voodoo. A criticism leveled against Evangelicals/Protestants is that personal salvation is often its only message. Both criticisms can be overplayed but are valid in their premises.

On Sunday mornings, Haiti's streets are filled with pretty girls wearing frilly dresses and colorful ties in their hair, and boys looking smart in their Sunday best. Along with their families, they are off to church.

Ministries to Note

The vital factor of today's church in Haiti is leadership. Bright minds, schooled in the academic and the world of experience, aren't looking for prosperity or the ease of living elsewhere. Neither are they naïve. Their analysis is clear, unapologetic, and unvarnished. They know the odds. They live in a catastrophic alley, where storms will smash over their world again. Corrupt politicians will rob their citizens blind. The power of voodoo will continue to mislead many.

Even so, driven by a call and raised in hope by faith, these young leaders create, build, lead, and comfort—moving forward, doing what good leaders do. Out of many possible examples, here are three.

- Parc Chretien Church, one of the largest evangelical congregations in Port-au-Prince, resides on a street designated for widening. One day without notice or compensation, the city hacked off the end of the church building, where some forty-six hundred gather for Sunday worship. Pastor Eliodor Desvariste, while deeply troubled for his people, began reconstruction, reconfiguring the layout to suit new possibilities. From the rubble rises a revitalized vision for ministry.

- Who would think of building a Christian university in Haiti? Jean Marc Zamour did. He knew that for the country to raise a new generation to engage in public leadership, they needed leaders who understand what it means to think and act in a Christlike way. Today, a young campus is being built on a two-hundred-acre site. This takes more than imagination. It takes faith.

- North of Port-au-Prince is Dessalines, a regional center. Its only hospital, Claire Heureuse, built and funded by missions, offers medical help. Chaplain Hyrouance Cadet invited me to accompany him on his morning rounds, asking me to pray for a baby just hours old; for a child with severe burns; for a young man barely surviving a knife attack just above his heart. They were all being treated in the name of the One whom we too love.

For over thirty years, Ian and Alice Van Norman have been coming to Haiti for up to six months each year, building schools, a hospital, centers of ministry, and churches, and now helping with a university.

Entrepreneurs in their own land, they have given from their resources and at times were matched by their business friends. As Lily and I drove the dusty roads and walked the muddy streets with the Van Normans, we watched as they arrived in places of their beneficence. They were greeted with wide smiles, bear hugs, giggles, and faces alive with recognition, as children sought to hold their hands. We stood by teary-eyed. They have brought much more than money to Haiti. They have given years of their lives to people they have come to love.

If you live in North America, plan on a visit to Haiti. Don't let your life go by without seeing firsthand the life and energy of Christian faith in this land of wide gaps. For holding the disparities together is the One who is before all things and in whom all things hold together. That's what the apostle Paul said about Jesus in his letter to the Colossian church. It's still true.

Today's Reading

Better is one day in your courts than a thousand elsewhere; I would rather be a doorkeeper in the house of my God than dwell in the tents of the wicked. For the Lord God is a sun and shield; the Lord bestows favor and honor; no good thing does he withhold from those whose walk is blameless.

Psalm 84:10–11

Items for Prayer

- There is danger that one tires of praying for a country with seemingly continuous disasters and unresolvable issues. Let us be faithful in our prayers for Haiti, specifically for those who provide education for children, that their efforts would bring transformation to this coming generation.
- For the many who are working in difficult conditions, providing medical care and comfort.
- For pastors and Christian leaders who are called on to help those wanting to find release from the prevailing presence of voodooism.
- For the missions and NGOs who deeply care about the many needs and are giving of their lives in service.

Prayer

Dear Jesus, you who gave your own life so we might live today, I pray for many in Haiti who struggle for the basics of life, and for children so wanting to attend school. I pray

71

for Pastor Desvariste and other pastors and churches through the land, and for President Zamour as he builds this Christian university. May those at Hospital Claire Heureuse and Haiti's other hospitals and clinics be enabled by good staff and supporting funds. Lord, we are so grateful for the Van Normans and their gift of love and development. May others take up their challenge to give of themselves as well. Here in this land, where joy and hardship live side by side, may your people, empowered by your presence, be bold in trusting you, honest in their commerce, and faithful in their worship, so this country will rise in strength and witness of you, Lord, whom so many love and wish to serve. Amen.

13

INDIA

Over a Billion, and Growing

India is the second most populated country in the world, after China. India's population is varied and complex: 22 official languages, 456 languages total, and 2,500 distinct people groups. Its constitution provides for religious freedom, but the rise of Hindu nationalism concerns both Christians and Muslims.

Christians make up 7% of the population. Many come from the most vulnerable sections of society, the Dalits and tribals, and mission movements are doing outreach among the higher castes. India was one of the earliest countries to receive the gospel. Thomas, a disciple, is reported to have come to Kerala in southwest India around the turn of the first century.

Location: South Asia, framed on three sides by the Indian Ocean
Population: 1.3 billion
Religion: Hindu 74%; Muslim 14%; Christian 7%; Sikh 2%; Buddhist 1%

Dispatch

India is a place of endless surprises—a tapestry finely woven over millennia, with wealth and poverty lying cheek to cheek. Drive down one street and you see prosperous high-tech firms; just a short distance from wealth is the entrenched culture of poverty—people scavenging for their existence. In all of its finery and tragedy, India is where the life and witness of Christ is pushing back in a way one would not have thought possible.

Complicated by a five-thousand-year history, plagued by its many Hindu gods, colonized by Germans, Portuguese, and British, this country of 1 billion-plus people is complex beyond a lifetime of study.

The Caste System

India's caste structure defines the person, his role, and where he can (and cannot) move. It is a religious vision of life that gives high privilege to only 5 percent; 25 percent receive favorable status, and the balance of 70 percent are relegated to OBC (Other Backward Classes), including the Dalits (the untouchables, or outcasts), who are part of no caste at all.

It works this way: Society is seen as a person. The "head" is the Brahmin caste (5 percent)—priests and academics who serve as the mouth of the body, providing spiritual well-being. Only men who are born into this caste can become priests. According to the Hindu idea of karma, a person continues to die and be born again until possibly reaching this upper state. When a Brahmin dies, he has no further need to advance. He is like a spark returning to the fire.

Beneath the head are the "arms," the warrior caste called Kshatryia (12 percent) who rule and protect society. Then come the "thighs," the Vaishya caste (12 percent), merchants and landowners who oversee commerce and agriculture. Finally, there are the "feet," the lowest caste, who are the Sudra (25 percent). These are peasants, farmers, and unskilled workers, those who do manual labor for the top three classes of Indian society.

The untouchables, or Dalits, make up the bottom half, and aren't considered a caste or even included in society's "image" of a person. Half of India, in effect, is considered "non-persons." Higher castes refuse to touch, eat with, or associate with untouchables. And although the government has passed a nondiscriminatory law, this age-old system is well entrenched. *Untouchable* means exactly that: You don't touch them or allow them to touch you.

With 700 million classed as servants or untouchables, the caste system hinders people's mobility to move outside the determined social structures and diminishes their capacity to rethink the very notion of a person.

Dr. Richard Howell, the general secretary of the Evangelical Fellowship of India, put it this way: When two Indians meet as strangers, he told me, "the encounter is often dual; everything—response, behavior, body language, social niceties, form of address, receptivity—depends on an assessment of where the person stands on the scale of power and influence." For an Indian, superior and subordinate relationships "have the character of eternal verity and moral imperative—and the automatic reverence for a superior is a nearly universal psycho-social fact." A person's entire worth depends on the position he occupies on a hierarchical scale. In Hinduism, identity is dependent upon worth, and worth is determined as people are born and reborn in accordance with their karmas, the quality of their deeds. This obviously affects human relationships.

The caste system was seriously challenged by the arrival of Christian missions. Schools were opened for Dalits in the 1840s, when missionaries began the slow process of treating untouchables as humans.

Much has changed, but the caste system is alive and well. In the IT sector, people are accepted on the basis of education and skill. But when marrying, families press hard to ensure their children marry from a class no lower than theirs, as property that moves intergenerationally is to be kept within the caste of its beginning.

Evangelism Within the Caste System

So how does the gospel advance in India's caste structure? It spreads like wildfire. Dr. Howell says two things characterize evangelism here. First is *fluidity*. Many come to faith without calling themselves Christians. They keep their traditional names, clothes, and customs, and meet together in something other than a typical church. These groups include the Allah Abad, the "church meeting" of about ten thousand in the Punjab, who meet Sundays on a field. Also, there is the Yesu Darbar, a group known as the "royal court of Jesus Christ." Another group is the Yesus Satsang, or truth seekers, most of whom would not be recognized as Christians, yet they trust in Jesus and follow his teachings.

Dr. Howell's second characteristic of evangelism in India is *spontaneity*. Gospel initiatives often break out in places where it seems there has been no strategy or anyone targeting the area for evangelism. These outbreaks of faith have a strikingly familiar pattern as we see in the book of Acts: teaching, healing, and casting out evil spirits.

Persecution is a growing factor in some areas of India. An underlying concern is that the government might shift toward religious fundamentalism and press legal penalties on religions other than Hinduism, deny opportunities for employment, or impose heavier taxation. Today in rural areas, churches are burned, pastors beaten, and Christians intimidated. As the gospel presses into new areas, conflicts increase.

Yet there are many reports of an acceleration of Christian witness, increased engagement, and unprecedented outreach. We visited an ashram ministry center outside of New Delhi. The director, who had been raised as an orphan, had a heart for lepers, so he persuaded the government to give land where lepers could build their shanties. At the same time he helped them fill out forms for government subsistence. Since lepers have children, the director wondered, *Where do they go?* So he built a home and school for them. Then he noticed mentally challenged women abused on the streets, and he built a home for them as well. When I asked about a new hospital nearby, I assumed he had done regular treks to North America or Europe for fund-raising. No, he didn't even have a passport, the director told me, and much of the financial support came from Hindus in the area.

That night, in the ashram center's church, I preached, and after I had finished, many lined up for prayer, including those asking to be set free from evil spirits. So I did as instructed in the New

Testament: I took authority. A pastor later said, smiling, "Well, Brian, welcome to India."

TODAY'S READING

The heavens declare the glory of God; the skies proclaim the work of his hands. Day after day they pour forth speech; night after night they display knowledge. They have no speech, they use no words; no sound is heard from them. Yet their voice goes out into all the earth, their words to the ends of the world. In the heavens God has pitched a tent for the sun. It is like a bridegroom coming out of his chamber, like a champion rejoicing to run his course. It rises at one end of the heavens and makes its circuit to the other; nothing is deprived of its warmth.

Psalm 19:1–6

ITEMS FOR PRAYER

- Give thanks for the remarkable growth of Christian ministry in India and for the creative means by which the gospel is spread.
- Pray for national leadership, for their integrity and boldness as they seek to plant and grow churches.
- Alongside those coming to faith is the need for economic well-being. Many agencies are offering micro-financing (small loans) to assist those who otherwise would not be able to do business or to care for their families. Pray for those agencies and those whom they assist.
- There is a continuing need for Bible translation for the many who currently don't have the Scriptures in their own language. What a gift for people to read the Bible in their own tongue. Also pray for those doing translation work.

PRAYER

Father, India is your world, and those who live there are your creation. Your son, the Lord Jesus, gave his life so they too would know of your gracious love and your daily provision. Today we especially remember those who are planting churches in the urban and rural centers of India. May their faith be resilient so that their words are alive with your presence and promise. As your gospel continues to move from village to village and city to city, protect your people from those who would intimidate or persecute. And may Bible translations continue to build so people can read your words in their own language. I offer this prayer because only in your name is there authority. Amen.

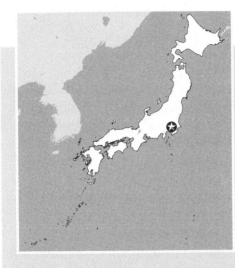

14

JAPAN

Punching Above Their Weight

Located in the so-called Pacific Ring of Fire, **Japan** comprises 7,000 islands and is subject to frequent earthquakes and tsunamis. Most Japanese live on the largest islands: Honshu, Hokkaido, Kyushu, and Shikou. A powerful economic force in the world, it has eschewed military buildup. However, tensions in the area over land rights are troubling.

While their religious faith is rooted in Shintoism, more than half claim to have no personal faith. The Christian community is small, less than 2 percent. The Christian message is seen by many as non-Japanese, even though the gospel has had a place there for 500 years.

Location: in the North Pacific Ocean, close to the eastern borders of North and South Korea, Russia, and China

Population: 126 million

Religion: Buddhist 70% with a strong overlapping with Shintoism, 24% "other" (hundreds of newer religions); Christian 1.5%

Dispatch

It was soon after the threefold disaster of tsunami, earthquake, and nuclear reactor meltdown that we traveled along the northeast coast of Japan. It's quite impossible to imagine what fifty-foot waves can do to a land and its people. It was in 2011 that twenty thousand people died, and areas contaminated by radiation are still unusable. Land sunk by the weight of the sea remains vulnerable to flooding on the cycle of each tide. People from the Fukushima area, the location of the nuclear reactor, for months following the meltdown were treated like lepers. Products manufactured in that area were viewed with suspicion; understandably vegetables, but steel bearings? Fear misconstrues logic.

A sports metaphor came to mind as I watched volunteers working to bring people hope. Boxers taking on another in a heavier weight class are said to be "punching above their weight," taking on more than one would expect.

In the middle of these sad and hopeless communities, Christians set about to do what most would never have believed they could do. Their numbers were considered too small to do much.

A small organization to help with disaster, ingeniously called CRASH (Christian Relief, Assistance, Support, and Hope), sprang into action hours after the earthquake, tsunami, and nuclear meltdown. In the wildness of those early days, as people and money and resources poured in, nothing productive would happen unless these resources were coordinated. Samaritan's Purse brought in a military 747 loaded with supplies. But unless these supplies were properly and efficiently distributed to those in need, they would sit in warehouses.

Aided by the Japan Evangelical Association (JEA), CRASH Japan brought together people from all streams of Christian life. When the disaster struck, the leaders of CRASH Japan quickly moved to serve the immediate needs. Seasoned missionaries dropped what they were doing and joined in. Young people arrived from around the world, over seventeen hundred of them. Japanese Christians set aside their work, and many moved into the five camps set up in the northeast to save lives.

As we traveled with the general secretary of JEA, Reverend Kenishi Shinagawa, and other leaders of CRASH Japan, we met pastors, Christian aid workers, and young people from around the world. Winter was arriving, and people were moving into resettlement camps. Machines continued the laborious job of cleaning up the carnage. Life was trying to get back to normal. But this is Japan, where family and community are everything. Now separated from friends and brutally cut off by death, many were lonely, completely unprepared to face winter without family.

It was then that CRASH Japan, led by Jonathan Wilson, moved into a new phase, providing emotional aftercare. While machines continued their work, Christians focused on the soft underbelly of human trauma—people living alone without hope. It was feared that the suicide rate (already high in Japan) would spike if people were not reached in time.

Japan, one of the most difficult countries in which to advance the gospel, is a curious mixture of intensely focused family and community life with a high regard for ancestors. Japan is also a materialistic culture. The prayer of Christian leaders has been that because of recent disasters, the people will give more attention to spiritual matters. Materialism inflicts a spiritual disease, which deconstructs the interior—one's spiritual life. The other prayer is that as younger leaders take their place, the paradigm of small cell-like congregations may break open into new models, especially in the urban areas, where people live far from their places of family ancestry.

For this we give thanks: In the midst of disaster, the Christian community is a witness of love and care. The soil has been prepared. May the seed of faith find a hospitable place, and with careful nurture, produce a great harvest.

"You Stayed"

A villager told a Japanese pastor, "I've watched you Christians. When people from other faiths arrived, they worked to clean up their temples and help their own people, but you Christians, you will help anyone. You didn't just stay with your own. And I've noticed now that most of the others have left. You Christians are still living and working among us."

Hurray to those who have punched above their weight!

Today's Reading

He reached down from on high and took hold of me; he drew me out of deep waters. He rescued me from my powerful enemy, from my foes, who were too strong for me. They confronted me in the day of my disaster, but the LORD was my support. He brought me out into a spacious place; he rescued me because he delighted in me.

Psalm 18:16–19

Items for Prayer

- Pray that there would be a breakthrough of strongholds that keep Christ from being known in Japan.
- As Christian young people come to Japan to study language and culture, they have an opportunity to give witness of Christ. Continue to pray and encourage young people to consider this as an intermediate educational experience. One never knows; their hearts may be caught and they will stay.
- Also, teaching English as a second language opens doors for witness. Pray that many will consider this option.
- Pray that this model for disaster relief will be used in other countries, providing a framework for effective response.
- And pray for the younger generation of leadership, that as they seek new models of witness and congregational life, there will be a move of faith and of the Spirit.

Prayer

Gracious Lord, in the midst of sorrow and disaster you are ever present. We also know that you use times of tragedy as a way to call people to see your offer of life and salvation. This is our prayer for Japan, a people of extraordinary competence and discipline. We thank you for the response of many following the tsunami to the "cup of cold water" offered in your name. May this witness continue to reverberate, especially through the communities that were most affected. As people continue to consider the ultimate reality of life after death, may the promise of your resurrection draw them to your love and salvation. Amen.

15

PRISON MINISTRY

A Beautiful Moment in an Awful Place

Today we see inside a ministry that most of us know little about: prisons. Society protects us from criminals, but also effectively protects us from even thinking about those behind barbed wire and concrete prison walls. It keeps us from them as well as them from us. Jesus knew what he was doing when he strongly told us to remember the prisoner.

Throughout our fifty-two-week journey through this book, we will visit prisons a few times, both because there are important stories to hear and people to meet, but also so that we remember the men and women for whom Christ died and for whom he deeply cares. The extension of that is that if their lives matters to him, they will matter to us.

Dispatch

Prisons are scary, dreary, cold, smelly, noisy, and confusing places.

After signing in to a Mexican prison, giving up our passports, and being frisked and checked over, we walked through a maze of corridors topped with rolls of razor-sharp fencing. We would be in two places: Section 8, the open block, and Section 7, the maximum-security block.

Prisoners crowded around us. We were greeted by hugs and handshakes. Roberto, leader of our visiting team (a theology professor and chair of Mexico Prison Fellowship), was a welcome sight to the inmates. I was an unknown, but they wanted to shake my hand too. I mumbled something in Spanish, then resorted to "Hi."

Around a corner we saw a tent-like overhang and a small table covered with a white linen cloth. A candle and crucifix adorned the table—the centerpiece of our upcoming service. In the corner some inmates were puffing on a crack pipe.

Handsome and muscular, Edgar, about thirty-five, took my hand. His eyes sparkled while his hug confirmed his welcome. Chair of the weekly worship service, he was energized by his assignment. We all stood, singing and praying with about twenty-five inmates who circled the worship table, a space as sacred and hallowed as one could imagine.

Christmas was coming, and the prison was celebrating. Edgar and his committee had put together a play about the birth of Jesus, using typical prison humor. When a male dressed as Mary, large with child, entered the scene, the men hooted.

Later we walked toward Section 7, the maximum-security block. We crossed an open area bright with plants and flowers. The gardener, now a believer, received our hugs; he was in for life—120 years for killing four men, although he confessed it was actually fifteen. After climbing some stairs, we came to a caged area divided into two sections. To the left, in an area about seven by a hundred feet, some eighty inmates were milling about. To our right were the cells, bars dividing the walkabout area from where the men lived—five to a cell. Gates opened and we moved in, brushing up against the cells, moving in and around the men. I was a stranger, but they saw the people with me every week.

Five men peered out through the bars. They smiled and stuck their hands out for a handshake. An inmate pointed to one of his cellmates: "He killed four." I turned and saw a smile and an outstretched hand. The rule here is that if one has a visitor (usually a wife or girlfriend), the other four leave to mingle in the open space, pulling a curtain across the cell to provide privacy. It was here that we were getting hugs and answering questions. Caged in with men in maximum security, some doing life for multiple killings, I looked around for a guard but saw none.

Then I saw Piedad, dressed in her red Prison Fellowship International golf shirt, her face up against the bars, praying with an inmate. She is a eucharistic minister, trained by the church to offer consecrated Communion wafers to believers. Fearless, she comes once a week and every day during Holy Week. Praying and ministering to those deemed too dangerous to be let out into the main prison, she has found her calling.

As we left, just outside the cells we saw a wooden case much like an altar, erected to the Virgin Mary. This one was different. We peered in, expecting to see figures of the mother of Jesus. Not here. Crowded into the cabinet were death figurines dedicated to *Santa Muerte,* the Angel of Death, a cult formed in Mexico that commands an enormous following—a reminder that the spirit of darkness finds an active place where darkness is the prevailing topic and reality.

Back in the main prison, two impressive and smiling young brothers gave us hugs of welcome. Victor and Julio, both in for life for armed robberies, had been locked in Section 7 for ten years. In time they came to Christ, and their conversion was so transformative that they were moved from maximum security into the main section, possibly for the rest of their lives. Yet joy radiated. No complaints, no asking for privileges. They just wanted to be loved and to love. Ironically, one was wearing a Wheaton College T-shirt (a Christian university in Illinois, USA). He knew nothing of the school.

Prison is a desert of spiritual and human emptiness. People dry up from the inside out. Hopelessness rules in bleeding hearts cauterized by time. With dignity cut off at the legs, men and women see themselves as the prison system sees them. Relationships slowly drift and then lose any strand of connection, as those outside feel the fatigue of visits, raising kids, and paying bills alone; or finding solace or friendship in another.

In this bleak desert a new kind of life blooms. Piedad, boldly going alone into cellblocks of violent men to lead them in prayer, transforms the landscape. Edgar, eyes filtering peace and joy from his inner being, makes no apology to his colleagues as to where he stands for Christ. Victor and Julio, still facing life in prison, are strong in their love for Christ, knowing that the Father loves them.

While these flashes of color and wafts of sweet kindness mitigate bleak, lonely, smelly places, millions are in prison, some not far from where you and I live. It is in those places that the Spirit is not absent. He works among people deemed untouchable and too often forgotten.

Jesus said it this way: "I was in prison and you came to visit me" (Matthew 25:36).

Prisoners, most of them guilty, are all created in his image. They are loved by him who calls on us to be the expression of that love.

A beautiful moment in an awful place.

TODAY'S READING

For you created my inmost being; you knit me together in my mother's womb. I praise you because I am fearfully and wonderfully made; your works are wonderful, I know that full well. My frame was not hidden from you when I was made in the secret place, when I was woven together in the depths of the earth. Your eyes saw my unformed body; all the days ordained for me were written in your book before one of them came to be.

Psalm 139:13–16

ITEMS FOR PRAYER

- Each country has its own judicial threshold that defines who will be incarcerated. Some people need to be locked up because they are dangerous to society. Others do not. Regardless, they are men and women in need of being touched by the gospel in real person-to-person terms. Pray for prison ministries in your country, city, or town.

- Locate who is doing prison or jail ministry. Learn from them what and whom you might pray for, and bring this to your church for their awareness and prayers.

- Prisons are in need of radical rethinking. Pray for ministries such as Prison Fellowship International (PFI) and others as they attempt to create new kinds of institutions. And pray for legislators who seek to find better ways to deal with crime in just and helpful ways.

PRAYER

Father, this very day as millions are confined in prisons with no seeming benefit other than being penalized, our prayer is that you will continue to inspire Christians to visit them, people like Piedad, who care for those so often forgotten by families and friends. We pray for Victor and Julio as they live out their time incarcerated. May mercy sustain them, and give to them, as well as other Christian prisoners, the grace and love needed to make you known to their inmates. Bring into the law and justice system creative people who will find new ways of serving both victims and criminals. And as inmates leave the prisons, may they find a community ready to receive them and love them. Change hearts so that all may live to the praise and honor of your name. Amen.

16

EGYPT

A First-Century Miracle in Twenty-First-Century Garb

Few countries can boast of a recorded history centuries before Christ as can **Egypt**. A walk through the Egyptian Museum, just off Tahrir Square in Cairo, is an introduction to a people proud of their past. The Pyramids and the Sphinx represent stories of conquest and fame, and a trip down the Nile River brings one face-to-face with its incredible history.

Location: North Africa on the Mediterranean. Half of its population lives alongside the Nile River, a meandering waterway almost 7,000 kilometers, or 4,250 miles long, the life source of the nation.

Population: 86 million

Religion: Muslim (Sunni) 87%; Christian 12% (Coptic 10%, Evangelical 2%)

Dispatch

Whether you travel the chaotic streets of Cairo or cruise down the flowing waters of the Nile, Egypt—ancient, rich in culture, sounds, architecture, and ruins—continues on its political, religious, and social journey.

Years since the revolution toppled President Mubarak's thirty-year reign, one can still feel the restless spirit in Tahrir Square, the downtown public plaza in Cairo and center and symbol of its revolution.

What began in the Arab Spring (a series of anti-government uprisings) had been a long time coming, and it will be a long time before it finds resolution. The move from a military dictatorship to some form of democracy is a bumpy road.

Some things are certain, and one is that Islam will continue to exert enormous power. The unanswered question is this: Will Egypt retain a secular-type structure so that Islam isn't able to enforce Sharia law? Here, its 121,000 mosques and imams have immense influence.

While Christians make up 12 percent of the population, this can be misleading. For example, listed companies show that 32 percent are owned by Christians. Also, mission agencies appear strategic and forceful, managed by creative and entrepreneurial leaders. Let's meet a few.

Mission Agencies

The Bible Society of Egypt is at the forefront of evangelism. It is large, creatively financed, and highly productive in new forms of literature. In the face of the pressure and abuse by the Muslim Brotherhood, they are strategic in planning for the long term and for increased witness. The vision and dreams of the society are amazing and challenging. They publish for both the Coptic and Evangelical communities.

Following the ISIS killing of twenty-one Egyptian Christians in Libya in 2015, the Bible Society printed a brochure made up of Scripture and a poem, which in days had more than one and a half million in circulation. A Muslim asked a Christian, "Have you seen this? You can read it, but please give it back, because I only have one and am sharing it with all my friends. I've never read such beautiful verses, and need it back because I am trying to memorize it!"

The Coptic Evangelical Organization for Social Service (**CEOSS**)—*Coptic* means "Egyptian"—has over five hundred staff and five thousand volunteers. Their range of ministry is amazing. Working with a $10 million (U.S.) annual budget, they have remarkable capacity to serve the poor. We visited one of their projects in the slums of Cairo called the Islamic Vision. The CEO described how CEOSS had convinced many imams that female sexual mutilation (FSM) and the marrying of children were both unhealthy practices. I asked an imam sitting to my left for his story.

The imam said he had met Christians who helped him understand the importance of treating women properly and protecting children from abuse. He told me how Evangelicals had changed his views, and now in his Friday services at the mosque he was preaching this new message of treating women properly. His gratitude was evident in a warm hug as we left.

Sat-7 is a television service throughout the Middle East and North Africa. They produce and distribute Christian programming via satellite to millions of Muslim homes. Carefully avoiding clashes with Islam, they produce programs that give an understanding of God's love.

Habitat for Humanity Egypt works closely with local community groups. A decade ago they were building twenty to thirty homes a year, and now almost three thousand are being built. Their vision is that for the twenty million now living in poverty, by 2023 they will lift 400,000 families—or two million people—into healthy and functioning homes.

Here is what amazes me: Habitat Egypt, a small organization founded by a religious minority, operates in a society where the dominant religion persecutes. Instead of complaining, they lead with this message: "We will work to make your life a better life, your home a better home, your family a better family."

The Evangelical Theological Seminary in Cairo, formed in the 1840s, is one of the oldest colleges in Egypt. With qualified faculty and three hundred students, this college has an important role in building congregational and mission agency leaders.

Garbage City

Garbage City is a place like none other. Garbage from Cairo is brought to this center just outside the city, alongside limestone quarries where material was cut for building the pyramids. Some years ago, a Christian businessman was convinced to help those in this most despised of vocations—collecting, sorting, and selling garbage. Father Simon, as he is now called, left his print shop and got to work. Schools, a medical clinic, and a church sprang up. They discovered they were working on top of an enormous cave. So they excavated and built a twenty-thousand-seat church in the cave. This led to other auditoriums being carved out. During the early days of the Arab Spring, seventy thousand Christians concerned about their country gathered in the cave churches for a twelve-hour prayer vigil and praise service while protests were going on in Tahrir Square.

This ministry in an Islamic world is a first-century miracle in twenty-first-century garb. If you want to visit one place in the world where the dynamic of caring for the poor, preaching grace, and the laying on of hands are all nestled in a spectacular and artistic facility, choose Garbage City, Cairo. You will be changed.

Being marginalized doesn't mean we are forced to live on the margins.

Today's Reading

In that day there will be an altar to the Lord in the heart of Egypt, and a monument to the Lord at its border. It will be a sign and witness to the Lord Almighty in the land of Egypt. When they cry out to the Lord because of their oppressors, he will send them a savior and defender, and he will rescue them. So the Lord will make himself known to the Egyptians, and in that day they will acknowledge the Lord. They will worship with sacrifices and grain offerings; they will make vows to the Lord and keep them. The Lord will strike Egypt with a plague; he will strike them and heal them. They will turn to the Lord, and he will respond to their pleas and heal them.

Isaiah 19:19–22

Items for Prayer

- The ongoing political upheaval in Egypt creates enormous tensions between various factions. Pray that Egyptian Christians will be proactive in their service to others and will show the way in reconciliation and peace.
- Given that Christians are often under attack, pray for the work of the government, that it will craft laws that afford liberty of faith to all.

- While many Christians seek to leave the country, pray that many will choose to stay as an ongoing witness. The country needs a solid Christian base for the continuing presence of congregations and mission agencies that speak to the heart of the Egyptian people. This country matters much to the well-being of the Middle East.

PRAYER

Dear Father, may this land of Egypt, to which you sent your Son to be protected from the wicked intents of Herod, know your life and salvation. As the political debates proceed and religious animosity raises its head, Holy Spirit, bring through your people a strong word of peace and reconciliation, so that they will be known more by the words and presence of Jesus than the latest argument or public defense. This is a people and land you love. May Egypt be receptive to your desire to bring life and health to their region and to the world. Amen.

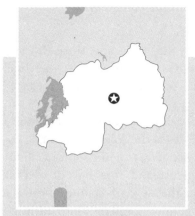

17

RWANDA

The Devil Never Travels Solo

Rwanda is a small African country whose people have borne unimaginable sorrow. This dispatch is about the genocide of 1994. In the next, we visit with a remarkable Christian leader who helped Rwanda respond to the crisis.

Much of the country is mountainous; its climate is among the finest in the world. Valleys are lush and green with lakes dotting the landscape. In 1962, Rwanda won independence from Belgium, and the next year the UN appointed France as its protector.

Location: Central and East Africa near the equator, bordered by Uganda, Tanzania, Burundi, and the Democratic Republic of the Congo

Population: 10 million

Religion: Christian 90% (Roman Catholic 45%, Evangelical and Anglican 35%); Muslim 5%; ethno-religionist 4%

Dispatch

I bit my upper lip and peered through misty eyes as I left the Genocide Museum in Kigali, Rwanda. That this postcard nation would have experienced a holocaust seemed impossible.

People-dehumanizing. Culture-destroying. Soul-demonizing. Life-demolishing. And all to a people whose history, prior to colonization, was a model of national harmony. In one hundred days in 1994, over one million were killed; 20 percent of all Rwandans died; 70 percent of Tutsis perished.

I had thought I understood what sparked the slaughter: tribal hatred and warfare, not unlike neighboring countries where inter-tribal animosities flare up in periodic raids and killings. But what stopped me cold was the historical basis of the genocide. This was not typical tribal warfare between the Hutus and Tutsis. It was a conflict between social classes, not ethnic groups. Yes, there had been rivalries, but nothing in Rwandan history could have predicted this savage butchery.

The key to trying to comprehend this horrific slaughter of a million Tutsis and moderate Hutus is the role of Rwanda's European masters. They drove a wedge between peoples who for centuries had lived as one. The Hutu and Tutsi have shared the same language and culture since the eleventh century when the Tutsi (cattle ranchers) came from Ethiopia and the Hutu (farmers) arrived from Chad. Today, it is impossible for most to detect the differences in dialect. Physical characteristics are so washed out by intermarriage that Rwandans themselves can't distinguish them by appearance. Genetics, I'm told, show no differences.

Then in 1919, Belgian colonial masters took control and ripped apart this historic merger. Some Tutsi were given government jobs and were generally more highly regarded, while the name *Hutu* became synonymous with "servant." Of the 7 million citizens, 85 percent were eventually classified by ID documents as Hutus and 15 percent as Tutsis.

Identity Cards

The Belgians divided and conquered with identity cards that registered each person by "race." While in fact just one race existed, the cards served to instill into their self-awareness that each person was of one of the "races." Why this procedure? By dividing them into social classes, and using their historic names Hutu and Tutsi, the colonists set one group against the other.

With the power of government, the Belgians used ID cards to press Rwandans to buy into this preposterous lie. The government had its list, a bureaucratic maneuver used by other countries as well to identify those they might want to either discard or promote.

Sadly, the 1994 holocaust in Rwanda wasn't the country's first. In 1959, 300,000 Tutsi were slaughtered, and a million fled into neighboring countries. In the 1980s and early 1990s, the ruling party manipulated public opinion. The Tutsi were increasingly seen as the bad guys. Radio station RTLMC was established for the sole purpose of instilling hatred among the Hutu, poisoning their minds against Tutsi families, neighbors, and co-workers.

In January 1994, in the French magazine *Kangura*, journalist Henry Ngeze wrote of the Tutsi: "We . . . say to the Inyenzi [cockroaches] that if they lift up their heads again, it will no longer be necessary to go fight the enemy in the bush. We will . . . start by eliminating the internal enemy. . . . They will disappear."

"Shaking Hands With the Devil"

General Romeo Dallaire, the Canadian head of the UN peacekeeping force in Rwanda, pled with his UN masters for authority to step in. He was refused. He later told us at a prayer breakfast in Toronto that when he shook hands with the leaders of the genocide, he knew he was "shaking hands with the devil." The French, who were tasked with military oversight by the UN, either disregarded the killing surge or had no idea of its severity. Then the fuse was lit.

On April 6, 1994, Rwandan president Juvénal Habyarimana, a Hutu, was flying into Kigali along with the president of neighboring Burundi, Cyprien Ntaryamira, also a Hutu. A mortar shell blew the plane out of the sky and both were killed. Current president Paul Kagame, who then ran the Rwandan Patriotic Front (RPF), claimed it was Hutu extremists. Who knows?

Within three months over one million Rwandans died. In Kigali, the killings were led by the Presidential Guard, an elite group of the army, and in the countryside, a militia called Interhamwe was responsible. People were raped, shot, ripped open, cut down, nails driven into skulls, heads bashed in. Today, thousands of skulls can be seen in the many places of memorial.

As numbing as was the visit to the Kigali museum, our time in the village of Nyamata showed the fury that evil can create. Here in one day, 12,000 had been slaughtered in a church and its surrounding compound. We walked between rows of church benches, piled high with clothes worn by those who perished that day. A similar scenario of people seeking refuge was played out in fifty-three other churches.

Impossible to Imagine

But our encounter with these unbelievable horrors was not over. Led downstairs at Nyamata Church, we stepped into a lower room near the back of the building. We first saw what we were becoming accustomed to seeing: rows upon rows of skulls and bones. About five feet down was a casket covered with white silk and a cross. Our guide Leon told us the story.

Annonciata Mukandoli was twenty-eight years old, reportedly a beautiful Tutsi woman who, though often invited to marry, had refused. As the wave of killings swept the region, she was targeted, but they had a special means of death for her. Sharpening a long stick, her murderers inserted it through her lower torso until it came out her neck. Then they left her to die.

In time, her death became the symbol of calculated evil, and in 2007, authorities gave her a special place of honor and rest. Our emotions were raw as we viewed her casket, imagining the utter terror and pain she endured. I could imagine her frenzied murderers, hungry for annihilation of a people they had been told were their enemies.

Within the shambles of Rwanda, peace and reconciliation gradually emerged. But let it not be forgotten that a European power, prided in its culture and religious heritage, crafted a social experiment and used it to undermine social unity with division. In so doing, it opened the doors to evil. The demonic never travels solo.

Tragically, Christians from all church communities were also involved.

Yet in time a seed forced from its protective shell shot out its rootlets and gathered strength, enriching itself from the soil of faith. Growing up is a people who reject the notion that they have been victims. Instead, they see their future through the paradigm of hope and reconciliation.

In this brief dispatch, I am reminded that this delta of horror had many contributing streams. Do your own reading and research. I continue to struggle with the age-old question: Where was God in all of this? What I saw was a people determined that hope would rule their lives and country. When we see tragedies developing, we need to pray for those whom God will use to bring restoration and peace.

TODAY'S READING

Righteousness and justice are the foundation of your throne; love and faithfulness go before you. Blessed are those who have learned to acclaim you, who walk in the light of your presence, LORD. They rejoice in your name all day long; they celebrate your righteousness. For you are their glory and strength, and by your favor you exalt our horn.

Psalm 89:14–17

ITEMS FOR PRAYER

- These vicious stories remind us that evil is not just an idea. Pray for Rwanda and other countries where hatred and vengeance break out.
- Over half of Rwandan parliamentarians are women, elected after the genocide. Pray for their leadership, as they attempt to give hope and organizational direction for the future.
- The justice process has been tedious and long, with many still not convicted. Pray for the wheels of justice, that they would serve the long-term needs of the people, bringing to an end this tragic and catastrophic event.
- The elimination of social distinction between the Tutsi and Hutu is part of the government's attempt to redefine the future. Pray for political leadership as it seeks to build a foundation as a basis for trust.

PRAYER

Dear Father and Lord of all, our hearts break as we read about the killing of people created in your image. We sorrow

97

over the loss of life, the terror brought into the lives of the survivors, and the many, many children who have grown up without parents and the spouses who now live alone. Gracious Spirit, continue to visit Rwanda with your grace, touching those still in grief. Help young people to envision a different means of solving social conflicts, and birth in their hearts your newness of life. In your name, which is above every name, we offer this prayer. Amen.

18
RWANDA— BISHOP JOHN

Guiding a Nation
in Finding Salvation

In the previous chapter, we learned of Rwanda's genocide. But that's not the end of the story. The Spirit had prepared one man to help the country wrestle with its demons of hatred and to teach trust in the power of the gospel to transform.

Dispatch

We drove with Anglican Bishop John Rucyahana north from Kigali, up, down, and around undulating hills. Streets were clean—no garbage bags in sight, no visual reminders of genocide, apart from the many memorials. Underlying memories and understandable tensions and fears linger, but for more than two decades, Bishop John's strong pastoral hand, matured in the service of caring for people and churches, has helped the country heal.

As the bishop shares in his book *The Bishop of Rwanda*, John was a teenager when 300,000 Tutsis were slaughtered in 1959 and he and his family fled to Uganda. As he grew into adulthood, he left his Catholic upbringing with a lingering anger over the Tutsi killings. In time, nurtured by a family friend, John "was arrested" by Christ, he wrote. He became a school headmaster and studied for ministry in the Anglican Church as a rural evangelist, serving in Uganda during the rule of Idi Amin, and eventually studying in the United States.

After 1994, John returned to Rwanda as a bishop and began a long and heart-stretching ministry of caring for the hurt and traumatized. In time, President Kagame recognized that someone was needed to bring grace into hatred, forgiveness into revenge, and hope to calm confusion and counteract paralyzing fear. Bishop John was appointed chairman of Rwanda's Commission of Reconciliation.

Even though the genocide was supposedly over, rebels continued to ravage the land. The bishop's own sixteen-year-old niece, Madu, was fearful after returning to Rwanda. She was afraid because her father was a Tutsi and her mother a Hutu. The bishop writes:

> I told her that I would take care of the provisions for the move, and they should come immediately. She thanked me and went back home to make preparations for the move. The same evening she arrived home, infiltrators attacked. They held Madu down and took their machetes and peeled the flesh off both her arms from the shoulder to the waist, and then they stripped her naked and raped her while she was in that pain and slaughtered her. They killed her brother and sister too.

How could reconciliation ever take place after such moments and accruing memories? How could Bishop John help Rwanda?

Some twenty years later, I am driving with Bishop John into a prison compound housing over nineteen hundred convicts—25 percent convicted of genocide with one-third of the total number women. Some seven hundred had gathered under a tin roof for chapel. As we arrived they were already into worship and praise, all led by prisoners. The music, prayers, and testimonies were riveting; we couldn't help but enter in. Their words of faith and forgiveness left us gulping for air. I spoke on Jesus' story of a loving and forgiving father. I ended with prayer, but Bishop John wanted it to go further. He stood and invited those to come to the front who wanted a prayer of forgiveness of their sins. The area around the platform was jammed. The bishop turned and said, "Time to pray again." And so I did.

A Testimony

We then visited a village of newly built residences constructed by Prison Fellowship International, bringing together both perpetrators and genocide survivors. The village people gathered in a meadow. A group of women danced in praise to the rhythm of the drumbeat. Chantal Mutuyimna, an elegant woman, told of her mother and father and six siblings being hacked down by those with whom she now lived side by side. She smiled as she spoke. "Now I can leave the village and know my goats will be well cared for."

This process of reconciliation began in prison as Bishop John worked with Prison Fellowship. I asked how different his commission was from the one in South Africa. He noted that there the focus was on learning what had happened and finding a way for the races to live together.

In Rwanda, he observed, it was about an earlier defined social class distinction, which had been deliberately fanned into flames of hatred and killing. Here, he explained, the goal was to encourage people to seek transformation, not coexistence. This for him was a moral and spiritual issue based on a vision for transformation of all, combined with forgiveness of those who had killed or were complicit. His goal was for them to live side by side. In this way both survivors of the genocide and its perpetrators would take responsibility for the past and the future.

Rwanda is still in transition. Even so, its collective courage is a reminder of how grace can triumph in the midst of calamity and sorrow. We learn again that in any place or moment of tragedy, the Lord raises up people to extend his peace, grace, and truth.

Over a second cup of coffee I asked Bishop John the basis for his ministry. He flipped opened his pocket Bible and began to read from Paul's second letter to the church in Corinth:

Today's Reading

So from now on we regard no one from a worldly point of view. Though we once regarded Christ in this way, we do so no longer. Therefore, if anyone is in Christ, the new creation has come: The old has gone, the new is here! All this is from God, who reconciled us to himself through Christ and gave us the ministry of reconciliation: that God was reconciling the world to himself in Christ, not counting people's sins against them. And he has committed to us the message of reconciliation.

2 Corinthians 5:16–19

ITEMS FOR PRAYER

- During the awful years building up to the genocide, the Spirit was preparing Bishop John to be a national pastor. Pray for a continuing nurture of godly younger leaders who will, in time, also lead the people of God, and indeed the nation, in peace and reconciliation.
- There is no end to bringing peace and forgiveness. It is a daily requirement and a step-by-step process. Hearts are still wounded in Rwanda, and while many are healed, the caregiving ministry continues. Pray for those who help both genocide victims and perpetrators in healing and reconciliation.
- The story of Rwanda does not stand alone, and neither will it be the last. The experience gained by Christians in this land can serve to assist others. Pray that what they have learned will be used to bring about peace and reconciliation in other lands.

PRAYER

Loving Father, whose heart we know is grieved by the horror and sorrow of this land and its people, give us as we pray a love for those who stooped to maim, violate, and kill. We know it is those who are sick who need a doctor. Your love is for all, including violators. As we pray today, may the love that flows from you transform our revulsion over this story into a breaking of our heart—not only for those who are victims but for the perpetrators too. Keep us from smug self-righteousness, and may we reach out in love to those who are caught in the downward spiral of evil. As well, strengthen Prison Fellowship, and others who minister to both survivors and perpetrators, that their hold on you will provide spiritual understanding in their important ministry. For your glory and praise we pray. Amen.

19

SOUTH KOREA

The Second Largest Missionary-Sending Country

South Korea was occupied by Japan from 1910 to 1945. After WWII, the peninsula was divided. The northern part, now called North Korea, was occupied by the Soviet Union, and South Korea by the United States. Before the Korean War (1950–1953), over 60% of Koreans lived in the north, but many fled to the south to escape Communist rule.

Location: in the southern part of the Korean Peninsula, South Korea borders North Korea and is separated from Japan by the Korea Strait.

Population: 50 million

Religion: Christian 31%; nonreligious (though linked to Confucian values) 31%; Buddhist 3%; ethno-religionist 7%

Dispatch

A newcomer may be amazed by the advances South Korea has made in economics and education. Even though crushed by foreign occupation (1910–1945) and then defended by the United States, this southern part of the China peninsula rose from the rubble of the 1950s war to become a showroom of industrial capitalism. It now ranks eleventh in world economies.

The capital city of Seoul is spectacular, and a visitor is struck by its life and energy. During a late autumn visit we saw trees of orange and red, showing off a city modern while quaint, with a retained memory of its past—a stunning contrast to its cousin in the north.

However, one shouldn't be blind to the soft underbelly of material success. Poverty does exist here. And so does sorrow over their inability to reunite with families to the north—a continuing undercurrent that shapes its policies and energizes its movements, all driven by a profound desire for reunification.

At night the glow of illuminated crosses dots Seoul's landscape. Christian faith is neither ridiculed nor rejected. Like reuniting with families caught in the web of North Korea's paranoia and seclusion, faith is core to the story of this little nation that defied the odds of postwar politics and moved away from socialism while refusing to buy into Western secular inclinations.

Growth of the Church

The story of church growth here is unprecedented. Bigness is neither always good nor effective, but the stories of stunning growth and evangelism in South Korea represent and embody the rise of a nation and voices of faith from which thousands leave this land to serve around the world.

In fewer than six decades, this modest nation leapt to the front in missions. As recipients of foreign mission input, they have ceased being a missionary-receiving country and have become a missionary-sending country. In recent decades they have sent out, each year, over a thousand long-term missionaries, as many as all the Western churches combined. Estimates are that twenty thousand long-term Korean missionaries are active somewhere in the world. Their goal is to have a hundred thousand by 2030.

Roman Catholics arrived in 1603, and in the 1800s, during a time of intense persecution by the ruling Joseon Dynasty, thousands paid for their witness with their lives. Protestants arrived (primarily Methodists and Presbyterians) in the 1880s. Korean religion differed from Chinese and Japanese religions in that they viewed God as monotheistic, a Creator God called Hananim.

During the Japanese occupation, seven million Koreans were either deported or killed. Rejecting calls to worship the Japanese Emperor and resisting the pressure of assimilation (including requirements to speak another language and not their own), Koreans embraced Christianity to save themselves and their nation, forging faith and nationalism as mutually reinforcing partners. Christian faith became friend and enabler.

During the Korean War, from 1950 to 1953, South Korean churches appointed chaplains to serve in the armed forces. Soldiers who turned to faith became a core of Christians who would lead in the evangelism explosion of the last few decades.

Challenges

The Korean church is not without its challenges. In a competitive society, relationships can be strained. With an estimated 150 Presbyterian denominations alone, plus other denominations, the potential for division is high. As well, the attaching of religion to nationalism can build into the practice of faith a politicization that too often divides people on matters of policy.

Christianity grew in South Korea based on indigenous leadership, that is, Western missionaries invested church leadership in the hands of Korean nationals, so the challenge now is that their own missionaries emulate this model in countries where they are serving.

Observe the convergence of South Korea's history, experience, theology, and world events. They were a people schooled in a religion with a monotheistic base, which may have predisposed them to a Christian view of life. Humiliated and subjugated by their occupiers, when liberated by the "Christian" West, their affiliation was naturally to the faith of their liberators. Hardworking and determined, freed from threat of communism and provided with working capital, their export products exploded. Today, whether the product is a Hyundai or a Samsung, their market skills take a backseat to no one. This vision for the world provided a model for evangelism: If you could take on the world in business, there is no reason you couldn't do the same in missions.

South Korea is a riveting story. Lifted by the dynamic of faith, they are a new center of vision and mission. In the 1800s the center of world witness was the United Kingdom and Europe. In the 1900s that center moved to North America. It is now shifting to the global south.

The apostle Paul heard from Macedonia and crossed the great geopolitical divide so that Europe would hear the gospel. Today, Koreans hear the call to move into closed and hostile cultures with the message that has changed their nation.

Today's Reading

The LORD is compassionate and gracious, slow to anger, abounding in love. He will not always accuse, nor will he harbor his anger forever; he does not treat us as our sins deserve or repay us according to our iniquities. For as high as the heavens are above the earth, so great is his love for those who fear him; as far as the east is from the west, so far has he removed our transgressions from us.

Psalm 103:7–12

Items for Prayer

- There is much to praise God for in the rise of the South Korean church. Their dynamic and witness is strong and resilient. Pray for their leadership, including those who lead large congregations.
- Given its amazing economic strength and vision to reach out culturally, pray for its missionary enterprise, especially that they will recognize the importance of being culturally sensitive and to cooperate with Christians already in the countries to which they are sent.
- Internally, given the growth of many large ministries, pray for a spirit of cooperation and humility among leaders so that they will model for their people a servant heart and replicate that in the many countries in which they minister.

Prayer

Gracious Father, Lord of all, we give thanks for the ways in which your Spirit has brought life to the South Korean people. We praise you for the energetic spirit of its leaders and people to witness and give to the growing of your church. As they expand their missionary enterprise to many countries, may wisdom and grace characterize their going, and a godly spirit of cooperation mediate their relationships. May the leaders discern the importance of allowing Christ to rule, keeping their patriotic emotion under the authority of Christ and his kingdom. In your strong and holy name we pray. Amen.

20

HONDURAS

Hope Matters

In the 1980s, the United States sent military personnel into **Honduras** to assist in the fighting against the Contras in Nicaragua. In 1998, Hurricane Mitch was particularly devastating to Honduras, destroying three-quarters of its crops. Floods in 2008, combined with a constitutional crisis in 2009 (the president was thrown out), have made it difficult to govern in recent years. A critical challenge is the high level of corruption in society, and for some years, Honduras has been considered the deadliest country in the world (outside of war zones) for assassinations and murder.

Location: basically between North and South America, in the region known as Central America. It is bordered on the west by Guatemala, El Salvador to the southwest, and Nicaragua to the southeast. It features Pacific Ocean coastline in the south and a large inlet in the north to the Caribbean Sea.

Population: 8 million

Religion: Christian 98% (Roman Catholic 79%, Evangelical 19%)

Dispatch

Jogging through the capital city of Tegucigalpa in the early morning seemed like a normal activity until my pastor friend frowned and said, "We are the number-one killing country in the world. Best you find another way to exercise." Even so, as I met leaders and pastors, I discovered that kingdom life, like salt, is doing its work in bringing transformation to this Central American country of Honduras.

Two years ago, in San Miguel, a barrio of 98,000, there were 115 killings a month; now that number is down to three or four a month. Too many still, but a stunning shift. Two years ago, 64 percent of the country's population experienced some kind of violence—from extortion to killings. That has been reduced to 34 percent.

Honduras was not always so violent. As a land bridge from the drug-producing countries of the south to the United States, it became a crossing point for drug cartels. High unemployment and few vocational or recreational opportunities made crime here a juggernaut of domestic life for this country.

But Christians, rising in faith, refuse to let this tide of crime and its accompanying violence wash over its people. In San Miguel, there is a youth center where young people learn skills from computers to music to barbering and cosmetology and physical fitness. World Vision, with a national staff of 500 and 75,000 child sponsorships, targeted violence in this barrio. Partnering with nine evangelical congregations and its one Roman Catholic church, along with USAID and community organizations, it has created a social inversion, upsetting the status quo of violence. They have introduced a sense of pride and highlighted human value. This is a clear expression of our heavenly Father's love and of the power of Christ to transform people and society.

Hope

Foundational to these changes is the embedding of a sense of pride within Hondurans. This represents a radical shift of thinking among people who know that their country is considered the murder capital of the world. There is nothing magical about what World Vision and its partners are doing. Money alone won't bring about change, neither will grand ideas. Instead, nestled into this world of violence, they are instilling incarnational hope to enable people to reach their dreams. They are determined to reject the notion that life has to go on as it was. Reducing violence calls for restoring pride and driving out fatalism. Crossing the Red Sea seems like child's play compared to the boldness this requires.

Speaking about World Vision, Pastor Galedro said, "They helped us get outside the walls of the church, onto the streets, and into the lives of teens. We had to recover the space we had lost with our youth. Church life robbed us of time with our children, and gangs filled what we had left empty."

Tegucigalpa sits among high hills, mostly populated by the poor. Our SUV shifted into four-wheel drive and ground its way up the mountainside, bouncing over lava rock, as Bolívar and Karla Sánchez took me to meet some pastors they love. Leaving paved roads, we drove into the barrio of New Capital. Here the homes are shanties, buildings strung along the hillsides. There is no running water, and dirt roads and rocky streets are the only means of travel. New Capital has one hundred evangelical churches and one Roman Catholic church. Most are small, and their pastors eke out a living caring for their flock and working side jobs. The churches are constructed by shiplap lumber and covered by tin roofs or whatever other material is available.

We met pastors, and sometimes their wives, in seven churches, hearing stories of conversion and faith along with joy and struggle among their flocks. Many have come together in what they call "Pastors United in Love," which began when Bolívar and Karla heard a pastor say, "I'm an orphan. I have no one who is a mentor to me." Some church leaders down in the city began to gather the often desperate pastors every Monday. A bus picks them up, and for the day they encourage one another and have a time of worship together. Also, they are taught how to teach the Bible and to preach, what it means to care for their own families, and to nurture their marriages—all issues core to their own lives and ministry.

Opportunity

Where does one start in a country wrestling with political infighting, suffocating corruption, extortion, out-of-control killings, and children recruited as drug runners?

Maria Alvarez knows. She and her engineer husband are church planters. As a volunteer, she serves on the national board of Opportunity International (OI), a micro enterprise ministry that helps people build their own businesses. Enthusiastic and passionate about those they serve, some OI people told me of Sofia. Wanting to change her life, she started making bracelets in her home, but knew the future was in making things men would buy as well. OI helped her with a small loan, enough to get started. When that was paid off, she moved to the next level: her own shop. Then came the economic calamity in 2009. She lost everything, but OI knew she could be trusted, so they refinanced her loan and she was off again, working with the loan counselor to rebuild her business.

Where money isn't available, where does a person go for help? Opportunity International now has ten thousand clients. It is built on a Christian understanding of stewardship and honesty, and 94 percent of its loans are to women. Records show their clients are good at working together with others; they pay on time and put profits back into their families. Once a week they meet to make payments on their loans and receive business training, including subjects such as accounting, how to treat their clients, and how to have a successful marriage.

In Honduras, I saw Christians who refused to give in to humiliation, instead investing their lives in the heart of their society and believing in the gospel promise that the gates of hell will not prevail against God's kingdom.

I saw World Vision at its creative best— influential and trustworthy—its ministry built upon on-the-ground collaboration. I saw Pastors United in Love linking hearts in the midst of poverty, caring for one another and living among their people. I saw Opportunity International lifting those with determination from poverty, offering start-up capital, and giving weekly nurturing for success.

Person by person, day by day, community by community, Christ's kingdom is a transforming presence in Honduras.

Oh yes, and I did take the pastor's advice and retreated to the hotel gym for exercise.

Today's Reading

The Lord reigns, he is robed in majesty; the Lord is robed in majesty and armed with strength; indeed, the world is established, firm and secure. Your throne was established long ago; you are from all eternity.

Psalm 93:1–2

ITEMS FOR PRAYER

- Knowing of the desperate situation in their own country, Honduran Christians are working and praying to overcome the evil of murder with the peace of the Lord Jesus. Let's pray for the vision, passion, and protection of World Vision and others in their work.

- Many small churches are right in the middle of cartel-infested barrios. Pastors are at the front edge of helping people live Christ-centered lives. Pray for courage and boldness in their leadership and witness.

- As in many countries in their region, unemployment is high and the means of beginning one's own business is tough. Opportunity International and others are helping to lift people in their personal and family lives. Pray for their leaders and clients that poverty will become something of the past for many of them.

PRAYER

Dear Father and Lord of life, we remember today Christians in Honduras who struggle in the awful mix of poverty, violence, and political instability. We know that many, in your name and in your power, are ministering, giving their best to raise a standard of faith, integrity, and peace in the midst of this chaotic world. We pray for Bolívar and Karla as they work with pastors on the hillsides. May they have ongoing love and a capacity to train and encourage these Christian leaders. We praise you for the work of World Vision and their years of experience, accumulating wisdom on how best to serve. May their leaders be graced with your love as they lift communities up in faith and hope. How important, Lord, it is to have a job, a means of providing for family. Opportunity International has such a strong reputation for helping. May they continue to have the funds needed to help people with vision and hard work to bring to their families what governments can't or won't do. We offer these prayers in faith and hope, in the name of Jesus our Lord. Amen.

21

COLOMBIA

The Way Forward

In 1499, **Colombia** was "discovered" by the Spanish. It won independence in 1819, and was declared a republic in 1856.

At times during the last half of the twentieth century, it experienced increased armed conflict. The 1950s were known as *La Violencia*—conflict between liberals and conservatives, in which 180,000 Colombians were killed. As well, in the 1990s, mainly in the rural areas, conflict increased between the right-winged paramilitary, left-wing guerilla groups, and government troops. Since the turn of the century, conflict has been on the decrease.

On July 4, 1991, a new constitution was adopted.

Located: on the northwest coast of South America, bordering Panama on the west, Venezuela and Brazil on the east, Ecuador and Peru on the south

Population: 48 million

Religion: Christian 94% (Roman Catholic 82%, Evangelical 12%)

Dispatch

Brutalized by wars of nationhood, guerilla chaos, landowners' paramilitary bands, and government armies, Colombia still travels a road of social upheaval. Known in recent years for its brutal and controlling drug cartels, Colombia is now on the road to recovery. In observing that recovery, I unearthed the story of one who faced guerillas in his own backyard and defended those of faith.

Colombia is not for the faint of heart. Its inner complexities and religious inequities are part of its fabric, and the conflict was not just because of the cartels. As in many countries with a religious majority, the minority often faces unusual and unfair practices. This was true in Colombia and has been in part corrected.

To understand the stories that follow, a brief explanation of terms and groups will help. To the outsider, Colombia seems like a snake pit of armed conspiracies and factions. FARC, a Marxist group, presses a leftist political agenda and, like their enemies, is armed to the teeth. The National Liberation Army mixes Marxist ideology with Roman Catholic liberation and is much less predisposed to arms. Another guerilla group, M19, attracted followers of former president Gustavo Rojas Inilla. Paramilitary groups were set up by right-wing capitalists to protect their investments. Cartels are mixed up in all the groups as they use, produce, and sell drugs to help fund their activities.

Persecution

First, we'll look at the persecution of Evangelicals. In the late 1990s, various gangs within the cartels killed some four hundred pastors. They assumed that because they helped guerillas when hurt or dislocated, Evangelicals were on the guerillas' side. Pastor Hector Pardo, working alongside the Mennonite Peace Initiative, went back into the highlands and met Salvatore Mancuso, second in command of the United Self-Defense Forces of Colombia (AUC) paramilitary group. Pastor Pardo, now seventy-five, was not unfamiliar with the power gangs in his country. His father was a founder of a guerilla movement in the 1950s. Pardo, having grown up among gangs, knew their ways. As he said, "I was with them until the Lord rescued me."

He faced Salvatore Mancuso with the question, "Why are you killing our pastors?" "Well, you support the guerillas" was the response. "Why do you say that?" asked Pardo. "Because when they are injured or hurt or their families are in trouble, you are there to help them," replied Mancuso. "Ah, now I understand. But that's what Jesus calls us to do. Everyone is made in his image. He died for each of us. He taught us how to love, even our enemies."

The two men made an agreement, and the pastors were no longer persecuted. But that wasn't the end for Pardo. He wanted to tell his story, so he wrote *From the Other Trenches*, an account of his life, making sure it got into the hands of FARC. His argument was this: Arms are not the way forward. Only Jesus can bring change and peace. The book did what he hoped it would. FARC leader Zacharias Valencia, nicknamed "The Old Man," read the book and turned his life over to Christ. Late one evening representatives from FARC, M19, and a guerilla movement arrived at Hector Pardo's home. Their request? That Evangelicals support their causes. While they never did get a promise, before they left, Hector led them in the sinner's prayer and they walked away, each with a new Bible. With a twinkle in his eye, Hector noted, "And no money exchanged hands."

Another Challenge

Evangelicals have faced a substantial challenge in a Catholic-majority country, especially on two issues. In the 1950s, the traditional parties, Liberals and Conservatives, faced off. The Conservatives teamed up with Catholics, writing plans to eliminate non-Catholics from the country. Of course, there was enormous pressure on Protestants to the point that they feared for their lives. Evangelicals in turn joined the Liberals, made up of progressive Catholics who viewed non-Catholics as legitimate citizens. Doing so positioned Evangelicals with the Liberals as political partners and served to antagonize the Catholics and Conservatives.

There was an additional problem. Article 53 of the constitution recognized the Catholic Church as the official religion and gave it statutory privileges. Hector Pardo knew this needed to be changed; in 1990, he and other Evangelicals formed the Christian Union Movement to win a seat at the table of the constitutional conference designed to rewrite the constitution. And for their efforts they won two seats.

As the debate on the constitution pressed forward, Hector and his associates argued that while Catholicism may be regarded as the official religion of the country, Article 19 (which was to replace Article 53) needed to define freedom of conscience and worship, offering not only religious tolerance but also religious equality.

Also, that special treatment given the Vatican by the government would be eliminated. That was passed, and now by law there is freedom of faith. Hector and his colleagues knew the way to bring about change was to be seated at that constitutional table.

Remarkable Growth

In 1990, there were approximately three million Evangelicals in Colombia. Today there are eight million—a statistic that prompted a quick "But why?" One pastor made this comparison: "In South Korea, after WWII, the church exploded in response to the good news of Jesus for the poor and those suffering from foreign domination. In Colombia, our people were collapsing under hopelessness—political infighting, guerilla movements, thousands upon thousands of people being killed every year, drug cartels ruining the economy and the nation, and four million Colombians, many from the upper middle class, leaving. We were drowning in hopelessness. The gospel of the good news gave hope, which set off a wave of conversions and ministries."

From this uplift of faith rose many mega churches, some of which have spanned offshoots in North America, Africa, and Asia. Not all are necessarily healthy, as we have found: The transplanting of a culturally valid and effective model into a foreign setting has its drawbacks.

In country after country, especially those that have experienced heartbreaking and spirit-crushing times, I hear stories of grace that defy even the writing of award-winning novelists. The Spirit, wending his way in and out of lives, writes of faith. Rooted in struggle and sorrow, these stories show how God intersects with the human condition as willing lives journal the great metanarrative of God's love. Hector is one such scribe.

TODAY'S READING

Great is the LORD and most worthy of praise; his greatness no one can fathom. One generation commends your works to another; they tell of your mighty acts. They speak of the glorious splendor of your majesty—and I will meditate on your wonderful works. They

117

tell of the power of your awesome works—and I will proclaim your great deeds. They celebrate your abundant goodness and joyfully sing of your righteousness.

Psalm 145:3–7

ITEMS FOR PRAYER

- We are grateful for leaders like Pastor Hector Pardo. Pray for the training of others who with courage and integrity will help lead the church in Colombia.
- Violence and war breed their own kind. Pray for a spirit of peace and reconciliation to permeate the church and from there to move into society. Pray especially for the Mennonite Peace Initiative and its partnership with CEDECO, the Evangelical Alliance of Colombia.
- As in other countries, there is a deep concern for Christian influence in civil society—in the government and all arenas that permeate society. Pray for Christians who seek to be salt and light, that they would be faithful in their living and witness.

PRAYER

Dear Father and Lord of Life, we lift in prayer today the people of Colombia, asking for your continued work in the lives of those leading the church. We know that embedded in its social fabric is the experience of conflict and retribution. Continue to give energy and public acceptance to the Mennonite Peace Initiative and the CEDECO as they seek to bring your call to peace and reconciliation to the attention of all. As the church continues to advance in faith and witness, deepen its understanding of your grace. May there be a spirit of cooperation, especially among its mega churches. In their proclaiming of faith, may you be understood as the Prince of Peace, through whom we all come to know of your love and experience new birth and inner transformation. In the mighty and loving name of Jesus, I pray. Amen.

22

NICARAGUA

Before and After

The Somoza family, a hereditary dictatorship, ruled **Nicaragua** for forty-three years. During the 1970s, the Sandinistas, led by Daniel Ortega, rebelled against the Somozas and finally deposed them in 1979. The contras then attempted to unseat the Sandinistas but lost; some 30,000 died during this period.

Location: Nicaragua is the largest of the Central American countries, with Honduras to the north and Costa Rica to the south, just north of the Equator. On the west is the Pacific Ocean and on the east the Caribbean Sea.

Population: 6 million

Religion: Christian 96% (Roman Catholic 70%; Evangelical/Protestant 29%)

Dispatch

Dorestela Medina Mendieta was a revolutionary even before she joined Daniel Ortega's fighters in 1973. While in seventh grade, she was already writing letters and organizing protests against the Somoza dictatorship. Her mother sent her on a student exchange program to the United States, hoping this would clear her head of this revolutionary nonsense. But after she returned, at eighteen, she left home and joined Ortega's forces. This young radical, steamed by the abuses of a dictatorship, was charmed by the ideas and personality of Ortega. It was heady days for young radicals. Initially, U.S. President Jimmy Carter supported Ortega, until he learned that he was helping to arm the Salvadorian rebels.

In 1979, when Ortega's Sandinistas took power, his new government called on the young revolutionary Dorestela to be part of the leadership team. She was appointed sub-director of immigration. Traveling back and forth to Cuba, she relied on Russia, Cuba, and Germany to help put an immigration system in place. Fighting broke out as the U.S. turned to support the contras fighting out of Honduras.

Now ranked fourth in the army, she was called to fire up the Nicaraguan troops as they moved to protect her government. Later she was put in charge of running prisons and combatting charges leveled against the Sandinistas about human rights abuses.

In 1995, after her soldier-husband died, Dorestela had had enough and left her government position. After working for various embassies, and struggling with a restless and peace-vacant heart, even testing New Age variations, she finally said yes to an invitation to attend a spiritual retreat. For three days they studied the passion of Jesus, his death and resurrection. She told me, "Brian, I cried the entire three days. Jesus touched my heart. When I faced who Jesus was and why he came, I knew then I could follow him. I felt much like the woman in the New Testament who poured perfume on the feet of Jesus even though those around her criticized her. I heard him say, 'Dorestela, I am your peace. I care for you. I will give you hope.' It was then my life was changed.

"My friends, and even my brother, said, 'Oh, you are now like St. Paul. You fought Jesus, and now you are loving him.'"

What led her from her conversion to her current vocation? I wondered. It's not surprising that the past is foundational for the future.

After her conversion, she had asked, "Lord, what can I do for you now?" *Take care of my children*, an inner voice responded. But that made no sense. She had children and family, but surely that wasn't what the voice meant.

For two weeks she prayed and stewed about the message. Suddenly it dawned on her. "Of course. He wants me to take care of those who as minister I was in charge of, but with a different feeling and attitude. Prisoners."

"So, what were your feelings about them when you were minister?" I queried. Her head dropped. "I had no feelings for them then. In fact, I had an uncle and a cousin in prison who had been there for ten years. I never once visited them—didn't even bring them a toothbrush."

Knowing it wouldn't be easy to show up visiting prisons as the former minister of prisons, she joined Prison Fellowship (PF) as a volunteer. At first, prison officials wondered what was going on. What kind of trick might she be playing on them? They didn't buy her story about spiritual transformation. But, in time, week by week, as she faithfully cared for those in prison, she built confidence in herself and trust among the guards, prison officials, and inmates.

Today, Dorestela is regional director of Prison Fellowship International for Latin America and Mexico, overseeing its ministry. How did this revolutionary spirit, caught up in throwing bombs and robbing banks, end up here? Another story of Spirit-intruding grace, catching a heart passionate about values and truth, transforming and shaping it to love and serve those she had earlier despised.

During our visit, we walked with Dorestela and Monseigneur Pena, head of the country's PF, into La Modelo Prison in Managua. Before we got through the gate, loud drum-driven gospel music filled the air. The service was in full swing. The band of rhythm and bass guitars, drums, bongo, and a creative keyboard were pumping out their beat. Latin music is wonderfully different. Then came three sermons—they were in no hurry. Father Pena, who could put the best of evangelical preachers to shame, offered the grace only Jesus gives. Ron Nikkel (who over thirty-three years founded 127 national Prison Fellowships) and I did our best to match his passion. No one wanted it to end until a guard walked in, and with a nod, gave the signal to finish.

Through Latin America and Mexico, Dorestela oversees sixteen countries with sixty-seven hundred volunteers working in many of the twenty-five hundred prisons that hold some 1.2 million prisoners. From a revolutionary teenager, loathing brutal overlords, to being a cabinet minister in a new government, young as she was, in time her restless heart wasn't at rest until it found peace in her living Lord.

As we see conflict breaking up countries, putting one at war with another, we pray, knowing the Spirit is there in the midst of difficulty, always at work where anger and revenge seem to rule, his eye on that one or two he can and will use in the future. There is no place he is not present. Praying for his entrance into such hearts is our cherished privilege and mandate.

There is no heart, regardless of its antipathy, resentment, or flat-out brutality, from which God is absent.

Today's Reading (Dorestela's life verses)

I thank Christ Jesus our Lord, who has given me strength, that he considered me trustworthy, appointing me to his service. Even though I was once a blasphemer and a persecutor and a violent man, I was shown mercy because I acted in ignorance and unbelief. The grace of our Lord was poured out on me abundantly, along with the faith and love that are in Christ Jesus.

Here is a trustworthy saying that deserves full acceptance: Christ Jesus came into the world to save sinners—of whom I am the worst. But for that very reason I was shown mercy so that in me, the worst of sinners, Christ Jesus might display his immense patience as an example for those who would believe in him and receive eternal life. Now to the King eternal, immortal, invisible, the only God, be honor and glory forever and ever. Amen.

1 Timothy 1:12–17

Items for Prayer

- The influence of Prison Fellowship has helped to change the conditions of prison life in Nicaragua. Continue to pray for its volunteers and leaders as they work every week, both with those inside and their families on the outside, who are often the forgotten ones.

- All of Central America is a conduit for drug smuggling. Young people waste their lives as they try to make a living or a fast buck, only then to languish in prison for years. It is to these, among others, that volunteers bring hope and life. Pray for the one-to-one visits so that the Spirit of Christ will reign and bring liberation.

PRAYER

Gracious Lord, we praise you for those your Spirit calls and draws from self-interest into service. Give wisdom and strength to Dorestela as she oversees the thousands of volunteers and leaders in Latin America. May there be a lovefest among Christians for those in prison. May your Word, your call to care for prisoners, be so strong, not only here but also worldwide, that prison officials will see the power of your grace and allow the effective ministry of those so called and gifted. Your kingdom come, we pray, for prisons in this part of the world and everywhere. In your victorious name we give thanks. Amen.

23

INDONESIA

A Jaw-Dropper

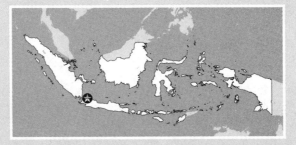

Indonesia is the largest Muslim country in the world. Its land mass is an archipelago, made up of more than 13,000 islands that are home to 700 distinct people groups. For over 300 years the Dutch were its colonial masters, a control broken after WWII.

Its national motto is *Bhinneka Tunggal Ika*—"Unity in Diversity" or "Many Yet One." While it promises religious freedom, with Muslims being 80 percent of the population, there are times and places where Christians are under attack.

Location: Stretched out over the Indian and Pacific Oceans, its neighbors are Papua New Guinea, East Timor, Malaysia, Singapore, the Philippines, and Australia.

Population: 245 million

Religion: Muslim 80%; Christian 16%; Hindu 1%

Dispatch

When I heard of radical Islamists burning down churches in Indonesia and killing Christians, I wasn't prepared to also hear stories of remarkable witness and of surprising enterprise in this incredibly complex country.

Mission work is tough, whether at home or half a world away. Media focus from Indonesia almost exclusively reports killings, persecution, war, and bribery. Little do we learn of what is advancing the Christian faith. Among its thousands of islands, here are two stories.

We visited Kirk and Shelley Kaufeldt, who are on staff at a university in Jakarta. I had heard it was a Christian university and assumed it would be struggling to survive since it is located in a Muslim-majority nation. I've been to Indonesia before and heard the sad stories of Muslim oppression and Christians losing their lives.

As we drove onto the campus, my jaw dropped. The university is stunning, with over 10,000 students. Clearly Christian in format and evangelical in emphasis, it includes a medical training hospital and even an Olympic-size pool. Its leadership has a strategy to build campuses across Indonesia. Capital costs come from the business enterprises of the family responsible for its creation and operation. It charges a reasonable tuition rate—not too high, but enough to ensure that its students are serious. The school is approved by the accrediting authority and has full university status with the Indonesian government.

Following Kirk into the student cafeteria, I asked, "So this is your average Christian center of education in a Muslim-majority world? How did this come about?"

A Family's Vision

It began with a businessman deeply committed to the spread of the gospel, followed by his son who has built a large business enterprise in Indonesia. They chose to make education and medical care their primary ministries. They support primary and secondary schools throughout the islands. The School of Education at the university is reserved for Christians. These students are given full scholarships with their promise that they will spend four years after graduation teaching in one of the associated schools. The Universitas Pelita Harapan (UP) stands for Hope and Light.

Hospitals are developed not as money-making enterprises but to encourage people to cross the barrier of fear of getting medical treatment.

Here, tucked away in the fourth most-populated country in the world is a vision driven by a Christian family and their enterprise to engage their world in the love and message of the Lord, focusing on two areas through which that witness can shine with hope.

An Improbable Requirement

Meet my friend Dr. Chris Marantika, whose story is one of a kind. Unique in its creativity and remarkable in its outcome, it reminds us that in places and times when it seems impossible, the Spirit is building Christ's church.

At twelve years of age, wanting more than what local education could offer, Chris left his island for Java, where through the witness of missionaries, he heard of Christ. After graduating from university, he wanted more and managed entry into the United States, where he completed his seminary training.

After hearing him at a pastors' conference in the seminary in Yogyakarta, a city north of the capital, Jakarta, I asked how the seminary had developed. When he returned home from his overseas study, he decided the best way to help build the church in Indonesia would be to plant churches. Since that plan needed pastors, he began the evangelical seminary.

Here is what I found to be ingenious. A condition of graduation was that each student would be required to plant a church of thirty new adult converts. No transfers counted. Under the banner of Vision Indonesia and the slogan "1:1:1," Chris called people to work and pray. The numbers stand for one church, in each village and town, in one generation. Thus the seminary's mantra: "1:1:1."

I visited a church planted by a graduate. Driving into the jungle, as we turned off the narrow road, we saw a newly built church. I asked the pastor how they were able to erect it in the middle of an Islamic community. Here was their creative strategy. They decided to work with criminals using this logic: If Islamic leaders saw criminals transformed by Christ and their lives changed, they might be more hospitable in allowing them to start a church.

And that's what happened. In time, Muslim leaders saw criminals reformed and living at peace, and so they welcomed the seminary students to build a church, and even gave them land. Wanting to foster a continuing and welcoming presence, they asked the Muslim elders if they could begin a midweek service. This was allowed.

"So, what about Sunday services?" I asked. "That will come," the pastor promised. "But why not now?" I asked. "We will continue to minister and see conversions, and in time the elders will want us to have our Christian Sunday services" was the response.

A reminder that the Spirit is always about his work in places we least suspect.

TODAY'S READING

How abundant are the good things that you have stored up for those who fear you, that you bestow in the sight of all, on those who take refuge in you. In the shelter of your presence you hide them from all human intrigues; you keep them safe in your dwelling from accusing tongues.

Psalm 31:19–20

ITEMS FOR PRAYER

- While it's important that we hear stories of effective outreach, please continue to pray for the protection and well-being of those in Indonesia who face danger at the forefront, leading churches and missions.
- Pray for these two centers of training, among the many sprinkled across the islands, and for teachers as they inspire their students to follow Christ.
- In a land so dominated by a religious majority, and given the danger of radical groups rising up in jihad, pray for wisdom and grace among its political leadership that the country will continue to foster peace among its many social, political, and religious groups.

PRAYER

Dear Father, as you cast your eyes across the wide expanse of this land of Indonesia, we know your heart is drawn to its people, so varied, kind, and resilient, yet so needy. Your call is for all to hear of the living and giving truth of your Son, our Lord Jesus. Today, as we visualize this land and its people, we pray for the training of younger men and women. Continue to bless the many training centers in Indonesia. Within this new generation, fire hearts of younger leaders with courage and a strong pull to be centered in you so they can lead the nation for your glory. Amen.

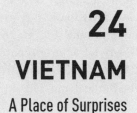

24

VIETNAM

A Place of Surprises

Vietnam became a household word because of its war.

For a millennium, Vietnam was part of China, but in time it became independent. Colonized by the French in the mid-1800s, Japan briefly was occupier (1940s) but was thrown out by France. In 1954, the French were expelled and the country divided into the north and south, two areas locked in deep conflict and hostility, with the United States intervening but forced to leave in 1975. Today, both the north and south are under an authoritarian Communist government.

Location: China lies to the north, Laos is to the northwest, Cambodia borders to the southwest, and the South China Sea is to the east.

Population: 90 million

Religion: Buddhist 52%; Christian 10% (Roman Catholics the majority); ethno-religionist 8%

Dispatch

Vietnam is a name and country that for many triggers memories of war, communism, control, persecution, and death. This land and people are complex and its stories many. We will spend two devotional chapters in this land. Vietnam is one of five remaining socialistic dictatorships ruled by Communist ideology, circumscribing its assumptions and demands.

Not surprisingly it is a country of contradictions that were made infamous by wars with the French and the Americans. The "domino theory" was the popular explanation for war in the 1960s and 1970s, an attempt to prevent the Chinese and Vietnamese from extending Communist rule throughout Southeast Asia. Being closed to Christianity for so many years, I assumed the gospel was underground. I found that it is and it isn't.

My first stereotype was shattered outside of Ho Chi Minh City, still called Saigon by many. We arrived at the campus of the Biblical and Theological Institute of the Evangelical Church of Vietnam-South (ECVN/S), a denomination still often called C&MA (Christian and Missionary Alliance). To the left I saw a multistory building housing classrooms and administration for 150 students. To my right was a seven-story student residence with a second under construction. In front of me was a three-thousand-seat church also under construction—all of this going on in a communist country that continues to enforce unpredictable and contradictory laws.

The other side of the story is the control the government has over all matters religious—a one-party government shaped by Communist-materialistic ideology. My prudent friends reminded me not to be lulled into thinking the government has gone soft on Christianity. They had many stories describing the quick and harsh reminders of who is boss.

Yet within these polarities, Christian faith is pulsating through varying contradictions: unease with government, conflicts and division within the Christian community, and a country seeking to emerge from the wars of the past. I was to learn from those who might be put in jeopardy if I mentioned their names.

Background

About two-thirds of the Protestant church (also called the Tin Lanh church) is made up of the Evangelical Church of Vietnam (ECVN). Started by the Christian and Missionary Alliance in 1911, it is, in effect, the traditional church. It has been divided into two separate operating denominations (north and south) since 1954. Although they want to reunite, the government interferes—a reminder of the delicate balance leaders must maintain in order to keep their people out of the crosshairs of governmental (police) action.

There are many small denominations, which reflect people's cultural mistrust, or choice, to create their own independent church or group of churches. At times these have been financially supported by well-meaning Westerners. There are eighty denominations; twenty-seven are members of the southern Vietnam Evangelical Fellowship; twelve belong to the northern Hanoi Christian Fellowship.

The term *denomination* is often an overstatement, as it may mean just a few house churches led by a strong pastor, and which may fade away once his presence is diminished.

Also, the term *house church* is often a figure of speech. We rode down a river in the Mekong Delta in a dugout to meet a pastor of a house church. We stepped onto the dock and saw a beautiful church building, seating over one hundred people. I exclaimed, "I thought we were visiting a house church!" We are, I was told. A Korean donor wanted them to have a chapel. Not looking like a house church to me, it still is counted as one.

The term *house church* does not always refer to where a congregation meets. Most often it means a congregation that is not registered with the government. Many house churches meet in a large house so as to avoid being shut down. Most house churches have 30 to 150 in attendance. Some build without government permission, while others work at getting it. There is a drive to build churches in order to give cultural presence to their faith. Usually it is only congregations worshiping in a church-type building that are shown to foreigners.

The soul of the Vietnamese people has not been lost. Its Christian witness is led by pastors and leaders, fearless yet wise. Their story is just being told.

Today's Reading

May the Lord answer you when you are in distress; may the name of the God of Jacob protect you. May he send you help from his sanctuary and grant you support from Zion. May he remember all your sacrifices and accept your burnt offerings. May he give you the desire of your heart and make all your plans succeed. May we shout for joy over your victory and lift up our banners in the name of our God. May the LORD grant all your requests. . . . Some trust in chariots and some in horses, but we trust in the name of the LORD our God.

Psalm 20:1–5, 7

ITEMS FOR PRAYER

- Living under a Communist regime creates mistrust and fear of others. Pray that within the leadership of churches and Christian missions in Vietnam there will be a spirit of peace and trust, so that the life of Christ will be manifest to the society and its political and social leaders.
- Bibles continue to be needed to advance the gospel witness and nurture the people of God. Pray especially for the release of Bibles in the various languages of ethnic groups in Vietnam.
- Among the mountain tribal people, there has been a remarkable growth of the church. While the government often harasses these people, pray for their protection and for leaders from these groups who would raise a dynamic and forceful witness for Christ.

PRAYER

Gracious Lord and God, we have learned that often out of suffering, deprivation, and persecution your church rises in strength. The people of Vietnam have not only known years of war, but continue to feel intermittent harassment by its government. First, we pray for Christians, that their faith would be strong and their commitment to Christ clear and uncompromising. We also pray for a reversal of government incursion that persecutes your people. Our trust is in you, that your Spirit will bring to this land a continuing flow of ministry that will surprise even the most agnostic. In your wonderful and mighty name, we pray. Amen.

25

VIETNAM— EVANGELIST NICK

Serendipity Redefined

In the previous chapter, we learned something of Vietnam's makeup and challenges. Today we visit a moment in time, serendipitous and remarkable, with evidence of the surprising activity of the Spirit in places we would think unlikely.

Dispatch

Early one afternoon we arrived at the Hanoi offices of the Ministry of Public Security (police overseeing all Vietnam). For two hours we exchanged candid and competing ideas with a corporal, chief of the division that oversees religion. This meeting was arranged by evangelical church leaders in Hanoi, seeking direct contact with senior police officials who handle matters related to religious freedom.

Attending the corporal was their translator and a party official, on hand to review what both sides said. We had our translator to ensure that our words were correctly translated. Cordially they shared tea and fruit, beginning with pleasantries and chatter about the country, the city of Hanoi, and our experiences as visitors. My being a Canadian helped in that my nationality didn't invoke feelings of historical conflict.

After the small talk, the corporal asked if we had concerns as to how Christians were being treated by his government. It was an inviting question, not defensive or protective. I pointed out that Christians (and here I spoke specifically of Evangelicals) in Vietnam were part of a worldwide body of more than 600 million. I noted that as Vietnam was entering into global trade associations, how they handled religious freedom was now in the open. They are now under the scrutiny of the United Nations, which would do due diligence on their laws and behavior and make those reports public.

Coincidently, that very week, at the United Nations, the Universal Periodic Review (UPR) presented its findings of Vietnam. The UPR challenged Vietnam's newly enacted Decree ND-92, which requires that before a religious group receives full legal recognition, they must have operated for twenty years with local approval, without any violation. This, of course, puts enormous burden on churches wanting to register.

Further, the UPR noted that a few weeks earlier, Hoang Van Ngai, a thirty-nine-year-old Christian, died while in police custody. Since he was an elder of the Evangelical Church of Vietnam-South, the commission noted that the probable reason he died was because he "refused to participate in corruption. . . . He was savagely beaten and tortured by the police." The police reported that the cause of his death was "suicide by self-electrocution."

I noted these issues with the corporal, and for two hours we discussed religious freedom and their obligation to bring fairness and justice to their own people.

A Surprising Event

In the middle of our conversation, another story was unfolding in this very city, a story that only a novelist's imagination might create—an event beyond what Christians in Vietnam could have prayed for happened.

As Lily and I drove to that afternoon appointment, we noticed billboards advertising public meetings with Nick Vujicic, an evangelist from Australia. Nick is not your average evangelist. Born with tetra-amelia syndrome, a rare disorder characterized by the absence of all four limbs, his physical feats are nearly unbelievable. Now a father, he has taught himself mobility and dexterity that you must see to believe.

The morning newspaper carried front-page coverage of his meeting the previous night in the Hanoi stadium. For a full week he had traveled throughout Vietnam, speaking to packed stadiums. All the while he was careful to follow the agreed-upon arrangements with the Vietnamese officials that he wouldn't speak about faith, only about hope and overcoming one's disabilities.

The night before, as he had done in cities and towns up and down the land, he told of his own challenges in growing up, having to overcome impossible physical circumstances. The nation was caught up in his story, buying his T-shirts and posters.

As he was coming to the end of his presentation, with the state television cameras broadcasting to millions, he asked a young girl on stage, who, like himself, had been born without limbs, "Do you know why I love God?" He answered his own question: "Because heaven is real. And one day, when we get to heaven, we are going to have arms and legs. And we are going to run, and we are going play, and we are going to race." Media reported, "Participants burst into tears." This moment of testimony was carried nationwide.

This surprise departure from the agreed-upon speech caught the television network unaware. His testimony found its home in millions of hearers.

How Did This Come About?

I asked a pastor how this could have happened here in Vietnam. It all began with Le Phuoc Vu, a devout Buddhist and one of Vietnam's wealthiest tycoons, chair of a business group called Hoa Sen that had partnered with First News and government-owned Vietnam Television (VTV). Joining in this venture was a Roman Catholic layman and a Communist party official. They invited Nick to speak across the nation to its young people on how to overcome disabilities.

Yes, here in a communist country, an Australian evangelist, funded by a Buddhist businessman, filled stadiums with his speeches carried on a state-run television network. To add to his public address, newspapers crooned his praises.

As we neared the end of our conversation, I asked the corporal of security what he thought of it all. He too knew what the newspapers had been saying about this remarkable young man. I asked, "Does that kind of faith in the risen Christ trouble you? Are you afraid of Christians being citizens? Wouldn't you want those who love to inspire and care for those in need to be your citizens?" Only a smile was forthcoming.

This state is tough and often unyielding. Officials allow scattered opportunities for faith to sprout, yet at will they deny religious freedom. However, in this moment the unexpected had occurred.

This land, fought over by the French and Americans and pockmarked by bombings, is alive today because of its hardworking people. Contradictions stand out. The church grows, yet is pushed off stride by police interference. While it is not a simple situation, the footprints of the Spirit can be seen in many places and lives.

Reg Reimer, author of *Vietnam's Christians: A Century of Growth in Adversity*, wrote a fitting epitaph to this most remarkable week: "Nick accomplished the goals of the event organizers and then some! From a Christian perspective, there could not have been any better preparation of the soil for the gospel. This evangelist tilled and exposed fields ready to plant."

TODAY'S READING

Blessed is the one who does not walk in step with the wicked or stand in the way that sinners take or sit in the company of mockers, but whose delight is in the law of the LORD, and who meditates on his law day and night. That person is like a tree planted by streams of water, which yields its fruit in season and whose leaf does not wither—whatever they do prospers.

Psalm 1:1–3

ITEMS FOR PRAYER

- As remarkable as this story is, life as a Christian in Vietnam can be tough and challenging. Pray for spiritual resilience and courage so that seeds planted will find soil, be rooted, and grow for multiple harvests.

- Young people are everywhere, business is growing, and optimism for the future seems strong. Yet such a small number of Vietnamese know Christ. Pray for a spiritual move in the land, a rising consciousness of the need for forgiveness, healing, and promise of eternal life.
- In Vietnam you can feel the energy and drive of its people. It will again become a dynamic country in the region. What a wonderful testimony it could be of the gospel and its power and ability to bring about transformation. Pray for those children and young people who soon will be leading the country, that the Spirit will foster faith and nurture them into strength and godly servanthood.

PRAYER

Father, I celebrate your special leading in Nick's witness, as he ably uses his disability as a powerful instrument of faith and hope. Bless him in his many appearances, keeping him safe and true. And for the young people of Vietnam, Father, I lift them in prayer, asking that you will raise up exemplary younger leaders, who, in knowing their own land and people, will be strong in their declaration of your kingdom life. Preserve them from harassment and persecution so they may freely make known your name and your love to all. Amen.

26

KAZAKHSTAN

Landlocked but Finding Freedom of Faith

Kazakhstan is the largest landlocked country and ninth largest land mass in the world. Since the 1700s it has been influenced and often controlled by Russia or the Soviet Empire. It was the last of Soviet territories to proclaim independence. Complicated by 131 ethnicities, the Russian language has equal status with the Kazakh language.

Location: south of Russia, touching Mongolia and China to the east, and bordered on the south by the many "stans" of central Asia

Population: 16 million

Religion: Muslim 54%; nonreligious 34%; Christian 12% (Orthodox 10%, Roman Catholic 1%, Evangelical 1%)

Dispatch

Chances are you haven't visited this central Asian country or heard much about it apart from seeing it on television as Russian crews land from the space station. Much like Alberta or Montana, sweeping wheat fields kiss high-peaked mountains. Huge in landmass, but with a small population, this country of crisscrossing cultures has survived invasions and domination of China and Russia for seven hundred years. Today it stands at the edge of a remarkable time of development.

Its life with and alongside Russia is a defining dynamic. While the country is Kazak, one-third of the population is Russian.

Indigenous Kazaks rub shoulders with Russian Kazaks, which creates its own kind of tension. These are not lessened by their 6,846-kilometer common border with Russia on the north. In the 1930s, hundreds of thousands of Kazaks died under Stalin's purge in gulags known as Karlags.

Their religion could be called "Muslim lite," since the prevailing influence continues to be shamanism (worship of ancestral spirits). During forty years of Communist rule, Christian faith was severely repressed. The fall of the Soviet Union in 1991, and subsequent independence for many of its satellite countries, triggered an outbreak of Christian growth. In Kazakhstan it is estimated that there were a hundred thousand Christian converts from 1993 to 1997, along with an inrush of seven hundred missionaries.

In 2011, the government enacted a bill, forcing missionaries out and requiring churches to regroup into larger congregations. This resulted in almost halving the number of churches. Colleges and seminaries too were closed. While there is freedom to live as a Christian, this law makes ministry more complex. Almost anything you want to do is inhibited by red tape. As I visit countries and cultures, most often people are my best windows to understanding.

Meet Two Pastors

Ahaman Egizbaev was born to Kazak parents, both senior Soviet apparatchiks (officials in the Soviet-run Kazak bureaucracy). Being Kazak, they were considered Muslim. After studying engineering in Moscow, Ahaman took a job in Kazakhstan. One day his driver gave him C. S. Lewis's *Mere Christianity*. Raised in a materialistic ideology, Ahaman had no clue on matters of faith. Yet when he read it, he said, "I dropped to my knees, confessed my sins to Christ. I got up not only united with God but freed instantly from my addictions."

When his father heard, he retorted, "You can't be Christian, you're Muslim"—this from a father who had never taken him to a mosque or introduced him to Islam.

Ahaman's curiosity led him to study at a local Bible college and then at ACTS, an interdenominational college in Seoul, Korea. He learned pastoral skills and English, and there discovered a deep desire to return to his homeland as a missionary. Even though he was with his own Kazak people, he didn't speak their language—he knew only Russian. Growing up in a communist home immersed in the Soviet/Russian culture, he had no occasion to learn of his Kazak heritage. Today he pastors a Kazak church with a vision to open a Christian university and seminary. He also serves as general secretary for the Evangelical Alliance of Kazakhstan.

Yerkin Khaidarov is a young pastor who also came from a non-practicing Muslim world, but his was radically different. He was a teenager in the 1980s, a time when drugs ran freely from Afghanistan north through his city of Almaty to Russia. By the time he entered college he was an addict. His father, desperate to free his son, tried every possible therapy and medical treatment. One day he heard of Teen Challenge, a ministry for freeing those trapped by drug addiction. Though it was Christian, he decided being a Muslim wouldn't stop him from grasping at any straw.

He met Doug Boyle, an Australian Assemblies of God missionary, himself a former addict, who had founded Teen Challenge in Kazakhstan. The first visit was almost too much for Yerkin, especially when he learned that he would have to go off drugs cold turkey.

He agreed, but mandatory daily chapel attendance was too much and he ran away, living for two years on the streets. Eventually his father confronted him: "Son, you either go back to Teen Challenge or leave our home. On the streets, you'll die an early death or end up in prison. Your choice."

Cornered, Yerkin returned to Teen Challenge, and eighteen months later left as a graduate. Today he pastors nine churches in which many are graduates of Teen Challenge and are in turn rescuing others. There he met his Armenian wife, Madlen, a musician.

What Lies Ahead?

This country of beauty, rough and raw in its early days of modernizing, has made a remarkable economic leap forward. Young and resourceful men and women are leading the evangelical church, learning to negotiate the tightrope of politics. However, the church is divided generationally. Both Baptists and Pentecostals are split between the older and younger: the older, reinforced by an aging fundamentalism, and the younger, charismatics, praying and pressing for growth and new churches and ministries.

While in Almaty, I met leaders from surrounding countries (Tajikistan, Kyrgyzstan, Uzbekistan, Turkmenistan, Azerbaijan, Georgia, and Iran). Many are facing the same kinds of issues as Kazakhstan, and they had gathered for their annual two days of prayer and fasting. They're joining in a common cause: building an evangelical alliance in their countries and creating a central Asia alliance. Their strength is that they share many common resources; their cultures have similar crossovers and most speak Russian. They all know what it was like to live under Soviet dominance, and they understand the rough-and-tumble nature of surviving in Islamic-dominant lands. The building of friendships, developing common training, exchanging resources, and mutually nurturing their churches make good sense.

Here kingdom possibilities grab my attention. This region might very well be on the brink of a major spiritual advance. Creative and prayer-bathed evangelism can bring life to a people hungering for what the old materialism failed to offer and what a nominal Muslim faith lacks. A modest amount of outside resources can make an enormous impact. Prayer focused on this country and its people will multiply as the Spirit brings a consciousness of the risen Christ.

TODAY'S READING

May the mountains bring prosperity to the people, the hills the fruit of righteousness. May he defend the afflicted among the people and save the children of the needy; may he crush the oppressor. May he endure as long as the sun, as long as the moon, through all generations. May he be like rain falling on a mown field, like showers watering the earth. In his days may the righteous flourish and prosperity abound till the moon is no more.

Psalm 72:3–7

ITEMS FOR PRAYER

- After the government's restrictive law in 2011, most missionaries left Kazakhstan, taking with them the support provided from their home-sending countries. This resulted in a precipitous loss of funds for nationals and their ministries. Pray for generosity of support from outside and a growing obedience of giving internally.
- There is a vital need for the raising up of training centers for pastors and leaders. It is important for a pastor to have a recognized certificate or degree. Pray for their initiative in building indigenous colleges and seminaries.
- It really matters that the Evangelical churches have official recognition from the government. Pray for wisdom for its leaders as they facilitate their ministries and churches in operating within a complex political and social world.

PRAYER

Father, Creator of lands where the beauty of nature and resources of the earth are magnificent reminders of your creative power, we lift our voices in prayer. Today we pray for our brothers and sisters in Kazakhstan, living in such a spectacular vista of land, yet often pressed on all sides by anti-religion forces and other faiths. We pray for institutions where coming leaders can learn of your Word and be trained in spiritual leadership. As well, give leaders grace and wisdom as they walk the winding, uneven roads of political and civic recognition, all for the sake of being free to make known your life and truth to the people of this land you so love. We pray this in faith, in the name of Jesus Christ. Amen.

27

THAILAND

The Power of Indigenous Leadership

Thailand (formerly called Siam) is a monarchy, the current king having served since 1946. Thailand has never been ruled by a Western power. Its political system is rife with inner conflict and division.

Location: Southeast Asia, as part of the Indochina Peninsula, surrounded on the south by the Gulf of Thailand, on the west by the Andaman Sea and the countries of Myanmar/Burma, Laos, and Cambodia

Population: 70 million

Religion: Buddhism 85%; Muslim 8%; Christian 1%

Dispatch

As I visit countries, meeting leaders, pastors, and people from all walks of life, I'm intrigued to learn each country's spiritual health, struggles, and some of their stories.

In Thailand one question kept surfacing. Speaking with pastors, educators, and mission leaders, I heard it time and time again. I wanted to understand the question in its context—a land of lush landscape, neighborhoods remarkably clean, and people incredibly respectful and kind. My question is this: After all the people, money, and years invested in missions, why is the Christian church here so small?

Thailand, one of Southeast Asia's "Tigers," while looking somewhat like Malaysia and Myanmar/Burma, is as different as Canada is from the U.S. or Sweden is from Germany. Never colonized, in the nineteenth century it negotiated land for freedom to keep out of the clutches of France and Great Britain, unlike Vietnam, Laos, Myanmar, and Cambodia. Today, its national personality avoids conflict, all the while keeping face and not losing position.

National pride is palpable. Pictures of the king—the longest reigning monarch—and the queen dot the landscape. Politicians may be vilified, but if one dares to offer criticisms of its royalty, the gentle Thai will rise in defense. Royalty is linked to nationalism. It didn't take but a few minutes in a major museum to hear their unqualified patriotism while describing the greatness of their nation, its leaders, history, and people. While national Christian leaders tend to be modest, that shifts direction when it comes to pride in their nation.

Completing the trilogy of national character, along with royalty and nationalism, is their religion, Buddhism. Thais are expected to be Buddhist. To adhere to another religion is viewed as rejecting one's nationhood, tantamount to denying one's identity. It's not surprising that evangelism has to buck this profound synthesis of nation, religion, and person.

Their fixation on Buddhism is powerful and overwhelming. More than the presence of temples and the role of temple attendance, what dominates is a consciousness of the spirit world. For the Thai, the presence and role of spirits is a profound influence. Everywhere there are spirit houses, small shrines outside of homes, offices, restaurants, and other places of business, and amulets hanging in taxis. Its core application is the appeasing of spirits.

But back to my question: After more than 180 years of evangelical missionary work, investments of thousands of lives and millions of dollars, out of a total population of 65 million, why are there only 370,000 evangelical Christians: one-half of one percent?

Since these numbers seem discouraging, I asked Dr. Wiracha Kowae, chair of the Evangelical Fellowship of Thailand (EFT), why he was optimistic. He noted five important changes.

- First, foreigners no longer run the Thai church. As in China, he sees the church having three mandates: self-governing, self-propagating, and self-funding. In China the Cultural Revolution regrettably repressed all religions; even so, the Christian church there became strong by the power and creative genius of its indigenous leadership to run its own affairs, to be the force driving evangelistic outreach, and to be responsible in funding their own efforts.

- As the Thai have moved from the rural areas to the cities, the old ways made rigid by a lack of education and loyalty to their religion are shaken, opening minds to other views and sets of values.

- Dr. Kowae noted that Pastor Yonggi Cho from South Korea helped them realize how much they were limiting what God could do. It became a wake-up call to pastors. In the past, in planning for their church buildings, they hadn't included parking lots, as it never occurred to them that their members would own cars.

- Critical to growth is the need to cultivate a culture of generosity. "Without that, spiritual renewal is unlikely," he said. Lacking generosity and little outward look for missions, churches remain moribund and listless. He noted that missionaries in the past assumed that Thais didn't have much to give, and so they weren't challenged. They came to feel that because the gospel was free, there was no need to give materially. Dr. Kowae links giving to a vision for missions. Resting in the comfort of being recipients of the generosity of others created dependence and kept the Thais from learning the art and practice of the gift of generosity.

- A curious development has given Christians a more visible place in the eyes of government. As Muslims in Thailand grew, they increased their cultural demands. Killings in three southern provinces by Islamists moved the government to be more supportive of Christians, now not seen as a threat to the nation. For the Christian community to be more positively viewed by a majority-Buddhist country helps to frame how Christians and their beliefs are understood.

The optimism of national church leadership is rooted in a reliance on indigenous leadership: national churches, colleges, seminaries, and missions led by Thais.

Enoch is an example. A former student communist agitator who was almost killed in the 1977 coup, he came to faith and today leads a national movement that trains volunteers to disciple others.

A Power for Living study found that Thais didn't find the names *Jesus* and *God* objectionable, one reason some had assumed the gospel has made only a modest impact. They then invited people to make a phone call to receive a book, estimating a couple hundred thousand would call. Surprisingly, 2.9 million did.

Thailand is a country to watch. Overshadowed by Buddhism and a culture that assumes being Thai and Buddhist are one and the same, how will this current vision break through barriers that have so bridled the gospel?

Thailand may be on the verge of a new breakthrough both in vision and witness, led by its own people, funded increasingly by its own people, and expanding by their own efforts—a challenging mission plan.

TODAY'S READING

I love you, O LORD, my strength. The LORD is my rock, my fortress and my deliverer; my God is my rock, in whom I take refuge, my shield and the horn of my salvation, my stronghold. I called to the LORD, who is worthy of praise, and I am saved from my enemies. . . . You save the humble but bring low those whose eyes are haughty. You, LORD, keep my lamp burning; my God turns my darkness into light. With your help I can advance against a troop; with my God I can scale a wall. As for God, his way is perfect: The LORD's word is flawless; he shields all who take refuge in him.

Psalm 18:1–3, 27–30

ITEMS FOR PRAYER

• Let's offer thanks for the many who over the years have served faithfully in this land. Thailand's leadership is in the hands of its own people today. Pray for the Spirit to destroy strongholds, backed in faith by men and women who, in prayer, will not be fooled by cultural missteps but will be wise in grace and truth.

- Christian education is critical in all lands for the advancement of the gospel. Thailand is a country of the young. Pray that universities, colleges, and other places of training will be vibrant in spiritual aptitude to equip graduates with knowledge of the Lord and his Word and experience in serving Christ in the church and the marketplace.

- Every country is challenged to discover the meeting place of culture and the gospel. Pray for wise minds and sensitive hearts that can help leadership and Christians understand how the life and word of Jesus speaks into their language, culture, and life experience.

- The presence of the spirit world inhabits the people. Pray for spiritual renewal to set people free from bondage and find liberty, which only Christ can bring.

PRAYER

Spirit of God, you bring the light of the truth of Jesus into our darkness. Your life-giving presence lifts us from our fears and releases us from cultural and spiritual containments. With this in mind, we pray for Thailand and its pastors, leaders, and king. We know the power of giving helps loose us from ourselves, as we see others and their needs. For Thai Christians, may this important gift of generosity become active and life-giving. May the seed sown over these many years find ready soil in which your kingdom will grow and bring peace and life to this great land. Amen.

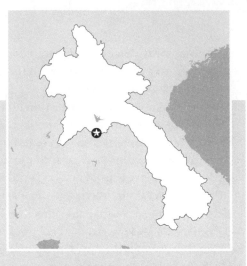

28
LAOS
Standing on Holy Ground

The **Lao People's Democratic Republic** is one of five remaining socialist states run by a single party with a distinctly communist heritage and ruling ideology. The others are China, Cuba, Vietnam, and North Korea. The Laotian government came to power in 1975 under the Communist Pathet Lao movement.

Location: in Southeast Asia, surrounded by Myanmar (Burma), Vietnam to the east, Cambodia on the south, to the west Thailand, and to the north China

Population: 6.5 million

Religion: Buddhist 66%; Christian 1.5%; Other 30%

Dispatch

Visiting countries with recent histories of dictatorships and war, I'm amazed that people live in hope even while suffering single-party governments and/or dominant religions, and in some cases atheism. There exist in these countries complex realities, which if described to an outside world might create hardship for those living in those countries and active in ministry. My calling is to discern the footprints of the Spirit, not to be an investigative reporter. Those who know more about what is going on here than what I am able to say will understand that often discretion conditions my preference for candor.

What makes this country distinct religiously is that all Protestant communities are grouped by law under one denomination called the Laos Evangelical Church (LEC), which was formed in

1956, and in 1960 given legal status. From 1975 to 1990, the LEC had little outside contact, as Laos remained a "closed" country. In 1990, that changed, and the LEC was given proprietorship for almost all Protestant denominations.

The government then permitted churches to form: the Roman Catholic Church, the Seventh-day Adventist Church (a thousand members), and the Laos Evangelical Church, now with a hundred thousand church members. The government requires churches to be registered under one of these three bodies.

Protestant ministries began late in the nineteenth century, and in the 1920s, missionaries arrived, mainly from North America. During Communist rule, 1975 to 1990, Christian activity was greatly curtailed. A law known as Decree 92, passed in 2002, outlines what religious groups can and can't do. Under this decree, the LEC has remarkable influence.

The LEC

What makes this country unique is that the evangelical group LEC has been granted by a socialist, one-party government the sole right to represent the Protestant world. Thus all Methodist, Anglican/Episcopal, Baptist, Assemblies of God/Pentecostal, and Lutheran churches come under its banner.

It is extraordinary that a government with its communist history gives official recognition to an evangelical group with authority to plant and operate churches within defined borders of freedom. The LEC president and his associates lobby on behalf of new church plants and speak on matters of religious repression. They provide political cover for their churches and people, ensuring a political tie to the all-important party apparatus. The significance of LEC was highlighted when I learned that it is a "red stamp" organization, which in essence makes it akin to a department of the government.

While this system has its own inherent weaknesses, many house churches often find their way into relationship with the LEC because of the political covering it offers. Operating within one of the five last surviving communist countries, this church structure is unparalleled.

Holy Ground

One evening over dinner, my wife, Lily, and I heard from a woman from the countryside, well educated and with extensive experience, talk about her passion to provide education in some of the most primitive villages. Living there alone, in conditions in which most of us wouldn't spend a night, her anticipation of this project was riveting. As we left dinner that evening, we agreed that we had been on holy ground.

We hear story after story of men, women, young people, and young and middle-aged couples with so much to gain by staying home who respond to the Lord's call to leave their homes for distant lands. Today the Holy Spirit is still selecting some of the finest. Their courage and seemingly reckless faith are beyond what most of us will experience.

As we pray for the world, let's keep in mind the wider picture of the work being done. New and creative approaches are being tested. Extensive use of technology now enables many to reach into the most obscure places. But it begins and ends with competent leaders who have a will to go. Only a small percentage can do so. In our prayer and giving, let's find those few and make them our daily focus of prayer.

Be generous. Support them before they have to ask. We will be changed as they become our means of being Christ to the world.

Today's Reading

Who may ascend the mountain of the LORD? Who may stand in his holy place? The one who has clean hands and a pure heart, who does not trust in an idol or swear by a false god. They will receive blessing from the LORD and vindication from God their Savior. Such is the generation of those who seek him, who seek your face, God of Jacob.

Psalm 24:3–6

Items for Prayer

- The political arrangement in which the Laotian government requires all Evangelical/Protestants to work under one denomination is a challenge. Pray for its leadership and the important work of planting churches and speaking out for those under the LEC banner.

- In 1975, when the communists took over, most pastors left the country. Pray for the recruiting and training of pastoral leadership.

- We met younger visionary missionaries who, in creative initiatives, are doing important work. Pray for those who must be unnamed (for their security), that their outreach will be given freedom by the government and that needed resources will become available.

PRAYER

Father, we know how small nations, without power or presence on the world scene, can easily get lost, forgotten in the noise and clamor of places of extreme need. Today we lift before you Laos, this small country in Southeast Asia, and pray for the pastors and the leadership of the various churches and mission agencies at work. For this teacher we met, protect her and overwhelm her with your love as she serves in education. Father, give wisdom and grace to the LEC, its leaders, and associated churches and ministries, that together they will exercise faith and spiritual discernment. May the redeeming presence of your gospel result in the planting of new churches and the coming to faith of many Laotians. Amen.

29

LEBANON

A Country Squeezed by Neighbors

An ancient maritime civilization, **Lebanon** was the home of the Phoenicians and later ruled by the Romans. In time, it was a major center of the Maronite Church. Arab Muslims moved in, and the Druze became a religious and political force.

The Turks (Ottoman Empire) ruled for over 600 years. After WWI, France took over until the country's independence in 1943. The Lebanese Civil War (1975–1990) brought great disruption. Since the beginning of the Syrian collapse in 2011, it has become a major center in caring for Syrian refugees.

Location: on the eastern shore of the Mediterranean, surrounded by Israel to the south and Syria to the east and north.

Population: 4.5 million

Religion: Muslim 59%; Christian 32% (mostly Roman Catholic Maronite, with a small minority Evangelical church)

Dispatch

Lebanon is a country of great beauty, lying between mountains to the east and the blue sea and sandy beaches of the Mediterranean on the west. Roman ruins, remarkable in their extent and preservation, sit alongside the sea just south of Beirut. It is one of my favorite countries, and I introduce you to this fragile country for your prayers.

A place of remarkable and turbulent history, it is a refuge for fleeing Syrians. In its southern region, it hosts one of Israel's enemies, the Hezbollah. Planted in Lebanon's flag is the historic reminder that the cedar tree and Lebanon go hand in hand. It was

Solomon who eyed its magnificent and resilient cedars for building the temple in Jerusalem.

While ancient, during the twentieth century Lebanon was rejigged following WWI, making it an uncertain political entity, as Syria to its east pushed its presence, operating as if Lebanon were but its extension.

As John Segarian, regional director for Youth for Christ, and I moved about, he was careful where he drove and cautious about what we said publicly. The Lebanese, having survived wars and many rumors, speak in quiet tones, wondering if listening ears are plotting nefarious schemes.

Prized as the jewel of the Mediterranean, Beirut is the choice city for money from oil billions in the Gulf. Until the civil wars of the late twentieth century, it was the city of choice for lifestyle, opportunity, and political freedom.

A Brief History

Centuries before Christ, the Lebanese were pioneers in coastal trading, their marine culture stimulating trade, bringing riches and envy. Conquered by Persia (Iran) and later Rome, in the first century AD, Lebanon became central to the spread of the gospel. When Muslim Arabs took over in the seventh century, the Maronites hung on. Because Lebanon was on the path of the Crusaders, in time the connection with France became a strong influence.

Following WWI, as European powers divided up much of the world, France changed Lebanon's borders, which shifted the religious mix. In 1926, Christians made up 84 percent; today they are closer to 30 percent.

Lebanon's constitution is based on religious powers, a remarkable feat—to build a country and its ruling bodies around religious sectarianism. The president has to be Christian and the prime minister always Sunni Muslim. The president can veto legislation. Even though Muslims now outnumber Christians, the earlier formula, based on a balance of Christians and Muslims, remains.

153

For decades Lebanon has been a political punching bag. Tens of thousands of Palestinians flooded in after the 1967 Arab-Israeli War. Between 1975 and 1990, civil war raged and 100,000 died. Syria then used Lebanon to get at Israel, supplying arms to Hezbollah in the south. Israel retaliated. The Syrian collapse has pressed over one million refugees into bulging camps in the north and throughout the Beq'ua Valley.

A new government led by Rafiq Hariri began rebuilding. But on February 21, 2005, a massive bomb killed Hariri, fingers pointing directly to Syria as the assassin.

In praying today for Lebanon, I wanted you to have this historical overview so that you might see what Lebanon faces. While Evangelicals are not implicated in the political trade-off between Maronite Christians and Sunni Muslims, the precarious environment requires strategic thinking in living between the factions. At any moment an unexpected move could destabilize the tenuous arrangements of life and liberty.

Its Important Location

Lebanon is strategically located and, given its strong Christian history, it has been a place from which the gospel has moved into other countries in the region. Today, as in Egypt and the West Bank, Christians are leaving in large numbers, looking for countries where their families can grow in peaceful and opportunistic surroundings. Estimates are that one-third call themselves Christians, with a small minority being Evangelical/Protestant.

Today, resolute and committed leadership presses outward the witness of Christ in church planting, pastoral training, youth missions, and extensive human care, especially with its large number of refugees.

The Syrian debacle will continue. Hezbollah in the south will be used as an irritant to Israel. Its Muslim divide of Shia and Sunni will add to its explosive nature.

The politics of this stubborn yet fragile region will come and go, expanding and contracting as its neighbors attempt to impose their will. But in the Middle East, Lebanon will continue as a location from which the gospel can be released. It is a region we must not forget in our prayers.

TODAY'S READING

Ascribe to the LORD the glory due his name; worship the LORD in the splendor of his holiness. . . . The voice of the LORD is powerful; the voice of the LORD is majestic. The voice of the LORD breaks the cedars; the LORD breaks in pieces the cedars of Lebanon. He makes Lebanon skip like a calf. . . . The LORD sits enthroned over the flood; the LORD is enthroned as King forever. The LORD gives strength to his people; the LORD blesses his people with peace.

Psalm 29:2, 4–6, 10–11

ITEMS FOR PRAYER

- With the steady stream of Christians migrating out of Lebanon, pray for those who stay, that a vision for missions will be strong as they live in the face of danger.
- Who of us understands the huge pressures associated with caring for refugees? Pray that those who have fled into Lebanon would not be forgotten, and that as Christians we will include in our prayers and giving the support of those who care for refugees.
- Pray for leadership within the churches and missions of Lebanon, that even in their precarious living situations they will continue to view the wider Middle East as a place where Christ chooses to build his kingdom.

PRAYER

Father, may this land of Lebanon, in which the early story of your church found roots, continue to be a place where you are made known. While many who call themselves by your name choose to leave, I pray there will be a resurgence of faith among those who stay. May your kingdom continue to impact this country that has known so much bloodshed, internal conflict, and outside aggression. Encourage those caring for refugees. Install wise political leaders who will lead with integrity and justice. We pray that peace will reign and your name will be praised. Amen.

30

THE WORLD PRAYER MOVEMENT

It Is Happening Around the Globe

Today's focus is not on a country but on the movement of prayer around the world. In this chapter, we try to better understand the contemporary prayer movement and to see how prayer is building in frequency and globally.

There are many global prayer connections available online and through conferences. However, this is just the tip of the iceberg, so to speak. Community- and business-based prayer groups are spotting the globe. Guides for prayer can be found on websites and in printed materials. Cities and towns everywhere are holding annual Mayor's Prayer Breakfasts. Behind the scenes of these public events, there is a new rising tide of prayer, a recognition of its need, and passion to engage in thoughtful and intercessory prayer.

Some web-based materials include these sites: globaldayofprayer.com; worlddayofprayer.net; 24-7prayer.com; globalprayermovement.org; and operationworld.org/prayermovement.

Dispatch

Jakarta was the site of the World Prayer Assembly, where we joined nine thousand people from sixty countries. We met in a facility owned by Christians in a country with a Muslim majority. On the last day, a hundred thousand joined in praying together at the Bung Karno Stadium.

Prayer is tough when taken seriously. Praying doesn't come easily. I can preach, organize, write, exhort, study, and create fairly easily, but praying is a discipline. For most, prayer is not our first choice—getting something done is, which presumes praying is not.

Yet people everywhere are gathering together for prayer: in homes, before the business day, online, and in parliamentary groupings. Towns, cities, and regions have annual prayer breakfasts.

Prayer gatherings are different and varied, noisy and silent, bombastic and reflective.

The World Prayer Assembly is a confluence of streams finding their way to a delta of prayer. This one was hosted by South Koreans—well known for their rigorous early-morning prayer gatherings—and by Indonesian prayer groups. It was a four-day pep rally on prayer. The music, dance, drama, and unabashed enthusiasm were all inspiring.

The genesis of today's world prayer was in 1984 in Seoul. Vonnette Bright, who with her husband, Bill Bright, founded Campus Crusade for Christ, led the Lausanne Movement in its late-twentieth-century prayer gathering. Here they were joined by the Global Day of Prayer, a focus triggered by Graham Powers of South Africa.

The underlying mood of the World Prayer Assembly matched my boyhood camp meetings. Joy captured the moment, for what could be more satisfying for those assembled from the troubled spots of the world? Those often living under the heel of a religious or secular majority, who are despised at best and persecuted at worst, are gathered in praise and prayer. I applauded with thousands as six hundred Christians from China stood to be welcomed. Those from Indonesia know what it means to pray in a Muslim-dominated country, where on some of its islands, Christians have recently been killed and churches burned.

It is within this burgeoning prayer movement that the gospel is unfolding in new ways. Sometimes its message is hopeful, other times disconcerting in the extreme. Even so, we are in the vortex of a spiritual windstorm. Spiritual activity creates it own spin-offs. Some of these spin-offs will raise concern by their style or theological assertions. However, it should not deter us from seeing the larger and more profound work of the Spirit.

Hunger for God and a Word-based faith know no bounds. I'm moved as I witness the breathing of the Spirit into peoples, regions, and vocational sectors. Where this all is going, we don't know. What occurs in the process of spiritual resurgence is beyond our predictions. However, in this global meeting of prayer, I note five clusters defining today's prayer movements.

Deep Personal Thirst

People, so thirsty for spiritual life, will go anywhere to alleviate dryness.

Who are these people? They come from all walks of life, from all kinds of life experiences, from profoundly activist religious groups, and from lifeless ones. I see old-line Protestants raised on the message "Be good and that will get you to heaven" desperate for a fresh infilling of the Spirit. Alternatively, I meet Roman Catholics and Orthodox eager to find new streams to quench their spiritual thirst. I also speak with Pentecostals tired of hype, looking for forms of spiritual journeys found often among the early church fathers, where quietness and silence brood in a mood to go deeper. Mainstream Evangelicals, whose spirituality is framed by doctrine, are prospects for the charismatic. In every group, at least some languish in the system at hand, longing not only for what is new but also for the Spirit life, breaking barriers of deadness and stopping the draining of the soul.

Evangelistic Passion

The drive to pray for the unreached has been part of our eschatology (doctrine of the end times) for hundreds of years. More recently, the focus has been on what has been called the 10/40 Window, the rectangular area of North Africa, the Middle East, and Asia between approximately 10 degrees north and 40 degrees north latitude. Heightened by 9/11 and increased awareness of the world of Islam, prayer groups have focused on reaching the unreached.

Living in Real Life-Challenging Faith

Religion offers the potential of two extremes: on the one side, a tightly scripted doctrine defining what to believe, and on the other, a watered-down faith, unsure of what to believe and what to ask for. Either extreme snuffs out life. In the wide middle is the offering of dynamic, life-changing, and God-intervening faith. We see this especially in the Global South, where people actually believe that what God promises, he will do. This may be for healing, solving troubling matters, or meeting physical or spiritual needs; they ask for an actual, observable action from God.

Engaging the Spirit World

Western minds often tend to operate as if faith were just an idea. The debate between liberal and conservative doctrine has been about ideas. The notion that spiritual war is waged in the "heavenlies" seems spooky. However, it doesn't take many conversations with church leaders in Africa, Asia, or Latin America before you understand that their environment of spiritual advancement is within the spirit world. We may be uncomfortable in identifying dysfunction or disunity as something other than psychological, but Christians in much of the world think otherwise. It is for them a battle defined as spirit warfare, and is often associated with intercessory prayer.

Embracing Culture

Prayer takes on the life and ways of the peoples practicing it. In my first service in a South Korean Presbyterian church, I was convinced I had ended up in the wrong place. When the time came to pray, I was expecting someone to pray while everyone listened. Instead, as they closed their eyes, everyone prayed out loud at the same time. The noise was deafening. After a few minutes, the minister rang a small bell and everyone stopped. Today, much of contemporary praying is closely linked to praise and worship, forms that fit the cultural world of those praying. While in the past, worship music in non-Western communities was often just a translation of older Western hymns and choruses, today indigenous music, dance, and forms have become the norm. These new words, melodies, and rhythms are eras away from the old forms.

Every sharp rise in spiritual interest carries with it extremes. Let's be careful not to be too critical of what is new or different. We can too easily dismiss expressions of prayer outside of our experience. It matters that we evaluate what is going on historically. New waves of spiritual life have carried with them forms of heresy,

160

but most in time do find equilibrium and normalcy. Listening to a text of biblical promise in a village void of clean water, and having no seed for spring sowing, will trigger prayer with different intensity and expectation than in a place where our biggest need is finding a new music minister.

As we made our way out from the prayer assembly, I knew we had felt the wind of the Spirit, heard the voice of our Lord, and embraced with joy and faith peoples from everywhere.

TODAY'S READING

Listen to my words, LORD, consider my lament. Hear my cry for help, my King and my God, for to you I pray. In the morning, LORD, you hear my voice; in the morning I lay my requests before you and wait expectantly. . . . But I, by your great love, can come into your house; in reverence I bow down toward your holy temple. Lead me, LORD, in your righteousness because of my enemies—make your way straight before me. . . . Let all who take refuge in you be glad; let them ever sing for joy. Spread your protection over them, that those who love your name may rejoice in you. Surely, LORD, you bless the righteous; you surround them with your favor as with a shield.

Psalm 5:1–3, 7–8, 11–12

ITEMS FOR PRAYER

- Let's be inspired by those new in the faith, and pray for their continuing joy and excitement in following Jesus.
- As we age in our spiritual journey, we can easily fall into allowing our prayers to become rehearsed phrases. Pray that the Spirit will bring new life so that as we pray, we will exercise a dynamic of faith for God to meet particular needs.
- As various prayer movements spring up around the world, let us pray for their leaders to have biblical wisdom and godly counsel in their leading.

PRAYER

Lord Jesus, in teaching us how to pray, you said that your will is to inaugurate your kingdom, your reign over all of

161

life. As we pray today, may faith rise in our hearts and may your presence fill us as we go to where we live, work, worship, and play. May what we expect in prayer be matched by a heartfelt belief that what you promise, you will do. In praying for others, here and worldwide, may our spirit engage with yours in a strong and lively belief in your promises. Help us, Lord, in our prayer life, that it will be a time of your infilling and an outflow of blessing to others. In your strong and holy name we pray. Amen.

31
TURKEY

Where Christian Faith Was Almost Snuffed Out

The historical role of **Turkey** has been enormous in shaping the church, both within its borders and in neighboring countries. The capital city, Istanbul (formerly Constantinople), was named after Constantine, the Roman Emperor who in 313 made Christianity Rome's official religion. The churches in the book of Revelation are located in Turkey, along with other sites visited by Christian pilgrims and tourists.

Officially a secular state, its majority religion is Muslim. And even though declared secular, the government funds much of Islamic religious life.

Location: Turkey links two continents, Europe and Asia, with the majority of its landmass being in Asia. Bordered by many European and Asian countries, it sits on the north side of the Mediterranean, east of the Aegean, and south of the Black Sea and the Sea of Marmara.

Population: 78 million

Religion: Muslim 97%; Christian 0.5%

Dispatch

A century ago, 25 percent of Turkey was Christian. Today it is less than 1 percent—and this in a country where the early church was planted. St. John's letters in Revelation were to seven of Turkey's cities. In the last one hundred years, the ancient stems of Christian life were not only cut off, but all of its roots almost torn up.

Walking the winding streets of Istanbul or riding the ferry from the Asian to European side, we recall that before the genocide of

Armenian Christians and the takeover by Islam 100 years ago, this city and nation were prime centers of Christian presence.

Today, an Islamic government with an odd kind of secularity is poised to join the European community. Under its current president, there is also movement to exert influence over the Middle East.

Turkey was the heart of the Ottoman Empire. In the late thirteenth century, its reach spanned the Mediterranean basin—southeast Europe, western Asia, the Caucasus, and northern Africa. This empire was intact until WWI, when it was defeated and its lands reduced to the current Turkish borders. Most infamous of Turkey's actions in the recent past was the genocide of 1.5 million Armenian Christians in the early 1900s.

Today, Turkey seems to be in an empire-revival mode, with emphasis on being Turkish and reestablishing their greatness as a people. Alongside this is an affirmation of Islam. Although it is officially a secular state, non-Muslims are viewed as infidels. A Christian businessperson said that even though he is on good terms with his colleagues, if he visits them in their homes, his dinner plate goes through a different process of being washed because he is considered unclean. In business or a public sector workplace, if one is known as a Christian, promotions are unlikely.

Still, today there is a small and growing community of Christians in Turkey—most of them newly converted Evangelicals. The Armenian Orthodox, who lived through a horrific century of death yet retain their ethnic identity, are strengthening their presence and community. Their churches, as well as the Roman Catholic ones, are all small and quite aberrant to Turkish nationalism.

Meet Levent

In 1985, there were an estimated thirty believers in Turkey who had converted from a Muslim background (Muslim Background Believers—MBB). Today there are over ten thousand. Levent Kinran, a church leader, is emblematic of the work of the Spirit. His parents' Muslim faith was at best nominal, and so as a teenager,

Levent looked elsewhere for a faith that made sense to him. He told me his story:

> I came to know Jesus in 1987. I was seeking God, and since I was a Muslim, my first steps were to take Arabic classes, worship five times a day, and try to become a better Muslim. However, as I was walking deeper in this direction, I began to question even the existence of God. I was feeling emptier and less fulfilled. At that time, I started reading a New Testament and was overwhelmed by Jesus Christ. His miracles, His teaching, His life, and His love touched me very deeply. I realized with amazement that His authority and His claims about himself were all true and that He was the Son of God!
>
> When I discovered His endless love for me and His dying on the cross—because of His love—I seriously considered responding to His call. However, being in the Muslim world, considering the call of Jesus is quite a challenge. There is a decree which commands that anyone who denounces Islam is to be killed. But the more I was convinced of Jesus Christ, the more aware I became that I could not live without His truth. As a result, I accepted Him as my Savior and my Lord. His love, His peace, and His joy have been unlike anything I had known, and are greater than any suffering.

Today, Levent is a leader in the Association of Protestant Churches of Turkey (here *Protestant* and *Evangelical* are interchangeable) and pastors the Anatolian Protestant Church of the Vineyard Christian Fellowship.

How Are Christians Faring?

In a country with such a complex history and intersecting social, political, and religious issues, the following may help our understanding:

- Turkey's declaration of being a secular state is curious. While Turkey doesn't allow religious symbols in government, the minister of religious affairs pays salaries of imams and other costs of the Muslim faith, making Christians through their taxes finance Islamic mosques and enterprises.

- The historical denial of the Armenian Christian genocide is legendary, although now there is the occasional public mention. Yet Armenians worldwide continue to grieve their loss as the government refuses to acknowledge its complicity.
- In recent months, the government turned one-third of public schools into Qur'anic schools. Thus Christians, and others not wanting such intense Islamic education for their children, either send them to private schools or submit.
- It is nearly impossible for a Christian congregation to get a permit to build a house of worship. This is of missiological importance. In the Islamic world, not to have a church building makes it difficult to sustain an ongoing public witness; it creates confusion among Muslims as to a Christian's identity if he or she doesn't have a place of worship.
- During the Ottoman Empire, Turkey was a world power. While this was lost in the early twentieth century, nationalism still profoundly affects governmental planning, with Islam intertwined with its national identity. Indeed, to be a Turk, one is assumed to be a Muslim. To be otherwise is unpatriotic.
- There was a slight increase in religious freedom following the 2007 killing of three Christians of the Zirve Publishing House. As the trial drags on, it gives advocates of religious rights increased opportunity to press their case for fair treatment. Also, international publicity is prodding the government to take note of the Christian community.

Looking Ahead

Certain factors provide opportunity for increased witness. Generations born after 1980 have grown up in a world of free elections, greater allowances to make their own choices, a shift from rural to urban living, and an explosive media. This generation comprises 60 percent of the population. They are better educated and not as aware of their past as are their parents. This makes them less rooted and more open to change. During a recent visit, it was announced that SAT-7, a media ministry across the Middle East, was awarded a channel on a Turkish satellite, a possible major breakthrough in broadcasting.

Turkey's religious majority too often treats Christians harshly. Even so, just to witness their joy in meeting together is deeply moving. Sunday morning in church I saw their uninhibited smiles and open displays of affection. I was awed by the sheer beauty of their fellowship and the telltale signs of love and enthusiastic conversation. Evident was a heartfelt thrill of being together with those joined by the love of Jesus.

Turkey, a geostrategic land bridge connecting Europe with Asia, is a place where many Christians are investing their lives as they seek a rebirth of the gospel witness. It matters that the gospel is again deeply rooted in this land of early apostolic activity.

Today's Reading

Let the morning bring me word of your unfailing love, for I have put my trust in you. Show me the way I should go, for to you I entrust my life. Rescue me from my enemies, LORD, for I hide myself in you. Teach me to do your will, for you are my God; may your good Spirit lead me on level ground.

Psalm 143:8–10

Items for Prayer

- Those of us who live in Christian-majority countries find it difficult to understand how Christians raise families, go to work, and move about in society where one is not only part of a tiny minority, but often marginalized and oppressed. Today, let us set aside any complaints we might have, which often are small compared to Christians in Turkey, and pray for their needs.

- These needs include the right to register churches, so important in their testimony to Muslims. Pray that attempts by the Association of Protestant Churches will get a fair hearing from the government and be given the right to build their own churches.

- Children often have no option but to go to Muslim schools. Pray for the raising up of Christian schools.
- Many Christians are working in business as a base for both employment and witness. Pray that others will join them in building a critical mass to strengthen their worshiping community and to spread the good news of Christ.

PRAYER

Loving Savior, here in Turkey, this land in which your church was planted, the light of your witness almost expired. The scourge of persecution and genocide reduced your faithful to just a few. Yet we know, Spirit of God, in such moments and places, your power is at work, giving strength and wisdom to those who love the gospel. Even though Christians are often treated unfairly, your Word continues to plant the seed of life. We pray for Levent and other Christian leaders that they would continue to experience the joy of your presence and in their study grow deeper in their faith. May the sweet savor of Christian love be evident in their witness, for the praise of Christ our Lord. Amen.

32

UKRAINE

Which Road Ahead?

The people of **Ukraine**, a vital center of Slavic culture, have lived under varying outside intruders: Lithuania, Poland, the Ottoman Empire (Turkey), Austro-Hungary, and Russia. In the twentieth century, much of its rule was within the Soviet Empire.

In a population of 42 million (which includes Crimea), 17 percent are Russian. While Ukrainian is the official language, a large number speak Russian as their primary language.

Location: Ukraine is bordered by Russia to the east. Other neighbors are Belarus, Poland, Slovakia, Hungary, Romania, Moldova, the Black Sea, and the Sea of Azov.

Population: 45 million

Religion: Christian 80% (Orthodox 61%, Catholic 10%, Evangelical/Protestant 7%); nonreligious 20%

Dispatch

As I pressed the buzzer at the apartment, I noticed a Post-it note directing me to the nearest bomb shelter. *How could this be?* I wondered. *In Kiev, in 2014?* People were moving about, living their lives, and yet here was a warning to protect us from what the government saw as a possible attack. Ukraine still plays out its historic intermingling of Slavic peoples in Eastern Europe.

Now twenty-five years after the fall of the Soviet Union, those who believed the collapsed Wall meant they were set free to become their own land and people once again were hearing drumbeats, reviving memories of empire.

The day the Ukrainian parliament passed a historic law voicing determination to work with Europe, I sat with leaders of the Evangelical church, hearing their concerns and hopes. One pointed to a map and noted a large eastern region above the Crimea. "This," he said, "is what they want to take." His lament was rooted in fear that the world would ignore this incursion; in world politics, what is denoted as "regional influence" means the dominant country can pretty much do as they please with whatever is within their "region."

The road to independence has been long and rough, especially as Ukrainians set their sails toward democratic statehood. The two communities, Russia and Ukraine, are linked in many ways. Under Stalin, 7 million Ukrainians died in the Holodmor (the Great Famine) of the early 1930s; nearly 700,000 senior Ukrainian leaders were purged during the occupation. After years of living under strict control, in 1991, Ukraine declared its independence.

Ukraine is very religious. One almost needs a lexicon to follow their religious tribes and links. There are three Ukrainian Orthodox Churches. The largest is the Moscow Patriarchate, with 11,952 churches, and the second is the Kiev Patriarchate, with 4,508 churches. The third is the Ukrainian Autocephalous Orthodox Church (UAOC), an independent denomination. There is also the Ukrainian Greek Catholic Church with 3,646 churches. Estimates put Evangelicals at about 7,500 churches.

Three Leaders

The witness of Christ flourishes through Ukraine's many peoples, churches, and communities. Meet three whose lives represent so much good in the land.

Oleksandr Babiychuk is general secretary of the Bible Society. We talked about strategy and ministry, and then he told me that in 1934, Stalin had his grandfather, a pastor, executed. Khrushchev imprisoned his father, also a pastor, for ten years.

In leading the Bible Society, Olexsandr's interest is in Bible translation and distribution. He knows the power political freedom has in allowing Christian witness. In 1982, the government allowed a one-time import of five hundred Bibles. In 2013, the Bible Society distributed 383,000 Bibles, New Testaments, and children's Bibles, a stunning reminder of the thirst—even among this most "Christianized" of people—for the Scriptures.

Denys Gorenkov heads up the IFES (International Fellowship of Evangelical Students), also known as InterVarsity. His story is timeless. His father, an intellectual and communist, filled their home with books. While in high school, Denys read a magazine with a long passage from the New Testament, but there was no context for the reading, which ironically was Jesus' message of turning the other cheek. The only place Denys could find biblical references was in Russian authors such as Dostoevsky. In time, while at university, he met Christian students, and through a Bible study he came to faith.

His Holiness Patriarch Filaret of the Ukrainian Orthodox Church (Kiev Patriarchate) is a courageous national figure. I asked what his daily prayer consists of. "We pray for peace, but not any kind. We don't need peace in slavery, but a just peace, which means peace and freedom."

Knowing the tension that often exists between Evangelicals and the Orthodox, I asked how they got along. He smiled and said, "There is a loving relationship between us. Yes, we get along well."

The Road Ahead

What does a Christian do when conflict stirs anger and hatred against your own citizens who are ethnic siblings to a border country? Denys Gorenkov told a story of how the Orthodox faced a crisis in trying to discern what was true during the rule of both Hitler and Stalin. People wondered, *Whom do we believe?* The conflicting propaganda out of Moscow about the work of Stalin, and from Berlin on the aggression of Hitler, gave them no objective means of determining what was true. So they configured this response: Since we don't know whom to believe, we will help the children; we will do what is good. When confusion reigns, we will help those in need. When clouds obliterate reality, we will care for the vulnerable.

What will come of the political and military infractions in Ukraine? We know from history that Christian communities, even those of considerable strength, can be strangled. Among the constraining opinions and national distress, I tried to distill from its Christian leaders what might guide us in support and prayer.

They admit an enormous opportunity was missed following 1991, when they might have advanced their political and economic worlds. But leaders driven by cronyism and consumed by greed allowed corruption to suck dry many initiatives. A lost moment. Then the political infighting, the intrusion of outside influence in its politics, and the incompetence of ruling parties set the country back.

The Orthodox, some with their patriarch in Kiev and others in Moscow, do not foster unity. Evangelicals, while significant in their numbers of churches, have not yet crafted an alliance, which would provide a vehicle for a cooperative voice and action.

Ukraine, with its brilliant culture and landscape dotted by domes and crosses, is a reminder of its historical and ubiquitous Christian witness. Today, it is going through another period of political agony.

Through the furtive years of Soviet surveillance, evangelicals were forced to live in obscurity. Yet they developed a core of leaders, and today a new generation is taking the lead. They are resolute. The fear of intrusion, while threatening, is not overwhelming. They are creative and outward looking, seeking ways to affirm their nation and people without allowing nationalism to define their faith.

I asked a student, "In this time of crisis, what do you want me to tell the world?" His response: "Yes, we are experiencing pain, fear, and hope. These are all big. As Christians we don't support violence or fascism, and we don't want to view Russians as enemies. We want Ukraine to be a nation where Christ is alive and helping people."

Keep these leaders in your prayers, that good will emerge from this moment of stress.

TODAY'S READING

Sing the praises of the LORD, you his faithful people; praise his holy name. For his anger lasts only a moment, but his favor lasts a lifetime; weeping may stay for the night, but rejoicing comes in the morning.

Psalm 30:4–5

ITEMS FOR PRAYER

- Many Christians know what it is like to suffer for their faith. Yet in the past years, Christians in Ukraine have experienced the joy of public witness. Pray that the government will remain intact, and that the freedom to design their own future will be kept in their hands.
- Divided loyalties can be destructive to communities. Pray for a strong move of the Spirit to break down dividing walls, keeping people from allowing old hatreds and national identities to erode the nation and embitter its people.
- There are strong churches and ministries. Pray for pastors as they lead their people in Christ-centered faith, guiding them to loving their world.
- Increasingly there has been a move among some evangelicals to engage in public-square leadership. Pray for these men and women, that their leadership and witness will give honor and praise to the Christ we love and serve and be the presence of our Lord in the places where they serve.

PRAYER

Dear Savior, you understand so well the hurt and sorrow of war. Bring to Ukraine your loving peace and presence. We pray for those who lead churches, especially those afflicted by conflicting national loyalties. May they voice your challenging words of unity for your church. Help them live out your calling and mandate. We know that calamity comes by war. Spirit of God, raise up a people to offset that which breaks down and destroys. Instead, may there be joy and celebration in this land as your people learn to sing a new song of Jehovah, even in the midst of political stress. We believe this can and will come, and in your name we ask and give thanks. Amen.

33

PERSECUTION AND MARTYRDOM

The Price of Believing

Their faces looked down from banners strung across narrow streets in Garbage City, Cairo, young men who days before had been killed by anti-Christian demonstrators. A mob of young Muslims, infuriated by ugly rumors, were sent to a neighboring community to kill young Christians and destroy property.

Our driver swung the car around a tight corner and parked. We walked up the stairs to meet Father Simon, the Orthodox priest for Garbage City. We talked with him of the young men who had been killed and the challenge they face as Christians when their beliefs are seen by some as worthy of death. He nodded, agreeing it was a problem, but said that living for Christ was what mattered.

Such issues were simply part of their daily ritual in giving evidence of the risen Christ.

Persecution, a word so associated with Christian witness, has not diminished in the twenty-first century. While most of us feel forms of cultural exclusion because of our faith or know the backlash our public witness may bring, the persecution I have in mind is the kind that kills, hacks off limbs, clangs shut the innocent in prisons, hauls them in front of courts, or burns down houses and churches.

Persecution is a fluid reality, breaking out in places we might think less likely. As wars and rumors of wars continue and disable people groups, Christians will inevitably be persecuted, some to the point of martyrdom for their faith.

Martyrdom. In a recent sixteen-month window, 5,479 Christians have been targeted and killed for their faith in Christ. Todd Johnson of the Center for the Study of Global Christianity estimates that some 70 million Christians have been martyred in the past two thousand years. And during the decade of 2000–2010, one million Christians were killed, or 100,000 each year.

The ten countries that top the list of Christian martyrdom are: Nigeria—2,073; Syria—1,479; Central African Republic—1,115; Pakistan—228; Egypt—147; Kenya—85; Iraq—84; Myanmar—33; Sudan—33; Venezuela—26. These numbers from Open Doors' World Watch List, representing a recent sixteen-month period, are conservative, registering only deaths confirmed. Many more occur without being reported.

Why this increased tension with more persecution and killings? Over the past century the world has gone through a religious whiplash. In the past fifty years we have seen the collapse of Communism and a remarkable expansion around the globe of Christianity and Islam. These two religions now make up two-thirds of the world's population. Escalating conflicts between these major faiths is marking today's world with increased tensions and resulting persecution of Christians.

Persecution takes place in many forms. A pastor in Turkey told of difficulties in buying or renting a building for their church. He said that in a Muslim country, people wonder what you believe if you don't have a place for worship. A man whispered to me of his faith in Christ but said that if his family knew, it would destroy them. A Christian leader in Kazakhstan told of their inability to get government permission to run a school for training pastors. Without a certificate or graduation, pastors aren't acknowledged. Their churches are burned to the ground, yet without a police investigation their insurance will not pay. The list goes on.

Often it's a mob that attacks a church or group. In countries such as Pakistan and Egypt, Nigeria and Syria, groups driven by fanaticism will bomb, burn, or chase out Christians. In other countries, such as Iran, the courts will be used to intimidate, charge, or imprison pastors, generating fear among congregations and giving a powerful signal to others, especially younger people, not to have anything to do with Christianity.

The actual accounts of killings and related persecution are underestimated. Many Christian ministries are still learning how to gather accurate data, to expose to the world which peoples and countries are at the fore of persecution. The most dangerous country statistically is the Democratic Republic of Congo, where the Islamic fundamentalist group Boko Haram is leading the war against Christians. While Muslim-majority countries are often places where Christians are most at risk, it would be unfair to say that Islam is always a threat. In Indonesia, the largest Muslim country, with 238 million people, there is relative freedom for Christians.

We do not have numbers for North Korea, Iran, or China. North Korea is the most closed country and the one in which Christians are thrown into concentration camps. Iran is known for legal constraint of Christians.

In China, the Christian community estimates range from 30 to 140 million. The government's concern is not so much that people follow Jesus, but that large gatherings may promote anti-government uprisings. China's history rises out of grassroots political movements, which over the centuries has resulted in the overthrow of governments, as with Mau and his Communist party in 1949. The fear of potential uprisings causes their concern over growing religions.

The China Christian Council and Three-Self Patriotic Movement (under the government department of SARA) attempt to register churches, and about one-third of them are registered. The reports of government harassment are often related to the provincial or local bodies of believers. The growing presence of Christians and the number of churches being built is giving strength to their freedom to live and worship.

Places of Greatest Danger

Open Doors—a ministry begun by Brother Andrew, serving persecuted Christians—in their World Watch have identified the eight most vulnerable places for Christians to live today.

- Pray for Christians in northeast Nigeria, where Sharia law rules; where Boko Haram, an Islamic insurgent group, operates and seeks to either force conversion or to kill, all designed to eliminate Christianity.
- Pray for Christians in Syrian villages or cities occupied by jihadi insurgents. Even though ancient in their faith and with their families having lived there for centuries, they face enormous danger. ISIL is engaged in the newest form of severe persecution and killing of Christians.
- Pray for Coptic Christians who live on the south coast of the Mediterranean in Egypt, especially those who live along the Nile, in places where the Muslim Brotherhood has enormous influence. Here Christians are kidnapped, and if a ransom is not paid, they are killed.
- Pray for women living in the Central African Republic, especially in towns populated by Christians that are raided by Muslim fighters.
- Pray for Evangelicals in surprisingly lawless areas of Mexico, where organized crime and powerful landowners hold sway.
- Pray for Christians in northern Pakistan. They are at particular risk of attack and death when they attend church.

- Pray for Christians living in drug-controlled areas of Colombia. The guerrilla group FARC is engaged in violence, persecution, and killing of believers.
- Pray for Christians with Muslim backgrounds in Saudi Arabia and Yemen. When a person converts and is open about his faith, his life is in danger. The belief that a Christian conversion "dishonors" the family or community is so primary that it makes killing that person a legitimate response.

TODAY'S READING

I will praise the LORD all my life; I will sing praise to my God as long as I live. Do not put your trust in princes, in human beings, who cannot save. When their spirit departs, they return to the ground; on that very day their plans come to nothing. Blessed are those whose help is the God of Jacob, whose hope is in the LORD their God.

Psalm 146:2–5

ITEMS FOR PRAYER

- In recent years, persecution and killing of Christians has been on the increase. A number of global organizations do research, follow, provide public information, and seek to defend those who are caught in legal battles in their countries. Some of these include Open Doors, Religious Liberty Commission (of the World Evangelical Alliance), and Jubilee Campaign. Pray for these ministries, especially for those who risk their lives by going into countries to research and verify conditions and the situation of Christians.
- There are websites that are up-to-date in providing information on critical places and situations. Check these out and keep yourself informed, both in ways you may help and for your prayer lists.
- While we will never know about most dangerous situations, the Spirit does, and praying is our way of interceding for people in danger, pressing in prayer for the many who today

languish in prison or are under surveillance, knowing that any day they may be attacked or arrested.

PRAYER

Jesus, Lord and Savior, you know the suffering and deep hurt of being taken, beaten, and killed. We intercede on behalf of Christians who are trapped, some behind bars, others in their homes, fearful of a mob, a secret security person, a neighbor, all because they worship you. I acknowledge that you didn't promise living for you would be easy; even so, we know you care. You know those of your church who are in need this very day. We offer three prayers. Break into their cells or place of confinement with your presence and give them protection from harm. Then for Christians living in harm's way in countries and neighborhoods where those who hate your name would endanger them, may there be protection as well. And then we pray for your leaders, pastors, and ministers who are fearless in making known your wonderful shalom—your peace—both for their hearts and their relationships. Give them courage and the will to be your living message. With the psalmist we pray, blessed are those whose help is the God of Jacob, whose hope is in the Lord their God. Amen.

34
VENEZUELA
A Country on the Edge

The **Bolivarian Republic of Venezuela** was colonized by Spain in the 1500s, and in 1811 became one of the earliest colonies in the Spanish-America orbit to declare independence. Ruled for decades by *caudillos,* military "strongmen," a number of democratically elected governments came to power, starting in the late 1950s. In 1993, the president was impeached for embezzling public funds, and in 1998, military officer Hugo Chávez was elected under the banner of the "Bolivarian Revolution." He died of cancer in 2013. Venezuela has the world's largest oil reserves.

Location: lying on the northern coast of South America, surrounded by Guyana, Brazil, and Colombia

Population: 30 million

Religion: Christian 98% (Roman Catholic 96%, Evangelical/Protestant 2%); nonreligious 2%

Dispatch

I sat looking into the brown eyes of a beautiful twenty-one-year-old university student, Sairam. Her face was framed by long, dark hair. She folded her hands and quietly said in English, "Dr. Brian, we are sitting on a time bomb."

Just out from spending six months in Helicoide Prison for public protest against her government, this fourth-year student had been squeezed into a small cell with five other students. Because there were only two small cots, they had to take turns sleeping.

Venezuela, a beautiful country with natural resources of enormous magnitude, is any day on the verge of collapse. The yo-yo effect of its huge oil reserves has contributed to a series of bizarre social and economic experiments that could push the country over the edge. In the government's anxiety to control, its

Marxist-minded political establishment has made it into what is akin to a police state. I was told that when I preached in churches and spoke in various social forums and interviews, I would be observed. Who was I? Why was I here? What harm might I do? These and other questions were being asked.

The wearing edges of this failing social experiment are evident: garbage not being picked up, police interspersed along the streets stopping drivers to look in cars for no reason other than control and intimidation. Days before we arrived, Venezuela's currency was devalued 300 percent. There are four-hour lineups for food basics. And in a strange twist of economic sense, gas for cars is one-half a cent per liter—two cents a gallon.

It has a five-hundred-year history of European and more recently indigenous dictatorial control. In 1999, President Chávez inherited a country wobbling on an uneven platform of social and economic inequities. His promise to bridge the rich/poor divide and reduce corruption secured his engine of political control, which in time he drove off the track. Some promises he could keep, as long as oil was floating around $100 a barrel. When that collapsed, it undercut his government's ability to fulfill its promises.

What is acknowledged are major crises at hand. It's as if a perfect storm is about to blow in on this South American people. As I met with economists, working people, professors, pastors, and politicians, I learned more about these crises.

The charismatic Chávez, with his ideas and presence, marginalized public institutions and their independence. By the time he died, they had been so eroded that civic powers such as the judiciary were under the thumb of political masters. Stories abound of justices penning decisions with the muscle of the military at their side.

Hour-long lines for bread and milk indicate that something is fundamentally wrong. The gyration of world oil prices has tumbled the country's economy on its nose. What is not known is what backlash civil strife might bring. It is feared that this may be a natural outcome as the poor get shoved further out of line by the powerful.

This speaks of the third crisis, which is social. The poor, lining up behind the government, believed that what Chávez and his political inheritors said was true and would be done. The people had had a history of quasi-slavery, as their economic masters had in the past kept them in mere life-existing poverty. Expectations rose, and for a time they were partially met. Refrigerators and washing machines were delivered as part of that promise. But when parts were needed, the shelves were bare. Countless billions passed hands, providing relief for some and a measure of economic help. Now that's gone. The country is bankrupt without a chance of even servicing the debt.

The cultural web has been woven with a mantra that says, "Depend on the state." With this underlying political philosophy, industries were taken over, and now most are in tatters. Newspapers, television stations, magazines, and radio companies have been bought out by those who favor the government. Now with no voice to help offset official propaganda, the social fabric is not only coming undone, it's dissolving.

These four rivers meet at the gorge of moral degradation, catapulting a society from its moorings into the unknown. In 2014, there were twenty-five thousand assassinations and killings. The number of kidnappings is unknown, and corruption is off the scale. Even the international study group Transparency International says it is no longer possible to measure Venezuela's level of corruption. Layer upon layer, handmaidens of the powerful—violence and corruption—rule. While these factors exist in various degrees in many countries, here corruption has become statecraft.

Why am I painting such a picture? Because Christian colleagues asked me to tell this story. While the standoff between President Bush and Chávez was dramatic, most assumed that with his oil-rich reserves, Chávez would bridge the chasm of possible social disorder. Now they say it has gone too far.

Stories of Faith

Yet here in the center of pending collapse is a common picture of faith. It is strong, joyful in witness, doing works of grace and kindness, wrestling with how faith intersects with political control, investing in the hearts and minds of its people. Let's visit two moments and places.

In the heart of Caracas, on the edge of a very poor area of Venezuela's capital city, I walked from the platform to sit in the front row with the congregation, alongside Sam Olson, native son, longtime colleague, and pastor. Fifteen hundred had gathered for the third morning service. A choir lively in Latin rhythm was carried by a twelve-member band—three trombones, three saxophones, two drummers, three keyboards, and a trumpeter from Cuba. Their mix of lilting Latin melodies was punctuated by jazz interludes as a horn or sax picked up the melody in a cadence of soulful peace. Preaching that morning, I was lifted in spirit by the warmth and enthusiasm of the people, something a preacher experiences only occasionally. Sunday night, in a much smaller church, there was the same sense of joy and trust. This was the first moment.

The second was Monday morning, meeting with people from the Christian Network for Social Interaction (CRIS). Their vision and purpose? To engage their crumbling world with integrity and a rebirth of social, economic, and political life. I asked for a quick bio: They are a mix of economists, professors, politicians, engineers, pastors, reporters, and lawyers. I spoke about the call of Christians to engage the public square, and then took questions: How to be a Christian in the various spheres? When to object? When to give in? I watched and listened to their honesty and fears, knowing they realized they were close to a precipice. Would some of these leave as thousands of their fellow citizens had?

I have met few groups in such calamitous moments, who, driven by concern and informed by their Christian faith, were searching for ways to work with a community in which they purpose to live out their faith.

Sairam, the young woman I mentioned earlier, is not a believer. When I asked if I could pray for her and her colleague, she smiled and said she wanted that. I asked if she had felt Christ's presence in prison, but such talk and the very idea of spiritual presence seemed foreign to her. But what she did know was that she had been visited in jail by a Christian who wanted to make sure she had water and food.

As you read this, Venezuela is not as it was during our visit. But today and tomorrow I will pray for Christians in this creative mix of Latin Americans. They too want a place of freedom where they can live and raise their children and be proud of the country of their birth or choice.

Days after we left, the mayor of Caracas, Antonio Ledezma, was hustled from his office into a black SUV and driven to jail. In the flow of events, who knows which might be the first domino to fall.

TODAY'S READING

The LORD is righteous in all his ways and faithful in all he does. The LORD is near to all who call on him, to all who call on him in truth. He fulfills the desires of those who fear him; he hears their cry and saves them. . . . My mouth will speak in praise of the LORD.

Psalm 145:17–19, 21

ITEMS FOR PRAYER

- The people of Venezuela have experienced many ups and downs of leadership and national well-being. Pray for the church leaders as they guide their people through days of difficulty.
- Pray also for the political leadership, whoever is in control, that they would refuse the option of corruption and civil strife, and instead bring to the people honest and fair rule.
- Pray for Christians who are trying to bring the salt and light of Christ into civil society. May they be wise and gracious, strong and loving—ever giving evidence of the Christ, who as a servant, taught us all how to lead.

PRAYER

Father, we pray on behalf of all Venezuelans, for their safety, protection from civil strife, economic health, and spiritual life. As this Latin America country rides the ups and downs of political intrigue and molestation, Father, bring into leadership those with a heart to care for their people, and wisdom on how to do it, politically and economically. Anoint Pastor

185

Sam Olson and his church and ministry colleagues as they seek to lead the people of God with courage, ever providing strength to those called by your name. May this land soon resound with freedom and opportunity for the gospel to affect all of life, ever giving evidence of Jesus of Nazareth, whose life we claim. In his name. Amen.

35
THE POPE
It Matters That He Is Wise

The Vatican is a sovereign country, embedded in Italy, and represents 1.2 billion Catholics. The head of the Roman Catholic Church is the pope.
Within the Christian world community, there are three basic groups: Roman Catholics, who make up 1.2 billion; the World Council of Churches (including Orthodox Churches) with 550 million; and the World Evangelical Alliance (WEA), comprising some 600 million.

Dispatch

The Vatican, splendid with priceless works of art, spectacular architecture, and resonating with historical and religious power, is the headquarters of half of the world's 2.4 billion Christians.

As a pastor's son from the Canadian prairies, it wasn't where I imagined I'd ever be—in a three-hour visit and luncheon with the Roman Catholic pontiff, Pope Francis.

Yet here I was with two colleagues from the World Evangelical Alliance with one purpose: to build a relationship and generate understanding with the pope so that Evangelicals might find ways of working with the Vatican in doing good. This includes releasing prisoners, confronting secularism, and facing the global challenge of militant Islam.

The historical and theological differences that separate us are profound. I am a son of the Reformation, its biblical framework providing an architectural structure for faith and life. I celebrate our understanding of the Scriptures as our only and final authority, the priesthood of every believer, the life-giving moment of rebirth, and the work of the Spirit in opening new churches and ministries.

Yet within the world of national and regional life, it matters that representatives from these three world Christian communities know each other, understand our differences and common objectives, and find ways to solve issues that complicate and distress the lives of Christians.

Reasons to Pray

I include this chapter in this book because, given its social, political, and religious significance, the well-being of the Vatican and the pontiff matter to us all. Half of those who call themselves Christians affiliate with Rome, and when its spiritual and ethical authority is diminished, this affects the entire world. When Rome loses her way, when corruption characterizes her financial dealings, when sexual scandals rob her of moral influence, when she fails to strongly declare the gift of Christ, secularism rises.

In considering this Christian community, I suggest prayers we might offer: First of all, that the Vatican, given its power and influence, would reflect the humility and love of the Jesus we serve. The danger of too much power is its misuse. In some countries, a religious majority can exert pressure, causing stress to other pastors and churches.

Let us also pray that the Vatican would reflect a common brotherhood in Christ and provide leadership in creating open and hospitable relations.

Pray that the pontiff would be wise and courageous. Given the Vatican's size, influence, and history, when children are violated and it appears that nothing is being done to correct sexual abuse, the world looks at those of us who follow Christ and condemns us all.

The role of the Roman Catholic Church matters to our common presence, especially in the face of Islamic dominance with its militants, who in some countries attempt to make conversion illegal. The gospel witness calls people to place their faith in Christ. It matters that these three world Christian bodies stand together in defending the right to make known the evangel and to be a faithful witness to others of the power of Christ in his resurrection.

It matters that we pray for the pontiff and the Church he oversees, because in many countries it is critical that we cooperate on issues concerning life. Evangelicals and Roman Catholics, as Trinitarians, have common ground on affirming life in all of its manifestations. Who is our strongest ally on defending the unborn? Who will stand with us on the arbitrary ending of life? Whom can we turn to in working together on issues of poverty, persecution, and martyrdom?

We are in the middle of a major religious shake-up worldwide. The Middle East is in uncertainty. Islamic fundamentalism is on the rise. The gospel witness permeates much of the global south. So, what of the future? The Christian community in many places is under attack. Where we can find common ground, we must.

My prayer that day in the Vatican was this: *God, enable this pope to be spiritually vital, that the Spirit would enable him to be tough in ethical leadership, and that you would give him wisdom to be competent in overseeing his world communion. What he says and what he does have a profound effect on us all. It matters to us that the Spirit rests upon him in wisdom and courage.*

Christians of our traditions and communions need not fear engagement. Working on human suffering and matters of injustice with Christians who have a different tradition and read the biblical text differently does not violate who we are or what we believe. International respect and cooperation among Christians is a worthy prayer and goal for today.

Today's Reading

I will give thanks to you, Lord, with all my heart; I will tell of all your wonderful deeds. I will be glad and rejoice in you; I will sing praise to your name, O Most High. . . . The Lord reigns forever; he has established his throne for judgment. He rules the world in righteousness and judges the peoples with equity. The Lord is a refuge for the oppressed, a stronghold in times of trouble. Those who know your name trust in you, for you, Lord, have never forsaken those who seek you. Sing the praises of the Lord, enthroned in Zion; proclaim among the nations what he has done.

Psalm 9:1–2, 7–11

ITEMS FOR PRAYER

- Globalization makes the role of the three major Christian groupings increasingly important. Pray for the leadership of each: the Vatican, the World Council of Churches (WCC), and the World Evangelical Alliance (WEA). (The Eastern Orthodox are included in the WCC.)
- Of the 196 countries in the world, there are many in which Christian communities are in either severe tension or open conflict. Pray that global leaders will have a heart for bringing about peace, even with differences that separate.
- Given the high visibility of the pope and his influence over the Vatican's members, pray that wisdom and grace, courage and faith will characterize his leadership, and that day by day he would be visited with strength for his momentous tasks.

PRAYER

Dear Father, today we lift in prayer those chosen in various global Christian communities, and especially the head of the Roman Catholic Church. Knowing how fraught we are with complex decisions, and being aware of the fragility of human emotions and well-being, bring strength and forti-tude to the pontiff in his task within the Vatican and those within that church communion. We confess our weakness and proneness to sin and ask for your wholeness as Chris-tians everywhere, for your empowerment to live your life with faithfulness and joy. Amen.

36

MALAYSIA

"Allah" Outlawed for Christians

Constitutionally, Islam is the state religion of **Malaysia,** and while the government declares freedom of religion, the power of Islam can be seen in public demonstrations, burning of churches, and a court decision that only Muslims can use *Allah* in reference to God. Formerly under the British Empire, Malaysia became independent in 1957.

Christian missions can be traced back to the seventh century. In 1810, Catholic priests arrived from Thailand and from the Philippines. The Plymouth Brethren came in the 1860s; Presbyterians and Methodists arrived in the last half of the nineteenth century.

Location: in the South China Sea, and consists of two major sections: Peninsular Malaysia located north of Singapore and East Malaysia or Malaysian Borneo

Population: 29 million

Religion: Muslim 62%; Christian 10%; Buddhist 6%; Hindu 6%

Dispatch

News of Christians being given the boot in Muslim countries tends to override other stories of remarkable opportunity, where instead of bowing to the pressure of religion and politics, Christians respond creatively.

Malaysia, an elongated landmass fingering down from the Indochina peninsula to the city-state of Singapore, is a complex grouping of peoples and religions: Malay—70 percent; Chinese—20 percent; Indian—5 percent; indigenous peoples—5 percent. Like Indonesia, it is predominantly Muslim, so much so that the government makes itself popular by assuming that to be ethnic Malay, one is automatically Muslim; and if Muslim, then Malay. Fixed in its statutes are regulations that make it unlawful to evangelize the Malay, and if Malay choose to convert, there is a protocol governing how they must register their conversion. Risks are so great that churches, if holding an event outside of their church building, must give an alert that it is a Christian event.

For years there has been conflict over Christians using *Allah* in Bible translation. The government took up the cause and ruled that *Allah* was only to be used by Muslims and their holy books. Christians objected, saying that they had used that name for years in their Malay translation. It went to court, and the high court ruled that it was permissible for Christians to use the name.

Riots broke out following the ruling. A flame fanned by government objection became real. Pastor Ong Sek Leang's church was broken into and Molotov cocktails thrown in. Before anything could be done, the church was destroyed. It was then that disaster invited a public inquiry.

When asked by a television reporter for his response, Pastor Leang said, "We forgive." And he followed it up, noting that they would not press charges. Within days, the leader of the opposition, a Muslim, toured the burned-out site. Following him, the prime minister, also a Muslim, visited.

While this was going on, the church had built another sanctuary some distance away. Even though they had completed the building, they still didn't have their permit. When the prime minister heard this, he signed their permit, authorizing the building of the new sanctuary, which was ready for occupancy. Political chatter soon included notations on issues with "Well, we should be like the Christians and forgive."

The government did appeal the court's earlier decision on allowing Christians to use *Allah*. On June 23, 2014, the highest court came back with a ruling that the former ruling was wrong and that Christians were not allowed to use the name *Allah* in any of their literature.

Calvary Church

With this controversy alive, I arrived at a conference in Kuala Lumpur. Musing about the challenges Christian face in this Islamic-dominated country, I wasn't prepared for the location of the conference. I asked the taxi driver, "Are you sure this is Calvary Church?"

"Well, they call it a conference center, but it really is a church," he added with a smile.

Here, in a country long a stronghold of Islamic faith and tradition and known for its opposition to Christian faith, a remarkable church exists.

Planted in 1968, after the attack, Calvary Church decided to redesign and rebuild. In reviewing their application for a permit with the neighbors, they learned that given the problem of sufficient space for parking, a new site might work better.

Their care in consulting with town planners paid off. They too agreed another site would suit everyone, and they even had one in mind, a five-acre property zoned for institutional use. If the church would build a "conference center," permits would be made available.

In its dedication, with Pastor David Yonggi Cho from South Korea preaching, I was reminded that circumstance is not the final arbiter. While spiritual life is never measured by architecture, size, or accomplishment, in this moment of dedication, I saw the brilliant logic in its construct. This large, creative, functional, and hugely people-friendly center will serve the wider community, building bridges to a society for whom the gospel message is foreign, if not threatening.

Built at a cost of $75 million (U.S.) , it is nearly debt free, with most contributions coming from Malaysia. Few dollars, I was told, came from offshore. Here, a country whose recent past included receiving missionaries and foreign funds, today has a missionary vision. Its expertise has changed from receiving and taking to giving and going.

TODAY'S READINGS

LORD, who may dwell in your sacred tent? Who may live on your holy mountain? The one whose walk is blameless, who does what is righteous, who speaks the truth from their heart; whose tongue utters no slander, who does no wrong to a neighbor, and casts no slur on others; who despises a vile person but honors those who fear the LORD; who keeps an oath even when it hurts . . . who does not accept a bribe against the innocent. Whoever does these things will never be shaken.

Psalm 15:1–5

ITEMS FOR PRAYER

- While Malaysia is Islamic by constitution, the size and energy of the Christian community has critical mass for both growth and witness. Pray for the pastoral and missional leaders who model faith and courage.

- Reports on encroaching Sharia law concern many who see an Islamic move to subjugate all under its rules. Pray that Christians will be wise and strategic in their public service, providing counterbalance to a force that attempts to thwart freedom and openness.

- As in all countries, cooperation among the various ministries, churches, and agencies is vital. Pray for the National Evangelical Christian Fellowship and the Christian Federation of Malaysia, two national associations that serve Christian communities and organizations.

Prayer

We pray today, our Father and Lord, on behalf of Malaysia and its many peoples. This prayer is given in the name that is above all others and in which we find comfort and empowerment. May your people in this land rise in strength and courage, ever giving voice to the life you gave in your coming, so that more people will hear your voice and know that you are calling them by name. Regardless of which name the government allows, Jesus, yours is the only one by which peace and life will come. It is in your strong name that we offer this prayer. Amen.

37
KENYA

A Canary in a Mine Shaft

Kenya is a Canadian prairie boy's dream. The wide sweeping savannah grasslands of the Serengeti, coming up from Tanzania in the south, give the eye a horizon-to-horizon view.

A gem of its British colonial masters, in the 1950s nationals rose in revolution, and in 1963, Kenya was given her independence.

As in any postcolonial period, the political and social road has been bumpy. The search for a multiparty democracy is hard to find in a country resting on centuries of tribal rule.

Christian faith is the religious majority. There is a strong Christian educational, medical, and mission community that serves as a pilot for many agencies throughout Africa.

Location: Northeastern Africa, on the Indian Ocean, bordering Somalia, Tanzania, Uganda, South Sudan, and Ethiopia

Population: 40 million

Religion: Christian 83% (Evangelical/Protestant 48%, Roman Catholic 21%, Anglican 9%); Muslim 8%; ethno-religionist 7%

Dispatch

I grew up knowing more about Kenya than any other country. When my friend George Macquarie and his family moved to Kenya, my many letters followed him to his boarding school, Rift Valley Academy. In the 1950s, our home in Saskatchewan became a missionary hostel, and for us a marvelous means of learning about the world.

Like so many African countries, Kenya struggled out from under colonial rule, with the Mau Mau Uprising leading to independence in 1963. I followed this story, learning the names of cities, villages, regions, political leaders, and combatants.

Late in the nineteenth century, the Christian story had come to eastern Africa by way of both Catholics and Protestants. As Kenya was brought to world attention through British colonial rule, missions from the United Kingdom and North America followed, building off the presence and organization created by the colonizers. In turn, missionaries opened the people to the rule of English-speaking whites.

Today, Kenya is predominately Christian in its faith. It is also the dominant African nation facing the influx of Islam, coming from the north and east.

Here the majority church is a collection of Evangelicals, making up 48 percent of the population. The church influence is enormous, with some seventy-seven thousand Christian congregations. The Evangelical Fellowship estimates that within their alliance there are forty thousand congregations, ten thousand schools, and five hundred hospitals and clinics, all founded and run by their churches and missions. Even so, Kenya's elections are marred by controversy. Its reputation of corruption at the highest levels of government is disturbing.

Kenya, rich and diverse in people and resources, is a land of remarkable beauty and of great importance to the presence and influence of Christian faith throughout the continent. The emerging presence of Islam is no secret. As it pushes its way down from the north, sub-Saharan countries are feeling the infiltration of its culture, laws, and mosques.

Unrest on Its Borders

The Somalian civil unrest relentlessly brews on Kenya's northeast border. Tens of thousands of Somalians have migrated south, reportedly being successful in accessing immigration. Islamic missionaries, funded by Islamic states rich in oil money, drive the growth of Islam at many levels. They strategically educate their brightest and find opportunities for them to rise in positions of influence, especially in the public sector, seeding Islamic faith into the country's future.

Just recently, the Kenyan government passed a law defining marriage, allowing Muslims to retain polygamy. Some see this as a foot in the door for Sharia law.

The dilemma facing Christians is this: The gospel opens society to other faiths, giving them the right to preach and freely make religious choices. We want others to enjoy this religious freedom even as we expect countries to allow us ours. However, in countries where Christian faith is not the majority, that often is not true.

So I asked, "Does it matter to Africa that Kenya—a country shaped by a strong Christian heritage—retains its Christian influence in society?" I heard a yes whenever the question was asked. Kenyans know Africans are intuitively sensitive and open to spiritual faith. Inevitably some religious faith will fill its life.

I then asked, "Does it matter culturally to the rest of Africa that in time, Islam might become the dominant religion in Kenya, forming the culture as it does in other Islamic-dominant African countries?"

Kenya's evangelical community historically has focused on evangelism, education, and medical care, and is not as much inclined to influence government and public-square interests, even though President Moi, an Evangelical, served as president from 1978 to 2002. Today, there is a voice of concern and it is this: If Christians don't influence public ideas and institutions, others will.

Kenya is a canary in a mine shaft. That is not to say that Christians in government automatically solve corruption, or that justice and fairness always flow from Christians being in leadership. However, the call of the gospel—to love your neighbor, to even love your enemy—nurtures justice that can flower into national life.

Kenya's many Christians are challenged to widen their influence so that, in decades to come, this critically located African nation will provide a strong Christian presence throughout Africa. By so doing, they will help protect African freedom, allowing its millions of people to worship and live in Christian faith.

TODAY'S READING

Whoever dwells in the shelter of the Most High will rest in the shadow of the Almighty. I will say of the LORD, "He is my refuge and my fortress, my God, in whom I trust." Surely he will save you from the fowler's snare and from the deadly pestilence. He will cover you with his feathers, and under his wings you will find refuge; his faithfulness will be your shield and rampart.

Psalm 91:1–4

ITEMS FOR PRAYER

- Amidst the many denominations, agencies, congregations, and leaders in Kenya, pray that grace will link them together in prayer and unity.
- The location of Kenya is strategic for Africa, and their strength in gospel witness has consequences for many. Pray for strong leadership, that they will provide godly counsel and guidance in building a strong nation.
- Kenya, large and historic, is an influencer. Pray that there will be a strong missional movement, sending Kenyans out into their region and globally.
- Christians have a significant presence in the country. Pray that their vision will include the call to justice in caring for the most vulnerable. Pray that materialism, the most seductive of gods, will not become the default of this strong Christian community, but that faithfulness to the gospel will prevail.

PRAYER

Gracious Father, we praise you for the work being done in your name in Kenya, this varied and populous land of northeast Africa, a country that has heard and known of your Son for generations. Even in the middle of conflict and tribal strife, we pray today for your people, that they will continue to move forward in your name, making known your love and goodness. We know that the influence of this land and its people is enormous in their region. May their skills and talents be used to construct a nation that will preserve the freedom of faith and stand as a model of righteousness to the world. Amen.

38

MUSLIMS

Why Rage Over Burning a Qur'an?

Muslims make up almost a quarter of the world's population. For most non-Muslims, it is confusing when we hear of reports of Sunnis killing Shias, when they both follow the prophet Muhammad and both highly revere their holy book, the Qur'an.

Like Jews and Christians, Muslims claim Abraham as their father and have a monotheistic belief in one God: in Arabic his name is *Allah*. For them, Islam is the only true religion, and those outside are apostate. Jesus, alongside prominent Old Testament figures, is considered a prophet, one to observe and honor. However, for Muslims, the Qur'an supersedes the Bible and any other religious text.

The major division between the Sunnis and Shias is about who is the true inheritor of Muhammad. This creates a fault line and a serious source of conflict, which is often carried over into national identity and politics.

Location: Indonesia is the largest Muslim-based country (13%). The Middle East comprises 20% of Muslims. In South Asia there are 20% and in sub-Saharan Africa 15%.

Population: 1.6 billion Muslims in the world

Religion: There are two groups within Islam: Sunni (75%) and Shia (20%)

Dispatch

We watched the video in horror as Islamic fundamentalists killed Christians after a "pastor" in Florida burned a Qur'an. In Afghanistan, explosive-filled trucks, suicide bombers, gun-firing civilians, and soldiers led murderous charges based on the reports. Why this outrage?

In today's devotional, in praying for the world, it is helpful to know what insults the Muslim faith, both for Christians living in places of Muslim majority, where their influence is growing, and in the West, where Muslim populations are growing and have become more visible. Increasingly, their public presence is more insistent, impacting our witness of Christ. So today we ask why their holy book means so much to them.

The Qur'an is at the very heart of Islamic faith and life. While the Islamic world is not monolithic in that it harbors deep and often violent internal disputes, Muslims are united when any disparaging word or act is directed toward their holy book or to the Prophet Muhammad.

Muslims believe Allah dictated the Qur'an directly to Prophet Muhammad between AD 570 and 632. Christians believe that the Bible is inspired and that it was written by a number of authors over time. A helpful way to see this is that our understanding that Jesus is divine is much like Muslims believing that the Qur'an is divine. As Muslims regard the Qur'an as holy, so Christians regard Jesus Christ as holy.

Devotion to the Qur'an

The devotion of Muslims to their holy book is quite extraordinary. They kiss it before and after reading it, and it occupies a central place in their homes. Many memorize it. The Qur'an contains 86,430 Arabic words, the equivalent of a 300-page book. Any translation apart from the Arabic is not considered the true word of Allah; the text is to be memorized in its original Arabic language. Simply put, to desecrate the Qur'an is viewed by Muslims as inflicting defilement on their souls.

Another comparison of Christianity to Islam is to see the Bible much as the Muslims regard the *Hadith*. Written by Islamic scholars during the eighth and ninth centuries, the *Hadith* is the record of what Muhammad said and did, and is used by Muslims to interpret the Qur'an, quite like Christians use the Bible to interpret Jesus. That's why some Islamic scholars say that burning the Qur'an is for Muslims is what desecrating Jesus or the Eucharist would be for Christians.

Christians read the Bible devotionally, as we rely on the Holy Spirit to help us understand our journey of faith. This provides trust in God's promise and provision of salvation and eternal life. Muslims leave interpretation of the Qur'an to their clerics, who then inform the faithful how it is to be experienced in their life and society. The linkage of their holy book and life is by way of Sharia law (meaning "path" in Arabic). Based on the Qur'an, Sharia law informs Muslim life, including their religion, family responsibilities, finances, and day-to-day routines.

Qur'an-burning episodes are like pouring gas on fire, fueling a population who view Western nations as Christian and therefore apostate. Our position is made even more onerous as Western forces have for years operated from some of their lands, such as in Saudi Arabia.

The Way Ahead

What is the way forward? Essential to our Christian faith is witness—telling others what Jesus has done. Inevitably, the conflict of faith will rear up in places where witness occurs, increasingly in Muslim-majority countries.

Within that mandate, it matters that we seek to know what triggers Islamic violence. Christian mission begins with a premise that we make every attempt to understand those to whom we minister. Appreciating how they think is what Philip did (Acts 8:29) when he took time to run alongside the chariot of the first minister of Candace, Queen of Ethiopia. By acquainting himself with the minister's world, he knew how to proceed.

What is surprising, however, is how some resort to extreme violence when their holy book is desecrated or burned. Do Christians do the same when their Bible is so treated? No, because our view of the Bible is different from the way Muslims view the Qur'an. *With this one caveat: Don't underestimate religious and political leaders as they use this issue to manipulate emotions and set off firestorms for political purposes.*

While the burning or desecration of the Qur'an is irresponsible and foolish, and the response of murder by Islamists has no justification, Christians seek bridges for conversation. It matters that we learn their ways and understand their beliefs. This is not only foundational to our witness, but it also exhibits the ways of our Lord.

Learning to pray for Muslims helps nurture our own heart of faith and serves to empower Christians who live in Muslim-majority countries so that daily, with tender love, their lives will give evidence of God being in Christ, reconciling the world to himself.

TODAY'S READING

All the ends of the earth will remember and turn to the LORD, and all the families of the nations will bow down before him, for dominion belongs to the LORD and he rules over the nations. All the rich of the earth will feast and worship; all who go down to the dust will kneel before him—those who cannot keep themselves alive. Posterity will serve him; future generations will be told about the Lord. They will proclaim his righteousness, declaring to a people yet unborn: He has done it!

Psalm 22:27–31

ITEMS FOR PRAYER

- In today's prayer, invite the Spirit to birth in us a love for Muslims. By faith, ask the Spirit to engender in our hearts compassion and understanding.
- Wars and physical disasters have loosened many Muslims from their homelands, sending them off as refugees. Pray that we will, in our own communities, locate a family, a man, a woman, a schoolmate, and build a friendship of help and care. And that in the right time and place, their minds would open with inquiry about the hope that lies within us.
- Many Muslims, through dreams, encounters, and visions, hear of the love of the Lord and are drawn in faith to a Christian community. Pray that the Spirit will engage many Christians to open windows of faith.
- It is an enormous challenge when a Muslim confesses Christ. The cultural shift for them is earthshaking. Pray for those in the throes of deciding for Christ, given the cost they will inevitably pay.

PRAYER

Father, one-quarter of our global peoples are Muslim, people for whom your Son came. Help us to see them as you do. May fear, emotional hostility, and indifference, which so easily can overcome our thinking, be challenged and changed. Lord, open our eyes to those in our communities who dress differently and even seem distant from our world. May we take advantages and look for opportunities in which we can befriend them and be to them your loving presence. In your holy and all-encompassing name we pray. Amen.

39

SOUTH SUDAN

Turning
Swords Into Plowshares

South Sudan is mainly agricultural based, and most people live at a subsistence level. Its civil wars have destroyed much: There is little infrastructure, passable roads hardly exist, and most of its daily necessities are imported from neighboring countries.

Before July 2012, Sudan was Africa's largest country. More than 2.5 million people were killed in two civil wars as leaders struggled to rule its sharply divided Arab and Muslim majority (mostly living in the north) and blacks and Christians (mostly living in the south).

In a referendum in the south, an overwhelming number voted to separate. South Sudan is now a distinct country with many of its historical issues continuing to vex both sides.

Location: located inland in northeastern Africa. To its north is its nemesis, Sudan; southeast are Kenya and Uganda, Ethiopia is to the east, with the Congo and the Central African Republic on the west and southwest. Vital to its history and economy is the Sudd, an enormous swampland linked to the Nile (White) River system.

Population: estimated 8 million (numbers hard to verify)

Religion: Christian majority (Roman Catholics 2.5 million, Anglicans 2 million, Protestant/Evangelical 1 million); some Muslims and animists

Dispatch

The problem in South Sudan wasn't that Muslims were killing Christians or Christians killing Muslims; it was Christians killing Christians.

Even as border disputes continue between Sudan and the new Republic of South Sudan, even more troubling to this new and fragile African nation are the intertribal killings and child kidnappings.

What surprised the Christian community was the hostility that escalated into killing between tribes, primarily in the state of Jongeli. Triggering these killings was an age-old problem: cattle rustling. Estimates are that three thousand South Sudanese died in two years from this internal conflict.

The nomadic tribes are rooted in centuries-old and culturally engrained habits and resentments. Cattle define life and measure their worth. This focus finds its way into the most central event of tribal life, which is marriage. Important in this cultural ritual is the dowry question: What will my daughter fetch? Thus the dowry becomes an arbitrator of social well-being.

The Dowry

The power of the dowry is extraordinary. The value of a daughter to be married is based on various factors: her characteristics—for some tribes, taller means more elegant and therefore more valuable—and the ability of the groom's family to pay. The South Sudan president's daughter, who married an Ethiopian, received a dowry of three hundred cattle. The average family may have twenty-five cows.

Translate that dowry into an annual income, and its value is enormous. While no money changes hands, and the dowry can be paid over time, getting your hands on new cattle is a prime matter, especially among young men preparing for marriage and wanting to build up their father's herd. Also, cattle rustling can enhance a young man's right of passage; looting another tribe's herd helps demonstrate his manhood. Linked to robbing and its retributive action of killing is child kidnapping. Children who are kidnapped become slaves, herding and protecting cattle.

Bishop Elias Taban, president of the South Sudan Evangelical Alliance, called together tribal chiefs, elders, government officials, and pastors to the Jongeli Peace and Reconciliation Conference hosted by the World Evangelical Alliance and Tear Fund, New Zealand.

None disagreed that peace was better for all. They affirmed Christ's call to love your enemy. Commitment to these values was loud and instant, even though many attending were nominal in their faith. Practical answers were less clear. Like many African countries, South Sudan's infrastructure is under-resourced, caught in centuries of tribal identity and ingrained attitudes, and deeply entrenched in its mores and expectations.

I listened to their stories, felt their sorrow, noted their analysis, and wondered about solutions. While the nation is fragile and new in its government, leaders such as Bishop Taban are key to finding resurrection-like initiatives. Taban, a civil engineer, is tall and imposing. Energetic and charismatic in public speaking, his entrepreneurial skills expanded beyond his congregation in Yei, and now the community runs schools and an orphanage, and has businesses, with a vision to open a university. His passion for the Sudanese to deal with their own social, religious, and economic matters was clear and pointed. He challenged them to build enterprises in the troubled state of Jongeli, creating rice farms along the flooding region of the Nile. In 2013, Bishop Taban received the Clinton Foundation Global Citizens Award.

What Will It Take?

Missions have been active here in Sudan for years. In the 1800s, Christian missions, both Roman Catholic and Protestant, were strong in the south. Today, while many practice tribal religions, Christian faith is accepted as the common point in securing peace.

Outside help is needed here to lift communities and to develop a promising future for their children. Big ideas, such as infrastructure, require major input from others. Health, education, creative training in agriculture, and husbandry are on the top of a to-do list—tough and daunting enough to stretch big-thinking philanthropists. Heroic efforts of church and ministry agencies, spotted about the countryside, are powerful testimonies to what can be done. Surely more of this is needed. The culture is responsive to Christian initiatives. They understand faith language, but the engrained culture and collective memories are hard to crack. While in some countries governments put in place policies to keep Christian agencies out, South Sudan is open and willing. No visa is required.

There is, however, a *however*: Their soil of development will lie barren until they themselves sufficiently want change and transformation. Finding ways to bring about peace is the formidable task for all: tribal leaders, NGOs, church and political leaders.

Investment boards of companies, strategy committees of mission agencies, and men and women looking for a place to make a difference may want to consider South Sudan. This people, generally handsome, tall, and dignified, are old in civilization and desperate to find their way. Making up the newest nation on planet Earth, they need our attention if they are to remake swords into plowshares.

TODAY'S READING

Make us glad for as many days as you have afflicted us, for as many years as we have seen trouble. May your deeds be shown to your servants, your splendor to their children. May the favor of the Lord our God rest on us; establish the work of our hands for us—yes, establish the work of our hands.

Psalm 90:15–17

ITEMS FOR PRAYER

- Mission groups working in various skills are so needed in South Sudan. Pray for those already on the ground, that they may be protected from civil wars and have sufficient resources to fulfill their calling.

- Being such a young nation, its need for infrastructure is critical. Pray that giving countries will be creatively wise and invest carefully but generously, so that this people will rise from their current state.

- While the country is understood to be Christian, it is largely a nominal faith, and its people are in need of our transforming Christ. Pray for its pastors and those in teaching, that the gospel story will be played out in their lives.

- The government, fragile as it is, matters to the people. Pray for wise and honest leadership.

PRAYER

Gracious God, creator of this people and its many tribes, you have walked these centuries down their paths. In this new political state, dear Lord, visit this land of South Sudan with a double-edged sword of spiritual harvest and economic well-being. Their heart is inclined to you, yet many are without knowledge of you. Burst in on this people so they may know grace and learn to live in your presence. May that collective experience translate into the growth of a nation that is good to its people, fair to its neighbors, and alive and well in you, our Lord. Amen.

40

GREECE

Few Countries Are More "Christian" Than Greece

Regarded as the birthplace of Western civilization, **Greece** experimented with the idea of democracy early. Here the Olympic Games were founded, and formulations of philosophy were birthed that would greatly influence the West. While the Roman Empire carried the Hellenistic (Greek) culture to the world, the ideas shaping the world 2,000 years ago can be traced back to this people.

During the twentieth century, Greece struggled within the European world: wars with Turkey and Italy and a stint under communism. In recent years they've been plagued with financial distress.

Most Greeks claim Christian affiliation in this country dominated by the Greek Orthodox Church. It was influenced by the apostle Paul and first-century Christianity.

Location: a peninsula in southeast Europe on the Ionian, Mediterranean, and Aegean Seas

Population: 11 million

Religion: Christian 92% (primarily Greek Orthodox, Evangelical 0.3%)

Dispatch

Not only is Greece Christian, but it can be difficult to navigate socially if one isn't Greek Orthodox. A professor, who is a publicly admitted communist, said, "Of course, we are all Christian. You can hardly register a child unless baptized by the state church. I'm an atheist, but I'd be a fool not to be a Christian too." A Christian leader in conversation happened to say he was evangelical. The other turned in surprise and exclaimed with puzzlement, "But I thought you were Greek!" Being both Greek and Orthodox, one is linked by the umbilical cord of history, tradition, and birth.

Countries in eastern and southern Europe, the Middle East, and northern Africa have historically been shaped by Christian Orthodox Churches whose people make up a 100 million worldwide, Christian groupings not under Rome.

A Note on Eastern Orthodoxy

Christians in the early centuries fought bitterly over which church would dominate: Eastern churches, centered in Istanbul (Constantinople), or Western churches centered in Rome. The Eastern churches refused to acknowledge Rome and rallied around a national or regional church. They had a similar theology to Rome's, but refused to submit to a Roman bishop or pope. The Orthodox churches include Coptic (Egypt), Greek, Russian, Ukrainian, Syrian, Antiochian, Czech, Armenian, Melekite, and Maronite Orthodox. They established their own churches with their own archbishops, giving tacit approval to the seniority of the patriarch of Istanbul. Some, such as the Coptic Church in Egypt, even have their own pope.

The Early Church

Greeks proudly declare, and rightly so, their early role in the worldwide church. The marvelous archaeological digs give evidence of this country's place in the founding of the Christian faith. A quick read of the book of Acts (chapters 16–18) describes those early days. The church grew not only by evangelism but also by force. Roman Emperor Theodosius pressed Christianity on his citizens. In the year 387, he announced chariot races in Thessaloniki, north of Athens. Once seven thousand people had assembled, he sent in his soldiers and all were slaughtered. Athenians, knowing he was on his way south in a matter of days, rushed to the sea and were baptized, demonstrating to the emperor their newly found faith.

Early in its history, Greece became solidly Christian, by conviction, fear, or accommodation, and today the Greek Orthodox Church remains a prime shaper of Greek life and politics.

Evangelicals recognize their minority status. They know that the majority faith can marginalize their witness whenever they choose. And further, there are social levers they can access to press civic authority and police to reduce religious opportunity.

Evangelical witness operates with two supporting expectations: that their witness of Christ will nurture within the Orthodox a deeper appreciation and love for Christ. In a country that claims to be Christian, their devotion and theology rest on understanding Jesus as an infant, the Christ child, and Mary as dominant. Most evangelicals admit their goal isn't so much to win over the Orthodox, but to inspire faith and spiritual renewal within the church and then to build a strong and credible evangelical presence by way of churches and missions.

Also, many feel that Western missions have overlooked Greece, assuming it is not in need of mission enterprises from Christians of other countries.

Proselytism

The Greek constitution declares it is a crime to proselytize. When Greece entered the European Union, they had to abandon this clause; yet the government prefers to pay fines when utilizing such a law rather than change it. One can appeal to the European court if religious rights have been violated, but costs for this are prohibitive. In effect, the continuing application of the old law has a dampening effect on Christian witness.

In a strange twist of language, the government uses an English word for Evangelicals, calling them *Protestants*, and refuses to use the Greek word *Dimartyria*, which carries with it an implication of being a martyr.

The use of the English term *Protestant* suggests that Evangelicals are foreigners.

The evangelical community began in the early twentieth century in part by the fall of the Ottoman Empire. This Muslim empire was centered in Turkey and had dominated Greece for four hundred years, ruling much of southeast Europe right up to the gates of Vienna. When the Ottoman Turks were defeated in WWI, Greeks living in Turkey were released to return to Greece. Many who had been living in Turkey prior to the war had been influenced by Evangelicals. When they returned to Greece, they kept alive their heritage and built churches, especially in the north around Thessaloniki.

Greece, a country rooted in the apostle Paul's missionary witness, is made up of a people who mostly identify as Christian. Yet this land is in need of spiritual renewal and the personal transforming presence of Christ.

TODAY'S READING

Rejoice always, pray continually, give thanks in all circumstances; for this is God's will for you in Christ Jesus. Do not quench the Spirit. Do not treat prophecies with contempt but test them all; hold on to what is good, reject every kind of evil. May God himself, the God of peace, sanctify you through and through. May your whole spirit, soul and body be kept blameless at the coming of our Lord Jesus Christ. The one who calls you is faithful, and he will do it.

1 Thessalonians 5:16–24

ITEMS FOR PRAYER

- In a country where Christian history dots the landscape and where symbols of faith are so visible, pray for increased freedom for public witness of the gospel.
- Pastoral leadership in Greece is in constant demand. Pray for the Greek Bible College and other places of training in their work of preparing pastors and Christian leaders.
- Financial severity creates difficulty for a government and its people. Pray for its financial well-being and for missions and churches.
- Because Greece is a refugee highway for many attempting to enter Europe, pray for ministries that bring food, clothing, and spiritual assistance to those living in bleak and trying circumstances.

PRAYER

Lord Jesus, for this people so early acquainted with your gospel, we pray for a revival of Christ-lifting presence within the hearts of the Greek people. As they wrestle with issues of finances, government stability, and the surge of tens of thousands of refugees, may they recognize that the message the apostle Paul brought so many years ago is as current and powerful today as it was then. By your Spirit, break in on their national consciousness so that in hearing your voice they will echo with Paul, "God is able to bless you abundantly, so that in all things at all times, having all that you need, you will abound in every good work" (2 Corinthians 9:8). Amen.

41

BURMA/ MYANMAR

As Wise as Serpents and Innocent as Doves

Burma, the **Republic of the Union of Myanmar**, is made up of eight major national races and 135 subgroups or tribes. Among its 116 languages, 26 have some Bible translation.

The cultural complexity and ongoing killings and conflicts come from ethnic tensions and divisions. Especially troubling is the ongoing issue with the largely Muslim ethnic Rohingya minority in the north.

Conquered by the British in the 1800s, in 1948, Burma became independent. Six months before independence, General Aung San, who led the struggle against the British, was murdered. (He was the father of Nobel Peace Prize awardee Aung San Suu Kyi.) After an interlude of Communist control and opposition forces, in 1962, there was a military coup that ruled until 2011. Then the military government declared democratization.

Location: in Southeast Asia, surrounded by Laos, Thailand, China, Bangladesh, and India

Population: 60 million

Religion: Buddhist 80%; Christian 9% (Evangelical/Protestant 7%, Roman Catholic 1%); Muslim 7%

Dispatch

Christian leaders understood well Jesus' advice to be "as wise as serpents and innocent as doves" (ESV). In a country best known as Burma, its citizens have survived fifty years of brutal military dictatorship. Inquiring as to how they emerged intact, one pastor noted, "We didn't put signs on our buildings. When we wanted to

215

build a church, we just built a house and made it larger. We kept our heads down."

A little history matters.

After a century of British colonial rule ended in 1948, Burma was given independence. Some saw it doomed from the start. Astrological readers interpreted that independence had occurred on the wrong day. Here, reading astrological signs is so important that governmental and business decisions will only be made when the Buddhist priest reading the astrological signs gives his okay. Even in building bridges.

During their drive to be freed from colonial rule, tribal antagonism was triggered when non-Burmese ethnic nationalities such as the Karen, Chin, and Rohingya sided with the British. Some were not Buddhists and were seen as traitors to the nation and its religion, especially the Karen tribe. They were targets of persecution by the government until 2012, when a treaty was signed. Only time will tell if the treaty is honored.

Burma's recent military regimes are seen as one of the most repressive in recent history. They have a record of crimes against humanity, torture, forced labor, and conscription of child soldiers. Much of the world community pressured the Myanmar military to stop the abuse of human rights. Driven by the courageous defiance of one of its daughters, Aung San Suu Kyi, they finally announced democracy would become the ruling system.

A few years later, changes in the country are mixed. Some are cosmetic, as the new constitution requires that 40 percent of elected members be military, 40 percent former military, and 20 percent civilian.

How is the church in Myanmar faring?

- Their ability to keep a low profile may seem to some a kowtowing to the military. Historians will give us a broader picture, but my sense is that their strategy of living out the gospel in ways that don't draw attention from the military is wise. This allows space in which churches and missions can survive.

- Their churches tend to be located in rural areas. The land is dotted with many small Bible colleges, everyone seemingly in need of their own school, reminiscent of other countries freed from military rule and dictatorships. As freedom becomes the new norm, learning to cooperate is a skill its leaders need to acquire.

- Leadership here in its churches and mission agencies is young and emerging with new freedoms under a new political mandate. These people are able and energetic, all boding well for the future of the church.

- The gospel witness faces distinct challenges in this Buddhist country. In contrast to Thailand, here Buddhism is more traditional than pervasive. In Thailand, spirit houses are everywhere: in front of hotels, restaurants, homes, and places of business. Amulets are hung from mirrors in taxis and sold in the open markets. In Myanmar, while temples are everywhere and used by citizens in their religious life, the religion is more cultural than personal, more traditional than operational. As well, there is a curious pattern of addressing spirituality. Education dominates life to age thirty, with the next twenty years focused on vocation and money. At fifty, spiritual matters are taken more seriously. This makes evangelism among young people crucial.

- The language of Buddhism is Bali Sanskrit, a rather distant tongue unknown by most citizens. While it is memorized, it is not understood, and so for young people their religion becomes even more detached.

- Concerns over human rights of the Muslim ethnic Rohingya in the north is an issue on which Christians must refuse to be pressured by Buddhist nationalism to overlook this human tragedy. It really matters that Christians take up the cause of protecting this people from killings and persecution.

Burma/Myanmar, known for the movie *The Bridge on the River Kwai,* is in a new moment of cultural transition. While moving toward a more democratic country, it still is very much controlled by its large army of 400,000. As well, there continues to be an issue of 140,000 war refugees in Thailand. With this is an unresolved request for a commission of inquiry into possible war crimes.

The church has learned to hold its opinion, keep its profile low, and understate its place and role. Its future will require diligence, humility, and the ability to be circumspect in witness and life. This is a great people who have known indescribable hardship; they have lived with a cruel government, yet have a continuing heart for the power of the gospel to bring personal and societal change. We prayed for its leadership, sensing great hope for its future.

Today's Reading

LORD, how many are my foes! How many rise up against me! Many are saying of me, "God will not deliver him." But you, LORD, are a shield around me, my glory, the One who lifts my head high. I call out to the LORD, and he answers me from his holy mountain. I lie down and sleep; I wake again, because the LORD sustains me. I will not fear though tens of thousands assail me on every side. Arise, LORD! Deliver me, my God! Strike all my enemies on the jaw; break the teeth of the wicked. From the LORD comes deliverance. May your blessing be on your people.

Psalm 3

Items for Prayer

- In newly emerging freedoms, there is often the inclination for Christians to go it on their own, without regard for others. Pray for Burma/Myanmar, that its leadership will see the importance of fellowship and cooperation in unity for a public witness of Christ and for strength of their common commitment.
- The persecution of the Rohingya in the north needs Christians who will stand up for their protection. Pray that Christians will be courageous in coming to their aid.
- Praise God for the movement of his Spirit. As the church grows, its need for trained pastoral leadership is critical. Pray

for these small and struggling schools, for their leadership, and for the required resources so needed.

• Within the strong Buddhist community, especially among its 700,000 monks, pray that the presence of Christ will infiltrate their leadership. Pray that many will come to Christ and be transformed by his presence.

PRAYER

Dear Father, Creator of all that is good, I give thanks for those in Myanmar who, through the tough times of persecution, emerged as having been faithful to you. Today, as some Christians face ethnic persecution, be at work among them. Give leaders boldness, humility, and a spirit of servanthood. For its political leadership, may their move toward democracy be more than window dressing. May the freedoms they have promised become reality. And in the midst of its rise in their standard of living, I pray that the church will defend the Rohingya in the north. May the church in this land become strong and viable, one that gives face, hands, and heart to their world of the Christ we love and represent. Amen.

42

NEPAL

A View From the Top of the World

With over a hundred ethnic groups, **Nepal** is dominated by a caste system that is endemic within its Hindu population. Ruled by a monarchy and historically isolated from the world, it has experienced no colonial masters. In 1962, the king took over direct power. Through the 1990s and early twenty-first century there was much unrest until Maoist rebels claimed power in 2008. Finally, a political formula was agreed upon, and in 2014, a constituent assembly was formed with an elected prime minister.

Location: This "top-of-the-world" mountainous country lies in Asia, on the southern slopes of the Himalayan Mountains, surrounded by China on the north and India on the south.

Population: 30 million

Religion: Hindu 80%; Buddhist 16%; Christian 3%; many identify as being syncretistic, mixing Hinduism and Buddhism

Dispatch

For many, Mount Everest and Hindu temples are the faces of Nepal. But peer behind that façade and you'll see another reality. In 1960, there were thirty known Christians; today, there are over 1.4 million. How did this come about? Quite simply, I was told. The Nepal story of Christian growth describes the power of indigenous (local) leadership and witness.

Christian faith rose within its own Nepalese culture. Isolated from other cultures, most foreign missions weren't allowed in, although the Bible societies had translated the Bible in the 1930s. The Hindu kingdom allowed only missions that were working in health and education, but refused permission to evangelize or build churches. Their witness had to be by the testimony of their lives.

After 1960, people began to convert to Christianity. Both India and Britain had recruited Nepalese to fight (including the famous Sherpa from eastern Nepal) in their respective armies. Many of them heard the gospel and came to faith. Returning to their families and villages, they told about the Jesus they had met, and soon churches flourished.

Because Nepal had little available university training, most who wanted further education went elsewhere. Again, as with the soldiers, students met Christians while studying abroad. After graduating, they too returned home and told their families and friends about Christ, and more churches were built.

In this country of 30 million, isolated from other cultural influences, a New Testament phenomenon was at work. When I asked if there was something within their life experience that triggered so many conversions, I learned two vital factors: physical healings and deliverance from the control of evil. Hidden in valleys behind mountain peaks, people are cut off from medical help. When they were sick they had only two choices: a witch doctor or Jesus. The former would add cost and bring no solution, while the second promised healing along with spiritual transformation for the person and community. The witness made visible by healings reverberated through families, villages, and tribes, and many confessed Christ.

I wondered what obvious impact the gospel has had on the people of Nepal. Six factors surfaced.

- People stop worshiping idols.
- Love becomes an obvious expression of relationship. In a family-structured society, love triggering concrete patterns of caring makes the value of this newfound faith manifestly obvious.
- Hard work. Wondering why this was a factor, I learned that in their culture not to have to work is a blessing: You have been cursed to work because your "karma" or fate is bad. The Christians taught that work is a direct gift from their heavenly Father.
- The gospel disregards the caste system, which degrades *untouchables* or *Dalit*. New converts of any class or distinction

can freely enter a church and eat alongside other Christians, knowing they too are beloved.

- Patterns of honesty and forgiveness become normative. Following the Maoist decade of killing and destruction (1996–2006) in which over eighteen thousand were killed, the government promised a truth and reconciliation commission. Years later, it still hasn't been implemented. When asked why, an official said, "Forgiveness is not part of our tradition. Without that understanding, such a commission is useless."

- Conversion to Christ brings economic change. Their many religious festivals require money to participate. The poor are often forced to borrow from landlords and friends. Once Christian, they no longer attend, eliminating that outlay of funds. Also, when a witch doctor was consulted, he might have told his client to do more at a festival, which again required money. Christians were taught not to gamble or consume alcohol; with their budget freed from those costs, they had more for food, education, and health.

A professor said, "I tell government leaders, the best way to improve the economic well-being of Nepal is to promote Christian faith. Christians work harder and save more. Women are well treated, and the national social well-being goes up. Christians make great citizens."

In this country, on the top of the world, there is a marvelous example of how Christians live out their faith: an unashamed witness, a heart to care for the handicapped and marginalized, and a determination to be present in the political system, affirming human rights and freedom to worship. The apostle Paul would have enjoyed writing a letter to this church.

Today's Reading

Answer me when I call to you, my righteous God. Give me relief from my distress; have mercy on me and hear my prayer. . . . Tremble and do not sin; when you are on your beds, search your hearts and be silent. Offer the sacrifices of the righteous and trust in the LORD.

Many, LORD, are asking, "Who will bring us prosperity?" Let the light of your face shine on us. Fill my heart with joy when their grain and new wine abound. In peace I will lie down and sleep, for you alone, LORD, make me dwell in safety.

Psalm 4:1, 4–8

ITEMS FOR PRAYER

- Recognizing the remarkable witness of Christians in Nepal, praise God for his working in this land and its people.
- The freedom permitted to people of faith to live and give witness is important in the building of churches and establishing of missions. Pray for the emergence of church leaders who will be characterized by peace and servanthood in their witness and outreach.
- Nepal is made up of an incredibly large percentage of young people. The need for economic growth and employment opportunities matters. Pray for Nepal as it builds a business sector.
- As a Hindu-dominated country, Nepal struggles with maintaining religious freedom. Christians still find it difficult, even though the law guarantees their freedom. Pray for Christians, especially those in public leadership, that they will be wise in their witness for Christ.

PRAYER

Dear Lord, I give praise for the ways in which your Spirit has enabled the church in Nepal to grow. Help us learn the lessons of mission and ministry in a place so isolated. May their story be told to encourage nationals in other countries where they too feel left alone. Your Spirit is ever present in all lands of your creation.

I pray that you would call up from Nepal's young population able men and women who love you, who are filled with the Spirit, and who are made wise by their experience and education. As they serve and lead, may the name of Jesus be regarded as trustworthy so that many will come to know you, whom to know is life eternal. Amen.

43

BANGLADESH

A Young Country
With Ancient Needs

Bangladesh, while ancient in culture, has a recent history as a country. Prior to 1947 it was a part of India. When India became independent from colonial England, what we now call Bangladesh became part of Pakistan, then named East Pakistan (even though distanced from West Pakistan by 1,400 kilometers). Disaster was written all over this arrangement, and after a fierce war in which some 3 million died, in 1971 it became independent and was renamed Bangladesh. While it began as a secular state, in 1988 Islam became the official religion.

The country's location makes it vulnerable to floods that wash down the mountains, swelling its many rivers and flowing into the delta, the Bay of Bengal. With a dense population of 170 million, Bangladesh is pressed into a landmass about the size of Greece, which has just 12 million people.

William Carey, father of modern missions, in 1797 left England and worked among the Bengalis, yet today this group is considered the largest of unreached people groups.

Located: surrounded by the northeast corner of India—it was formerly part of India

Population: 170 million

Religion: Muslim 89%; Hindu 9%; Christian 2.5%

Dispatch

As the plane veered to the right to land in Dhaka, I could see the many fingers of rivers crossing green fields, a reminder of how vulnerable Bangladesh is to rivers, monsoons, and floods. This country, carved out of northeast India, is built on a delta, a young nation established after a bloody war. This is a people not only struggling to keep their head above the ever-rising floods, but vigorously seeking to find their way into the modern world.

After defeating the British and then separating from Pakistan, Bangladesh has an enormous gap between a very small upper layer of the wealthy and a much larger layer of those living in poverty. While fashioning itself as a secular democracy, it really is a Muslim-majority country, incited by modern Islam.

What is overwhelming is to see people everywhere—170 million in a small landmass. Imagine that number living in one-third of Manitoba, or half the U.S. population forced into Florida. In Canada, population density is 3.3 people per square kilometer. In Bangladesh it is 1,086 persons per square kilometer. Its packed world must be experienced to be understood.

The people are loving and generous, and we felt at home. Their life is tough, and they know their share of suffering. Politically birthed in a bloodbath of 3 million dead, its nationhood withstands floods washing away everything they own. Christians feel the snubs as a religious minority, but not once did I hear the suggestion from them that life is too tough. No complaining, no wishing for what others have. Though they have so little, their celebrations opened our hearts. They were easy to love.

While their hospitality and generosity were genuine and greatly appreciated, Bangladesh is laden with enormous burdens of poverty, ignorance, and life-choking bribery. Literacy is, at best, 50 percent. Many live in homes so primitive you wonder how they survive. A government rife with corruption is so brazen it has become a way of life—institutionalized. Starting at the top of government it works its tentacles through all of public life. When working with anything official, nothing happens without greasing the wheel. Getting a job requires upfront payment. To land a job in the police force, for example, an applicant pays a major bribe and then works for ten years to pay back the loan.

Cheap labor attracts manufacturers of everything from T-shirts to lawn mowers. A twelve-hour day, six days a week, earns $100 a month. The Gross Domestic Product (GDP) has grown rapidly, driven by this labor market, but economists warn that the burden of corruption is disabling the country.

Leadership

Younger leaders here are the kind you could drop into any country or situation and know they would land on their feet. They are bright, wise, creative, courageous, and deeply committed to the Lord Jesus. And they are indigenous. The world has changed, and the period of foreign missions leading national ministries is over.

The Christian community here is still small: 2.5 percent. With approximately six thousand churches, the relief and development side of agency work is large and growing. For example, the Canadian Food Grains Bank works with the Nazarene Church, and World Relief Canada with Koinonia, a division of the National Fellowship. Each denomination builds its own residential schools to serve children of Christian families discriminated against in the public schools.

I saw maps, plans, and statistics—Christian leaders are careful in their planning. They explain their strategy of introducing Christ to villages, communities, and regions. The *Jesus* Film has been a particular accelerator in conversions. One pastor working with Hindus focused on entire families and villages. In one day he said he had baptized four thousand Hindus.

The vast population allows for all kinds of evangelistic groups to come unannounced and stay on their own, moving about (also leaving quickly), causing some to wonder why foreign engagement is so independent. However, this isn't the first country in which Evangelicals have been guilty of allowing entrepreneurial evangelism to run unchecked.

The city of Dhaka is a photographer's dream. Colorful, idiosyncratic, anything you imagine you might see you probably can find. Traffic is fascinating. Cairo, Bangkok, and Nairobi are wild, but this city holds its own madness. Drivers are bizarre and brilliant. Deft at missing one another, in a strange way they look out for each other. Tens upon thousands of rickshaws moving around motorcars, trucks, and cycles, all on a decrepit and broken infrastructure, make a simple journey an adventure.

One day we were to go northeast to meet some Christians. They wanted to meet us—most had never seen a white person. We wanted to go too, but "stomach revenge" had exacted its price—we were immobilized. Even so, that evening, a young man from the village arrived with gifts they had prepared for our visit. Since we couldn't come to them, they came to us. Lovely handcrafted gifts, from those with so little, all with words of gracious love. As the young pastor was leaving, I asked, "How long is the return bus ride?" "Four and a half hours" was the reply.

Why did it matter that they meet us? I recall as a boy hearing Nicholas Benghu from South Africa, in our Saskatoon church, telling of God's love. There are times when hearing it from another, one outside of your world, has a great impact. The missionary enterprise is important and alive and well. But I learned in this dynamic and busy world that the sustaining development of the Christian life comes ultimately through the strength of its national pastors and leaders.

Please get this message out: Your prayer and monetary investment in these men and women are worth every moment and every dollar.

TODAY'S READING

The Son is the image of the invisible God, the firstborn over all creation. For in him all things were created: things in heaven and on earth, visible and invisible, whether thrones or powers or rulers or authorities; all things have been created through him and for him. He is before all things, and in him all things hold together. . . . For God was pleased to have all his fullness dwell in him, and through him to reconcile to himself all things, whether things on earth or things in heaven, by making peace through his blood, shed on the cross.

Colossians 1:15–20

ITEMS FOR PRAYER

- As younger leaders increasingly guide the church in Bangladesh, pray they would be wise, finding ways to cooperate in spiritual unity, retaining boldness and creativity.
- While technically there is freedom of religion in Bangladesh, intimidation and discrimination are often used to corral the

gospel witness. Pray that Christians would be fearless in their testimony of Christ, and pray for political protection for its pastors, churches, and missions.

• Many leaders require support from outside, especially during flood times. The large number of Nongovernment Organizations (NGOs) is important for the well-being of the country. Pray for these many Christian missions.

Prayer

Gracious Lord, in Bangladesh, this country of great need and amazing opportunities, our prayer is that younger men and women showing here such dedication to your call will be encouraged as they continue in faith. During the rainy season and regular occasions of flooding, the work done in your name resonates with the love you want these special people to know and feel. May those of us with more than enough be generous in our help and support to ministries in Bangladesh. And may our children and grandchildren find ways and means of helping in the building of this country, which in time will know that Jesus is Lord. Amen.

44

PALESTINE

Political Complexity Is Not Its Only Story

Palestine includes the West Bank and the Gaza Strip. The Palestinian Authority is given the responsibility of overseeing their area. The political party Fatah won the election to lead both the West Bank and Gaza, but Hamas defeated them and currently controls the Gaza Strip.

Palestinian Christians are descendants from the ancestors who lived in the geographic region we know as Palestine. They include Oriental Orthodoxy, Anglican, Eastern Orthodoxy, Catholic (Eastern and Western rites), and Evangelical/Protestant.

In total, Christians make up less than 4% of Palestinians in the region: 8% in the West Bank and less than 1% in the Gaza Strip.

Location: This landlocked area includes what we know as Judea and Samaria, bordered on the east by the Dead Sea and Jordan, and on the north, west, and south by Israel.

Population: 5 million—80% are Palestinian Arabs and 20% Jewish Israelis

Religion: Muslim 88%; Jewish 8.5%; Orthodox 1%; Evangelical 0.2%

Dispatch

If you've been to Israel as a tourist, there is a good chance you have gone to Bethlehem to visit the Church of the Nativity but not stopped to visit Christians there in the town.

Here in the very place where Jesus was born, Christians live in ever-decreasing numbers. This neighborhood, in which Jesus entered earthly existence, is surrounded by religious and political pressures, resulting in a vacating of Christians. Of all the places in the world to pray for, it is here, for our brothers and sisters whose presence is being daily eroded.

The Middle East is a riddling complexity in its decades-old struggle. This isn't the time to solve this battle, but it does give occasion to introduce two ministries that speak Christian witness into this important land and people.

In Bethlehem

Bethlehem Bible College, located just off the main road to the Church of the Nativity, really matters. Over the years I got to know its former president Bashar Awad. Each time I visited, I asked our driver to stop so I could introduce my friends to both the president and the college.

Now called Bethlehem and Galilee Bible College, it was founded in 1979. Within the stress and misunderstandings that its complex community experiences, a ministry has developed, a credible and vital ministry of training and education. Awad saw Christians leaving to study in other countries, never to return. He knew he had to stop the outflow. Beginning with a modest gift of support, in time they bought the Helen Keller center, built additional facilities, and expanded from Bethlehem to a center now in Galilee.

Within this small but highly visible world, presence matters. Even though this Bethlehem is the very one of our Christian beginnings, over the centuries Christians have lost their place here. As in Turkey, the erosion of a Christian population gives way to Muslim dominance, snuffing out both influence and witness and often leading to outright persecution and exclusion. The West Bank is a place where this attrition continues at an alarming rate.

Christian Palestinians have dropped from 2 percent to 1 percent since 2000. Even though the Palestinian Authority claimed it was committed to equality for all, the Second Intifada impacted many Christians who had hotels and tourist companies. Many left.

Bethlehem College sits in the middle of this loss. The strong will and bold faith of its leadership are about more than retaining a remnant, but missional in vision, training pastors, helping in the planting of churches, and raising visibility of the gospel among people whose theological rationale is to rid themselves of

Christians. Recently the New Student Centre was dedicated with a new chapel, cafeteria, and lounge areas.

Musalaha

Musalaha, an Arabic word, means "reconciliation." The organization was founded and is led by Dr. Salim J. Munayer, an Israeli-Palestinian (a Palestinian born in Israel). He moves back and forth between Jerusalem and the West Bank.

The unique mission of Musalaha is to break down hostilities between Messianic Jewish Christians and Arab Christians. The political divide is so deep, one only needs to walk along the fence to feel its hostilities, resentments, hatred, and implied violence. Here is their vision statement: "Musalaha is a nonprofit organization that seeks to promote reconciliation between Israelis and Palestinians as demonstrated in the life and teaching of Jesus. We seek to be an encouragement and facilitator of reconciliation, first among Palestinian Christians and Messianic Israelis, and then beyond to our respective communities."

Dr. Munayer started putting together Palestinians and Israelis, taking them into the desert. Here in isolation, away from symbols and reality, it was a time and place to reflect, pray, and discuss.

Wisely, he knew that what could not be done was to try to solve locked-in feelings and views. First, they had to build fellowship and relationships, one by one, learning to trust one from the other side, hearing what they were saying rather than assuming what was intended. Salim notes, "I came to the conclusion that the theology of reconciliation was the best theology to deal with all these issues, and that more than anything else, the Jewish and Palestinian believers needed to be brought together, face-to-face. Anything less would not work because of the dehumanization and demonization going on from both sides."

Brother Andrew of Open Doors noted, "Of all the ministries in Israel, I found myself drawn most to this one. It seemed the most ambitious but also the riskiest. It wasn't an idea promoted by foreign missionaries but was birthed in the local Christian community.

It didn't just talk about the problem between Palestinians and Jews. It brought the two sides together and provided a means for them to reconcile."

Salim and I sat one evening, just outside of Bethlehem, eating dinner in a restaurant overlooking the Shepherd's Field. And to fill out the picture, just behind me was the field Boaz bought so he could marry Ruth, a Moabite, and daughter-in-law to Naomi, recently widowed. Boaz, whose name means "kinsman redeemer," is an Old Testament precursor to Jesus, our Redeemer.

We talked about wars, prisons, and words. He noted that one couldn't live in either the West Bank or Israel without being engaged some way in politics. In his book *Seeking and Pursuing Peace*, he wrote, "Everything we say and do has political implications. . . . So we do have a political agenda. We want to see nations in the Middle East, and especially the Israeli Jews and Palestinian Arabs, being reconciled by the gospel. What does that mean? It simply means to be reconciled to one another."

In this land of Jesus' birth, may we as Christians from other lands see the witness of Christ through these and other ministries, central to our prayers and support.

Today's Reading

Create in me a pure heart, O God, and renew a steadfast spirit within me. Do not cast me from your presence or take your Holy Spirit from me. Restore to me the joy of your salvation and grant me a willing spirit, to sustain me.

Psalm 51:10–12

Items for Prayer

- The seemingly impossible roadblocks to peace frustrate Christians on both sides. Pray for grace in living, that Christians in Palestine will model what it means to be peacemakers, ever showing the true spirit of Jesus of Nazareth, whom we confess.
- The role of Bethlehem and Galilee Bible College is strategic to the work of the gospel in the West Bank and beyond.

Pray for its leadership and students and for those the Spirit is calling into service.

- The reconciliation ministry of Musalaha, bringing people together in creative interchange of ideas and building of friendships, is vital in creating contacts across the divide. Pray for Dr. Salim Munayer and his team, that the effect of their efforts will bring a harvest of the fruit of peace and love.

PRAYER

Father of our Lord Jesus, Savior and King, we continue to pray for the peace of Jerusalem, knowing that in the midst of political battles, your Spirit is at work. We pray that there will be a chorus of peacemakers to manifest your ways, bringing this land of your first coming into harmony, so that your life will be reproduced in those living there. Prosper Bethlehem and Galilee Bible College. Fill it with students eager to be your servants. May Musalaha be strong in connecting Israeli and Palestinian Christian young people in learning to love one another, as we are clearly called to do. In your name we ask these things. Amen.

45
THE CZECH REPUBLIC

In the Heart of Secular Europe

The Czech Republic, formerly known as Czechoslovakia, was invaded in 1939 by Germany. In 1945, aided by the Russian army, they threw off their Nazi masters and became a Communist state. In 1989, as the Iron Curtain fell, democracy took its place, and in 1993, the Czech Republic "divorced" from Slovakia.

Location: A landlocked country of central Europe, the Czech Republic is bordered by Germany, Austria, Slovakia, and Poland.

Population: 10 million

Religion: Christian 26%; nonreligious 71%. While the country was historically Protestant, Roman Catholics today are the Christian majority.

Dispatch

What more enchanting place might one visit before Christmas than St. Wenceslas Square, lit with decorative lights and filled with festive crowds, and just around the corner from the statue of the great Protestant reformer John Hus. In the country now bearing the simple name the Czech Republic, Christians face challenges in a society infused by a materialistic philosophy and driven by a government rooting out vestiges of the gospel.

The "Velvet Revolution" of 1989, responding to a half million people demonstrating in the streets in Prague, ended forty-one years of Communist rule, transforming the country into a parliamentary republic. Václav Havel, a hero and poet, was installed as president in a nonviolent overthrow that was remarkable in communist history. This city of inspiring sites and rising spires, preserved from WWII bombings, has begun to rebuild.

The Czech and Slovak societies live with a history of two anti-Christian movements: the anticlerical 1928 nationalist movement, and the pushing underground of the church by the Communist takeover in the 1940s. Compounding these is the legacy of corruption inherited from former regimes. This accepted hands-in-the-till mentality was challenged when a Christian public servant took on the establishment.

Libor Michalek, who worked in the government, refused to follow orders to stop exposing an embezzlement scheme. Seeing that Libor was unwilling to exploit the public purse for political gain, the minister said, "Destroy it or it will destroy you." When he informed the Interior Minister that corruption was against his Christian convictions, he was told he was on his own. Even journalists were afraid to pick up the story. Eventually it broke, strengthened by taped messages vindicating the authenticity of his claims. It landed in court, where it stalled, but not before he became a household name. He then served as a senator, his evangelical faith intact and his public witness unfiltered.

Influences

A few factors impact the current state of public witness in this country: There are 50,000 liberal Protestants (down from 100,000 in 2001), 35,000 evangelicals, and 450,000 Roman Catholics (down from one million in a decade).

As communism took over in the 1940s, the government set up a system whereby all workers, including Catholic and Protestant clergy, were paid by the state. The state also took ownership of all church property. Only in 2013 did the government agree to give the property back to the churches. The government continues to pay clergy salaries, although this will be eliminated over time. The battles between the church and state over property ownership reinforced in the public's mind that churches too are corroded by self-interest.

Jiri Unger, general secretary of the Evangelical Alliance, lamented that the combination of the government controlling assets and also being the paymaster of clergy salaries has had a psychological impact of discouraging stewardship. The people's dependence on mother government for funding released them from individual responsibility to be generous in support of charitable work.

Unger said there was another influencing factor: Pre-1998, the government controlled what course of study a person could take. Known Christians were confined to the sciences, which kept them from majoring in the humanities, including communications and philosophy. If Christians didn't follow their instructions, they might be prevented from studying anywhere. The result is that a generation of Christians aren't schooled in social and philosophical study. This has hindered their development in ideas and skills critical to a Christian public witness.

A culture nurtured by cradle-to-grave government fosters a generational mindset. It was described to me this way: "A slave generation, unable to step out of the shadows of the ghetto of dependency, losing not only an understanding of taking risk, but of volunteering and giving: Giving disappeared as a value."

In its new freedom after the fall of the Soviet Union, Christians and others seemed unwilling to launch out into business, a vocation demeaned by the socialist government and frowned on by society at large. After the fall, the government attempted to offload state-run enterprises, but they couldn't be sold. There was simply no available capital to make a purchase. So ownership was given to government cronies, reinforcing the clouded view that business is not only social robbery because of the profit motive, but also has corruption as its handmaid.

The Future

I was curious to know how Christian leaders viewed the future. Two factors stood out. Today the younger generation of Christians are stuck, in need of door openers to help them move into places of service. Marginalized from getting an education, they were turned away from some vocations. They need models of what it looks like for a Christian to be successful. Libor Michalek was a stellar example of integrity.

Second, there is a prevailing skepticism. Prior to WWII, the country had agreed to Hitler's demands for territory in the Munich Agreement of 1938, with the understanding that France and England would support them. Both countries reneged, unwilling to defend Czechoslovakia against Hitler. This was demoralizing, stamping skepticism on their nation and people.

Czech Christians ask for prayer that the gospel will lift this generation, trusting in the power of the Spirit to make alive their witness with energy and expectation. Beyond wanting both spiritual and personal optimism, they ask the Lord for a fresh baptism of Spirit boldness. The struggle to witness needs an undergirding of prayer from friends in and out of the Czech Republic.

TODAY'S READING

The LORD is gracious and compassionate, slow to anger and rich in love. The LORD is good to all; he has compassion on all he has made. All your works praise you, LORD; your faithful people extol you. They tell of the glory of your kingdom and speak of your might, so that all people may know of your mighty acts and the glorious splendor of your kingdom. Your kingdom is an everlasting kingdom, and your dominion endures through all generations.

Psalm 145:8–13

ITEMS FOR PRAYER

- The erosion of faith is profound. Pray for a spirit of interest in spiritual matters, that Czech citizens will be inquisitive about their inner lives and eternity.
- Churches are small, yet eager to build new places of worship. Pray for leaders and those doing church plants, for young people to engage, and that a spirit of generosity will provide the means.

- Younger leadership is vital for churches to grow. Pray for the various venues of witness among young people, that there will be a spiritual breakthrough, infecting the entire nation.

PRAYER

God and Father, we lift to you this small and important country, the Czech Republic. Recognizing their history of faith, their sad stories of violence and brutality, and the ongoing lack of credibility with church structures, we pray that a deep hunger from among its youth will create a desire for life beyond a material explanation for what is true. Spirit of God, bring to their hearts an explosive understanding of Jesus Christ our Lord, in whose name we offer this prayer. Amen.

46
THE PHILIPPINES
Missions Take Many Forms

The Spanish arrived in **the Philippines** in 1521, bringing the Roman Catholic faith. Following a nineteenth-century revolution and a short-lived twentieth-century Japanese occupation, after WWII it became independent. A turbulent struggle for democratic rule continued through much of the last part of the twentieth century.

Location: Located in the western Pacific Ocean close to the equator and sitting on the Pacific Ring of Fire, the Philippines is made up of 7,107 islands, which are vulnerable to typhoons, earthquakes, and floods.

Population: 100 million

Religion: Christian 92% (Roman Catholic 77%, Evangelical/Protestant 13%)

Dispatch

As I walked up to a counter in a shopping center in Manila, I heard singing. It was the clerk. While waiting for her next customer, she was happily crooning a favorite tune. This was my first meeting with Filipinos in their country. Back home my elderly mother, while in a Canadian hospital, was cared for by a nurse from the Philippines, who lovingly and thoughtfully did all that was required and more, with humor and compassion.

These are people uniquely gifted, with pleasing cultural qualities. Their community, culture, and predisposition to serve and care is a story being written in the history books of Christian witness and outreach.

Twelve million Filipinos live outside the Philippines, over 10 percent of their population. Working in fields of medicine, domestics,

239

caregiving, and entertainment, this is one of the largest diasporas in the world. Unique by the services they offer, they get into places where mission agencies can't. Think of an Arab state. Who can sit next to a child, reading stories from the Bible to one who in time will be a prince? The stories of Filipinos slipping into closed-door countries is daring and charming. Wanted because of their loving spirit and capable skills, they are recognized as a valuable resource, recruited and paid for by people in lands where the gospel is banned.

What makes them so uniquely positioned? I asked Bishop Efrain Tendero, Secretary General of the World Evangelical Alliance. He started with this summary: "We are adaptable, available, and accessible."

Family

Filipinos love their families. Their close ties, which create emotional bonding, are huge factors in their work. They use *kapwa* or "togetherness." On Sundays, their day off, I noted that in Hong Kong they congregate in parks and grassy areas, meeting family and friends. This ability to create friendship reaches out to others; when they live in foreign countries, those they care for too become like family.

The American occupation provided the means for them to learn English. Given that it is such a desired language where Filipinos work, their fluency is important. For example, many are nannies, and the parents want their children to learn English. Most Filipinos speak at least three languages.

The bishop noted that Filipinos aren't easily thrown off by difficulties. Living cross-culturally, loneliness and cultural complexities can lead to anxiety and depression. Their emotional skills in managing these challenges makes them ideal as foreign workers. A common phrase is *Bahala Na*, meaning "Leave it up to God." Christians interpret this as literally trusting in God in the situation, giving them space to cope.

As Asians, they easily move from one Asian country to another, familiar with customs, clothing, food, and congestion. If you can hold your peace while driving in Manila, no traffic jam is too much.

The Philippine nation isn't big enough to hurt anyone. They aren't a threat and are not especially influential. They allow people to easily travel in and out of their country, making their national persona hospitable.

Their International Witness

In today's expanding Christian witness, Filipino leadership sees their strategic value. *Kairos* is a course designed to help Christian workers orient themselves in cultural transition, to be sensitive to religious issues and learn ways to live out the gospel. The course begins with "Why are you going?" preparing them to see going abroad as more than an economic venture. It helps them to understand that as followers of Jesus, everything they do is missional. To date, 25,000 have gone through the *Kairos* program; there is a goal of 200,000.

Today, over 500,000 Evangelical Filipinos live in 197 countries, from Nunavut in the north to cruise ships sailing the seas, from Saudi Arabia to the United Kingdom. Petrodollars, ballooning in the 1970s, drove the need for workers in the Middle East, drawing Filipino males. Then a demand for women in the Middle East, Japan, Hong Kong, Singapore, Malaysia, and South Korea became strong. Today, over 60 percent of Filipino missionaries are women.

A Filipino serving in the home of a Saudi prince went with the family on a vacation. During a party she was asked to sing, and so she sang, "Jesus loves me, this I know, for the Bible tells me so." The prince got into trouble over this, and she was reprimanded. When the time came for her permit to be renewed, she was refused reentry. But the child of the prince was so upset that they relented, and she was invited back to his home.

The bishop recognizes the Philippines as one of the most influential mission-sending bodies in the world. As Jochebed was "hired" by the Egyptian princess to raise Moses, so the Spirit employs those adaptable, available, and accessible to serve his global purposes.

TODAY'S READING

One thing I ask of the LORD, this only do I seek: that I may dwell in the house of the LORD all the days of my life, to gaze upon the beauty of the LORD and to seek him in his temple. For in the day of trouble he will keep me safe in his dwelling; he will hide me in the shelter of his sacred tent and set me high upon a rock.

Psalm 27:4–5

ITEMS FOR PRAYER

• The Filipino International Network was formed to coordinate activities and training for those in the Philippines and in global service. Pray for this body and the services it provides, especially to the diaspora.

• The challenges of this mobile society are many, including lonely and broken homes in the homeland, and the abuse of workers in foreign lands. Pray for the Lord's protection, especially over those made vulnerable in countries where human rights are at a minimum.

• As Filipinos intermarry in the lands in which they work, pray for their ongoing witness.

• As well, as they live away from home, there are many opportunities for witness among their communities. Pray for these activities and churches that spring up to meet the spiritual needs of lives in Christ.

PRAYER

Father, your ways are unique and surprising, yet all located within your wisdom and creativity. We praise you for the heart and soul of the Filipino people, for the ways that they dispense goodness and charity worldwide. We especially ask for your overshadowing presence in the lives of those who serve in difficult and complex situations in which they are vulnerable. Give them wisdom and courage to know what to do and when to offer your word of strength and loving witness. Amen.

47

LITHUANIA

Resisting the
Skeptical,
Believing the Impossible

In 1918, **Lithuania** declared itself a republic. However, for much of the twentieth century, it was occupied by both Germany and the Soviet Union. Church attendance here, as in much of Europe, is low.

Location: Northern Europe, one of the three Baltic states on the Baltic Sea, east of Sweden and Denmark, bordered by Latvia, Belarus, Poland, and a Russian exclave Kaliningrad Oblast

Population: 3 million

Religion: Christian 85% (Roman Catholic 73%; Orthodox 5%; Evangelical 5%)

Dispatch

Who would have guessed that this rather modest country would be the first to push out from under the crumbling Soviet Union and declare independence? They did, even though the not-yet-fallen Soviet system sent in troops to intimidate the bold and brash who had determined enough was enough.

In my visits, I'm amazed at countries where greatness, peace, tragedy, sorrow, and unvarnished beauty mingle. For many Evangelicals, we may not take into account places where Christian faith has had early beginnings. The farther one goes into eastern regions of Europe, Central Asia, and the Middle East, the more obscure the names are, and their historic Christian presence seems rather vague. To learn of those people and places awakens understanding and connects us with those we may have never met. My interest is to observe those works of the Spirit as he sparks faith and ignites service.

During the fourteenth century the Grand Duchy of Lithuania was Europe's largest, including land which is now part of Poland, Russia, Ukraine, and Belarus. In the late 1700s, Russia claimed most of the land of Lithuania. Declaring themselves independent after WWI, both the Nazis and Soviets took turns in occupation. As WWII ended, the Soviets took full control. During the Soviet occupation, Christians suffered imprisonment and torture, and many were sent to Siberia. On March 11, 1990, she declared herself the state of Lithuania.

A Challenging Idea

After the Soviet system collapsed, an idea was born, a seed at first, which grew to become the Lithuanian Christian University. It was constructed by visionaries who defied the odds and created a remarkable institution, linking people, skills, and opportunities. This story shows what can be done as people take risks and push beyond what most believe to be possible.

Soviets, even after losing control of Lithuania, tried to clamp down on this young upstart. The brash go-getters of the young government quickly moved ahead. The twenty-seven-year-old Minister of Culture and Education, Aurimas Juozaitis, met with German evangelist Johannes Reimer, at the time ministering in Lithuania. Aurimas had said to Johannes, "Our country needs a window to Europe, to the world, if democracy is to be given a chance. The external freedom from the Soviets is only the first step; the true freedom will have to happen in the heads of the people. We need a Protestant Christian university."

Johannes returned to Germany but could find no one interested. Next he met Art DeFehr, president of Palliser Furniture in Winnipeg, Manitoba, Canada. Art, a Harvard grad, was interested in Christian education and listened. He promised no money but showed interest.

In the 1970s and '80s, Mennonites had settled in Lithuania, a midway point in their emigration to Germany. Otonas Balciunas was a musician and teacher, struggling under the oppressive eye of the police. Even so, he and his wife, Raimonda, founded the Lithuania Christian Fund, nurturing their vision for university education.

After the conversation between Reimer and the minister of education, the idea moved into action. On October 31, 1990, Juozaitis, DeFehr, Reimer, and Balciunas met in Vilnius, Lithuania's capital. Here they signed an agreement with the newly formed republic to develop and build a Christian university.

It was just the beginning, but what a start. Within months of the hammer and sickle being lifted, the three pledged with the government to set in motion building the first Christian university of its kind, located in a former territory of the "old" Soviet Union.

Its Beginning

The university opened the next summer with a hundred students taking an English-language program. The government explicitly wanted it to be in English, and to build within it values that Juozaitis saw as from the West. They had to remind him it wasn't Western but Christian values that would bring the kind of education he saw his country needing.

Then followed a winter school. In the city where it was first held, there was fear that a Protestant school, especially Mennonite, would upset this heartland of Catholic conservatism. So the newly formed school was moved to Klaipeda, a beautiful city on the Baltic coast.

Today, fewer than half of its six hundred students are Lithuanians, many coming from other European and central Asian countries. North American students use credits toward their own university degree. The university, now called LCC International University, is a member of the Council of Christian Colleges and Universities in North America.

My sessions with students gravitated toward how one is led by the Spirit. Even those with no Christian experience were interested, for this was new and intriguing. Their questions reminded me how critical it is to build faith while they are young. Many of these students are from regions where for decades atheism has debunked faith.

This university didn't just happen. The Spirit works hand in hand with those who are already there, those with experience, and those willing to take a risk. It required an enormous giving of talent, time, and finances. Hundreds, at their own cost, traveled to teach, cook, build, manage, and love it into reality.

Today, a handsome campus, first-class facilities, qualified faculty, and able administrators are making it work. Take this as inspiration to pray when it seems there is no future. God is already preparing his people to step in at the right moment as catalysts. Also, ask what you might do to resist skepticism and accomplish what most think to be impossible.

Today's Reading

The law of the Lord is perfect, refreshing the soul. The statutes of the Lord are trustworthy, making wise the simple. The precepts of the Lord are right, giving joy to the heart. The commands of the Lord are radiant, giving light to the eyes. The fear of the Lord is pure, enduring forever. The decrees of the Lord are firm, and all of them are righteous.

Psalm 19:7–9

Items for Prayer

- For the president, faculty, and staff of LCC University as they press their boundaries to include an increasing number of students in their region.
- For the development of the Evangelical Alliance in Lithuania as it seeks fellowship and cooperation among its leaders in a country that has long lived with division and fear.
- For young people, many spiritually impoverished by a heritage and system that made knowing Christ difficult, that there will be a rising cadre who are passionate in their faith and witness.

PRAYER

Gracious Father, we give praise to you for the boldness and faith of those who took the risk to begin the college in Lithuania, for the hundreds who traveled there in its development to give of their time, expertise, and finances to see it launched and now sustained. We pray for its leadership and students. May there be a profound nurturing of faith in the lives of its young people, and in the land a flowering of fellowship and cooperation among its church and pastoral leadership. May your Son be known and followed, giving life to families, institutions, and the entire land. For your glory, and that alone. Amen.

48

FINDING NEW PLACES OF SPIRIT EMPOWERMENT

A Surprising Saga

Today we explore a ministry of Christians with a passion to pray and work on behalf of the poor and in places of conflict. As part of praying for the world, we move away from focusing on a country and instead think about and pray for a sector of people who work globally. This group will be new to most. It was to me. But my learning with and from them has been an important model for me, and I trust it will be for you as well.

Dispatch

It was on a visit to Assisi, Italy, that I first met Leonardo Gialloreti, a medical specialist in neurology. I was intrigued by his interest in matters such as how I read the Bible, and did I have anything he could learn about how the Holy Spirit works in my life and in the places and people I visit and work with?

Over a long Italian meal, he and his friends explored with me the work of the Spirit in the worldwide community. The passion of faith in his life and those of his colleagues seemed different from what I thought would be in their world. But nothing was off the table. Concerns and questions were all invited. There was, at least for me, a readiness to hear what the Lord wanted them to hear. And who are "they"? First, let me give you a little history.

It was the 1960s. Teenagers in Rome were as much into psychedelic music, mind-tripping drugs, and hippie music as they were in LA or London. But not all of them. Countering the counterculture, a group of young people in Rome eschewed the activities of their friends and sought a closer walk with Christ. Hungry for learning of the Bible, in a quest for meaningful prayer, and convinced that caring for the poor was a Christian mandate, they began to gather around able and critical thinker Andrea Riccardi, himself then only in his teens.

Today, the Community of Sant'Egidio has spread its influence and ministry to many in several countries, numbering some seventy thousand associates. It is made up of professionals who believe personal conversion is a beginning step to this walk of faith. It is not a religious order, and being Roman Catholic is not a requirement, although most are. They sign no covenant and make no explicit promises, but all understand that daily prayer, Bible study, and regular time spent with the marginalized and poor are what make them as persons and communities vital in their walk with Christ and effective in their witness to the life of the gospel.

As it grew out of its early beginnings, peacemaking naturally blossomed from its spiritual roots. The savage civil war of Mozambique—a Portuguese-speaking country in southeast Africa—lingered with over one million dying and 5 million displaced. Andrea Riccardi and others turned their attention to this country, and over painstaking negotiations brought the two sides together. On October 4, 1992, sitting across the table from each other in the world center of Sant'Egidio in downtown Rome, the government and rebels signed a peace accord that lifted that country from its many years (1977 to 1992) of bloodletting.

There are times when one's fences are pushed, staples are snapped, fence wires are strained by way of new ideas and an expanding fraternity. Let it be understood: I am rooted in an evangelical faith; I've been shaped by the Spirit's new birth. Yet I've met new friends who also envision Christ as our center and the Spirit in his power. They press me to see beyond what I've been willing to see or embrace.

It was this community to which Leonardo Gialloreti made the introduction. A heart for praying, studying the Bible, caring for the poor, and peacemaking community fills his life. Watching and listening to him and his colleagues gave me a learning moment of how the Spirit builds in places and with people whose hearts are hungry and open.

Their annual conference, held sometimes in Rome, is framed by the most impressive backdrop one might imagine and given pomp and circumstance as no other city affords. But such embellishments, or what some might call distractions, could not keep me from feeling the power of their vision and mobility of their strategy.

The opening night, leader Andrea Riccardi put me on the edge of my seat:

> Our horizons have become incredibly wide with globalization. This widening questions religions. If the Latin etymology of the word *religion* derives from "tying," the opposite of *religion* is not disbelief, but loneliness. The self-sufficiency of believers turns into blindness. But also avarice: not to make the spiritual and human resources growing in the womb of a religion available to others. And laziness: sometimes, when you can trace your own history far back, you feel you have the right to be lazy in today's history.

During days of prayer, dialogue, conversation, and public worship, I observed a few elements among them.

First, there was no obscuring of their hearts. They love Jesus, and often and loudly confessed this. Second, they showed no hesitation in reaching to the highest political levels to enact their vision of peace and spiritual well-being.

While patient in process, they expect results. Their dialogue isn't an end in itself. They look to substantive changes, work toward that, and refuse to abide in the ambivalence of words.

Also, they are unafraid of ideas—from wherever and from whomever. They invite people of all faiths, ideas, and perspectives to lay it out for all to see. Defensiveness has never been a fruit of the Spirit, and they surely don't intend to try to make it so.

They refuse to be confined by liberal/conservative rubrics. They claim the canopy of creation and all that is good and worthy as their inheritance.

To my surprise, they lifted the word *dialogue* to a new level. I've tired of the word, especially as used in hazy theological conversation, when it seems others expect me to reduce biblical commitment to a common denominator, making everyone happy, but with no Christological presence or transcendent power. Many of the dialogues I run into seem like replays of ineptitude, a pretense of progress and much bureaucratic bumbling, leaving more dead on the roads of war, avarice, and corruption.

These people are different. They leave me with a new vision of what honest conversation—yes, *dialogue*—can do: attracting people with divergent views and refusing to let differences of life, belief, and practice stall us in finding solutions.

As Abraham was invited to dialogue with God on sparing Sodom, he did. Paul learned of his hearers, and by so doing got a hearing in Athens.

My friends at Sant'Egidio give open and clear demonstrations of how the Spirit engages people to solve real problems—a worldwide witness to the presence and workings of the resurrected Christ.

TODAY'S READING

A shoot will come up from the stump of Jesse; from his roots a Branch will bear fruit. The Spirit of the LORD will rest on him—the Spirit of wisdom and of understanding, the Spirit of counsel and of might, the Spirit of the knowledge and fear of the LORD—and he will delight in the fear of the LORD. He will not judge by what he sees with his eyes, or decide by what he hears with his ears; but with righteousness he will judge the needy, with justice he will give decisions for the poor of the earth. He will strike the earth with the rod of his mouth; with the breath of his lips he will slay the wicked. Righteousness will be his belt and faithfulness the sash around his waist.

Isaiah 11:1–5

ITEMS FOR PRAYER

- In our world of faithless secularism and unbelief, we celebrate the work of the Spirit in so many places. Pray for this global ministry of laypeople in the Community of Sant'Egidio, who covenant to study the Scriptures daily, pray, and care for the vulnerable.

- Further, that their influence will powerfully affect us all, so we too will desire and cherish our time in prayer and study, and further, that our lives will practically demonstrate to others the love of the Father, the resurrection presence of Jesus, and the enabling power of the Spirit.

- Harsh and brutal conflict spots our world with its blood-spattering effect, showing how incorrigible hearts need the interfacing of those gifted with the presence of peace. Pray for the many ministries whose calling and expertise is to find ways to settle disputes and resolve wars and their many rumors.

PRAYER

Lord Jesus, our hearts break as we hear, day after day, of killings and physical- and soul-desecrating maiming in so many places. We know that only your life-transforming presence will bring about peace. Today I offer a prayer, a strong prayer, on behalf of ministries such as the Community of Sant'Egidio, the Religious Liberty Commission of WEA, the International Justice Ministry, the Jubilee Campaign, and others who give themselves to intersect hostilities and help broker peace. Lord, we know this is dangerous work, and so we offer this plea that your Spirit will employ those so gifted to put themselves in harm's way if necessary to stop the killing and life-destroying ways of those who believe the only way to get ahead is to harm and destroy. In this world of such conflict, Spirit of the risen Lord, help those who engage, giving them wisdom and grace, protection, and courage, for and in your name. Amen.

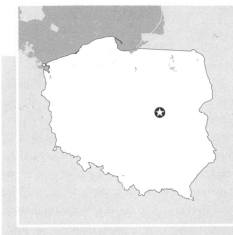

49
POLAND

Where the Church Held a Country Together

Poland's Roman Catholic community is particularly known for its devotion to Mary. The shrine of the Black Madonna in Czestochowa is considered the country's most important religious shrine, and was crowned by King John II Casimir Vasa in 1652 as Queen and Protector of Poland.

While pulverized by invading armies of WWII, Warsaw rebuilt an old section that looks very much like its prewar city. In 2010, the president and senior officials were killed in an air crash, which continues to raise concerns over outside influences.

Location: bordered by Germany, the Czech Republic, Slovakia, Ukraine, Belarus, Kaliningrad Oblast (Russian), Lithuania, and the Baltic Sea

Population: 40 million

Religion: Christians 90% (Roman Catholic 85%; Orthodox 1.5%; Evangelical/Protestant 1%)

Dispatch

It's impossible not to see paw prints marking each country residing alongside the Great Bear. Like others in the region, Poland is shaped by her historic relationship with Russia.

Poland has been Christian since its founding in AD 966, and yet it has a history of being pushed around. After WWI, the Paris Peace Conference restored Poland as a second republic, and in 1919, Poland bested Lenin in a war named the "Miracle at the Vistula." As the noise of war intensified on September 1, 1939, Hitler arrived and conquered. Seventeen days later the Soviets did the same. Poland then split between two occupying armies and lived with this overbearing dual presence. In 1944, she was made a satellite state of the Soviet Union. In 1989, the Wall fell, and the Soviet Union ceased to exist, as Gorbachev released its many territories.

During its occupations, Poland sought to define its national identity, refusing to give in to either of its occupiers. While Marxist-Leninism ruled during the Soviet influence, a pastor said that as a university student he could find none who believed. They called themselves "radishes"—red on the outside and white on the inside. For his required university course in communism he, like his colleagues, held his nose to pass the course. His rationale was that Poles wouldn't let anyone tell them what to believe. For him, stubbornness is one of their supreme and self-saving qualities.

Polish identity runs deep, strengthened as outsiders attempted to uproot them. Key to retaining their identity has been the affirming presence of the Roman Catholic Church, for centuries its cultural fortress.

John Paul II

Highly influential in the late twentieth century was Poland's beloved son, Karol Jozef Wojtyla, Pope John Paul II. Of all the factors that cracked the Wall and undermined dictatorial powers, this priest from Wadowice was key to its demise, a lesson on the influence of a spiritual leader. He faced brutality and power with weapons of language, not guns.

> The pope won that struggle by transcending politics. His was what Joseph Nye calls "soft power"—the power of attraction and repulsion. He began with an enormous advantage, and exploited it to the utmost: He headed the one institution that stood for the polar opposite of the communist way of life that the Polish people hated. He was a Pole, but beyond the regime's reach. By identifying with him, Poles would have the chance to cleanse themselves of the compromises they had to make to live under the regime. And so they came to him by the millions. They listened. He told them to be good, not to compromise themselves, to stick by one another, to be fearless, and that God is the only source of goodness, the only

standard of conduct. "Be not afraid," he said. Millions shouted in response, "We want God! We want God! We want God!" The regime cowered. Had the pope chosen to turn his soft power into the hard variety, the regime might have been drowned in blood. Instead, the pope simply led the Polish people to desert their rulers by affirming solidarity with one another. The communists managed to hold on as despots a decade longer. But as political leaders, they were finished. . . . Pope John Paul II struck what turned out to be a mortal blow to its Communist regime, to the Soviet Empire, [and] ultimately to communism.

Angelo M. Codevilla, Polish writer

Years later, as its economy has grown, Christian faith as central to its life has declined profoundly. When communism ruled, its cultural glue was the Church. She provided identity, relationships, moral certitudes, and hope to its citizens. Also, after John Paul II's first visit to Poland as pontiff in 1979, the Solidarity Movement was birthed. Aided by his presence and encouragement, and rightly naming what the Church had fostered, they stuck together.

Today, that glue is coming unstuck. While 85 percent claim to be Roman Catholic, regular church attenders have dropped to 39 percent. In this Catholic-majority country, Evangelicals view their influence as encouraging Christians of any stripe into life-transforming faith, pressing forward in church planting, creating mission agencies, and cooperating in outreach.

Also, Evangelicals are interested in finding common understanding and cooperative action with the majority church in public life. It doesn't take long to hear of visions of Evangelical churches and missions to launch social services in the name of Christ. There is a deep reservoir of spiritual vitality fueling hope and activity among its churches and people.

A recent Festival of Hope linked strands of churches and missions. The planners wisely invited and received support from the bishop, a historic marker in their journey. In Poland, as in other Catholic-majority countries, Evangelicals wrestle with their role in public witness. This theological divide is not stopping them in finding common platforms of witness.

Evangelicals have opportunities to test how a Christian minority can work with the majority. I met wise and courageous pastors and leaders with no fear of moving outside of bunkers that understandably had been protecting enclaves during the communist years. They are candid about the majority/minority reality. However, there should be no misunderstanding of their zeal as they pray for a Spirit-caused revival. Pivoting around that aspiration are galaxies of activities: church planting, missions in camping, and media initiatives. These are all fueled by a desire to strengthen Poland's national identity and push back cultural and spiritual clouds that shadow her history and darken her hope for the coming days.

Poland could model how churches, rooted in disparate histories, are able to foster hope and find areas of cooperative action as they press out from the past, refusing to allow a divided Christian witness to allow a secular presence to rule.

Today's Reading

The LORD reigns, let the nations tremble; he sits enthroned between the cherubim, let the earth shake. Great is the LORD in Zion; he is exalted over all the nations. Let them praise your great and awesome name—he is holy. The King is mighty, he loves justice—you have established equity; in Jacob you have done what is just and right. Exalt the Lord our God and worship at his footstool; he is holy.

Psalm 99:1–5

Items for Prayer

- The loss of church attendance in the dominant Christian church breeds faithlessness. Pray for spiritual renewal within all Christian communities, for an increased love for the Scriptures, a hunger for an infilling of the Spirit, and a passion for living out the life of Jesus.
- There is a movement to plant churches in both urban and rural areas. History tells us that often new life emerges when younger and unaffiliated churches are formed.
- There are millions in the Polish diaspora coming into contact with life-giving Christian communities in their new lands.

Pray that these Polish Christians will continue to find opportunities in their homeland to help those who are in desperate need.

- The Polish Evangelical Alliance brings leadership together, framing a vision for their collective ministries in a country where they are so much in the minority. These leaders need wisdom, grace, and courage.

PRAYER

Gracious Lord and Savior, today we lift before you Poland—its people, churches, and their spiritual needs. Out of anguish and struggle of past decades, the country is experiencing an economic renewal, but as this happens, people's hearts seem to beat less with passion for you. We pray for those leading churches and ministries, that they will manifest your presence and live within your power, making known your name. May the people of Poland be renewed in their personal faith and become effective in public witness. May you, the only Christ of salvation, the only name under heaven whereby anyone can be saved, become the focus of this people. Grant that Poland will be religious more than in history and in name, and that they will be vibrant with your presence. Amen.

50

RUSSIA

Search for Identity

The **Russian Empire** existed as a state from 1721 to 1917. The largest country landmass in the world, its empire touched three continents. The 1917 Bolshevik Revolution, led by Lenin, turned it into a communist state. In time, the empire expanded to become the Soviet Union, a territorial control lost in 1989.

Today, with a sizeable population and vast natural resources, Russia continues to seek its place in the changing political landscape.

For centuries, the Orthodox Church was its established faith. During Communist rule, they, along with Evangelicals, were persecuted: 200,000 Christian leaders were martyred, and Evangelicals were not allowed to build churches or conduct services. Today, the church has considerable freedom, although there is concern that the relationship between the government and the Orthodox Church may blur the separation of church and state.

Location: It shares land borders with Norway, Finland, Estonia, Latvia, Lithuania, Poland, Belarus, Ukraine, Georgia, Azerbaijan, Kazakhstan, China, Mongolia, and North Korea, and maritime borders with Japan and the United States (Alaska).

Population: 144 million

Religion: Christian 67% (Orthodox 64%, Evangelical 3%); Muslim 12%

Dispatch

I walked up the many steps to the preaching pulpit in Central Baptist Church near Red Square in Moscow. As I looked down to the congregation, I recalled a picture of Billy Graham preaching from that same pulpit when the Soviet Union ruled.

What I didn't know was that the church had been kept open by a curious historical circumstance. It was 1941, and Stalin was doing his best to persuade U.S. President Franklin D. Roosevelt to enter the fray of the war and create a second line of defense for the Soviets against Hitler.

Negotiations shifted from side to side. Finally, Roosevelt agreed. But included in the agreement was a promise by Stalin to keep open Central Baptist, the only Protestant church allowed.

Today, much has changed. While KGB surveillance continues, churches are being planted and ministries initiated. Now it isn't a carryover of atheistic communism that proves to be a challenge. Instead, it's living as a Christian minority. The Russian Orthodox Church, founded by Greek Orthodox missionaries in the 900s, implanted their vision of religious hegemony. Infringement by another Christian community, be it Evangelical or Roman Catholic, is viewed as predatory. Other forms of Christian faith are considered sects at best and cults at worst.

This sense of proprietary presence was triggered after 1989 with the breakup of the Soviet Union. Western missions booked their flights and arrived to evangelize. Seen as a Western religion, Evangelicalism crossed a border deemed sacred. The fear among the Orthodox was reinforced as Evangelical agencies recruited short-term missionaries, operated with little or no language skills, and proved deficient in cultural sensitivity.

I asked a group of Christian leaders how and when they came to faith. Most did so in the early 1990s from these very missions. The arrival of Western groups brought results, but as the excitement of ministering in a formerly closed country waned, fewer came and there was less support. The initial flurry of people and resources had created a bubble of expectation, and when it burst, Russian Christians were left on their own.

A Complex Culture

Russia is a land of contradictions with a deep and rich history. Some of the world's greatest writers are Russian: Tolstoy, Dostoyevsky, Solzhenitsyn; and also composers: Tchaikovsky, Rachmaninoff, Stravinsky. In sports they stand atop the world podium. Canadians know our greatest twentieth-century sporting moment was the 1972 world hockey series, when Paul Henderson scored a goal just before the end of the final game of the Russian/Canadian series.

Recall twentieth-century Russia and how its political leaders—Lenin and Stalin—used mass starvation and slaughter to protect and advance their ideological formulations.

Russians have an amazing sense of self-awareness, described to me this way: There is a heaviness and weariness of the soul, and for good reason. In the past century, some 20 million died by war, killings, and forced starvation at the hands of the government (actual numbers vary according to the source). They were taught that their ideology was superior, only years later to realize its deficiencies. For decades, they lived under surveillance and fear, not knowing who, even among their own families, would report words or actions deemed offensive to the secret police. Within the soul of the Russian people, there lingers heartbreak from decades of dictatorial control.

Today, its search is for national identity. Nurtured by the Orthodox Church for a millennium, its identity was overturned and rudely redefined by a Marxist/Leninist vision, only then to see its socialism morph into a mixed form of capitalism. Follow their history: Wrenched from the brutal rule of Czarist regimes in the early twentieth century, they were strong-armed by a Communist regime unmatched for its destructive powers. Now that their ideal has been broken, they ask, who are we?

Moving Ahead

What is the way forward for a Christ-centered witness? There is no simple or singular answer. Russians are Asian and Slavic, not

Western. They evaluate matters of faith slowly, and tradition is powerful. A primary means of evangelism is to understand others in their pain and suffering. I was told, "If someone knows you to have walked the valley of sorrow, they will listen, for they know you understand." The message "Jesus makes one happy" isn't as convincing as identity in suffering. Of course, the hope of the Lord's return is reassuring to them.

Leadership is central to shaping the future, but what kind of leadership? For centuries they've lived under the dictatorial, untrusting elite, who resorted to secret surveillance to maintain power. The culture has been so polluted by secrecy that it will take a spiritual revolution among its leaders if they are to govern in the manner of Christ.

It is important to pray for the coming generation of Russian Christian leaders, that the servant paradigm, the Jesus model, will direct their witness; also, that this influence will find its way into central Asia and the many "stans." Can you imagine the impact such a community will have when fashioned not by mistrust, secrecy, and brutality, but by the love of the risen Lord? Into other parts of the world they will in time go as the Spirit uses their experience of faithfulness in tough and hostile environments.

The apostle Paul knew it, and Russian Christians know it well.

Today's Reading

How long, LORD? Will you forget me forever? How long will you hide your face from me? How long must I wrestle with my thoughts and day after day have sorrow in my heart? How long will my enemy triumph over me? Look on me and answer, LORD my God. Give light to my eyes, or I will sleep in death, and my enemy will say, "I have overcome him," and my foes will rejoice when I fall. But I trust in your unfailing love; my heart rejoices in your salvation. I will sing the LORD's praise, for he has been good to me.

Psalm 13

Items for Prayer

- Christians in Russia are naturally supportive of their own country and people. Pray that they will have wisdom and freedom of heart to also pray for governments other than their own in whose countries Russian influence is historic and where it continues.

- Russians have survived much in their recent past. Pray for church leaders as they navigate the political shoals, that integrity will reign and the joy of servanthood will characterize their leadership.

- Given the dominant place of the Orthodox Church, pray that their leadership will foster a spirit of freedom and opportunity so that the name of Jesus will be known in the land.

- There is a severe lack of funding and training for pastoral and missional leaders. Pray that as the economy grows, indigenous leadership will be strong with a clear voice for the gospel.

PRAYER

Gracious Father, we pray for the Russian people, so creative and with such a rich culture, yet living through such trying times, learning to survive. May those of us outside their world appreciate and understand and be sensitive to their feelings of national pride and hope for the future. We pray for their young people and the various ministries reaching out to them. We pray for churches and pastoral leadership as they create the setting for faith and loving friendships. Holy Spirit, visit this land and people in your special way, bringing them joy that comes with your presence. May they know your fullness and, in the spirit of your mission, be spiritual benefactors to countries in their region. Amen.

51

PRISON MINISTRIES

In the Darkness, Light Shines Its Best

Leadership is core to effective ministry. In praying for the world this week, we walk with a person I know well, **Ron Nikkel**, whose vision and leadership is giving global opportunity and transformation to people we hardly think about. As we come to prayer, you may pivot from this story to other people you know, and direct your prayers to them. Never forget that ideas need legs, hearts, minds, and leadership skills to move vision into reality. That's why leadership matters. What we read of today was birthed and then brought to maturity by one willing to follow God's call.

Dispatch

In the dark halls of prison cells, I saw grace spread its presence. Today, in 128 countries, volunteers—Orthodox, Evangelicals, and Catholics—weekly line up at prison gates to be checked in and then go where some citizens can't get out. These hundred thousand Christian volunteers enter worlds Jesus warned we'd likely forget. But it doesn't happen by chance.

I traveled with Ron Nikkel to seven prisons in Central America, meeting leaders, volunteers, and boards, and praying, hugging, crying, and talking with inmates, families, and children. Ron and I have known each other for years. In 1972, I recruited him to work in Youth for Christ, focusing on young offenders. His passion for justice and his evident leadership skills and vision set him apart. Ten years later, when Chuck Colson needed skilled hands and a tender heart to take his newly founded Prison Fellowship Ministry worldwide, Ron was chosen.

He is shy and modest. He has cared for national prison leaders for years, and being with him was like watching a love-in. Rooted in this affection for him, however, is a shared and deep-seated conviction that justice is really a restoration of relationships. Not a program, not funding, not more jails. Prison Fellowship International volunteers know it well: It is weekly visits to forgotten citizens to bring Christ's love and power, knitting strand by strand and visit by visit, viable connections to bind together hearts and lives.

A Big Story

This is a big story with many subplots, heroes, and victims— some reclaimed, but most not; some healed, but many not; most hurting, and some searching. Yes, it would take a book to tell it all. Yet the story is profoundly simple, so obvious you want to smack your forehead with "Why didn't I think of that?"

Chuck Colson was Nixon's "hatchet man" before and during Watergate. After his time in prison, he birthed Prison Fellowship. Then his bestselling book *Born Again*, by its very name, became a cultural mantra. Anyone who would listen to him heard, in effect, *God didn't choose to use my political success, academic achievements, or status as a marine, but rather my single and biggest failure. He took me from the White House to the jailhouse, and if he can do that in me, he can do that in you.* Prisoners especially love that line.

After news spread of the start-up of Prison Fellowship in the U.S., requests poured in from around the world, and this is where Ron entered. He traveled the world, helping national leaders with a heart for those in prison to build an indigenous work. PFI didn't offer money; each national ministry was to be self-funded, self-developed, and self-led. That remains one of its core operational values.

When we visited Preventivo Prison in Guatemala, Father Gonzalo said, "Brian, I'd like you to meet Father Mario." He was dressed in street clothes, and I wanted to know more about him. I learned many years ago he had been ordained a priest. One night, another priest living in the same center was killed, and because Mario was in the area, he was charged and convicted, even without evidence. He spent fourteen years in this very prison. As we walked about, he talked with many he knew by name. His calling now? To visit daily the place where he spent almost a decade and a half. Joy radiates and laughter rings out. He is now "Padre Mario."

In Costa Rica, we saw evidence of how PFI works in ways that are refreshingly new. After being frisked and having our passports confiscated, we walked through the gates of the San Rafael prison. Instead of continuing on into the main prison, we took a sharp right, following a path around the fenced perimeter. A few minutes later, to my left I saw a separate section with fields of flowers. Eighty men divided in parallel lines were waiting for us to run the gauntlet. There were high-fives, handshakes, and hugs as we moved into the center area under open-sided tents for morning chapel. The music rocked. (Traditional hymns and quiet songs are not their fare.)

Later I was proudly shown the woodworking shop and then the vegetable garden. When I noticed a netted area, I lifted the net and entered a jungle butterfly garden. Its guardian showed me various stages of butterfly development and their many varieties. It was fitting to me that next door to the state institution, men who were finding the grace and love of Jesus were also discovering part of his beautiful creation in the fragile butterfly and learning about the elements of God's good earth. Here recidivism is 3 percent; in the regular prison, just across the fence, it's 65 percent.

Prisons—a Failure

So what is a traditional prison for Ron Nikkel? It is the point of deepest failure. It's a human intersection where personal moral failure meets societal failure, where society shows its inability to change fallen character. Why did Jesus point out visiting prisons as a demarcation between the sheep and the goats? Because here,

265

the need to work with his creation from the inside out is not only self-evident but also possible because here, sinners know what they are. It's a matter of helping to lift burdens, acting as spiritual midwives in the process of new birth. Prison is where bonding relationships can restore victim and victimizer and help to bring about *shalom*—God's peace.

Beginning in Brazil in 1972, in partnership with local prisons, PFI created faith-based units called APAC—in Portuguese, "Loving Christ, Loving the Prisoner." These units are for inmates who want to explore and grow in their faith. Designed to encourage spiritual growth, develop social skills, and prepare them for reentry into society, they are built within existing prisons but are separate and self-contained. All internal activities are run by PFI with only external security. In the San Rafael APAC of eighty-one inmates, there was one guard. There are ninety of these APAC units in Brazil, caring for some 13,500 inmates; in Chile, there are forty with 4,000 offenders.

For Ron, traditional prisons don't make sense, because they provide no lasting answers. They've become easy-solution warehouses, packing in more and more where there is less and less interaction between those who could help and those who need help.

"They put people with a moral infection into a place where moral disease is rampant and then expect them to be cured. It is irresponsible to put offenders in places where their choice to be responsible is taken away, because in prison all responsibility is removed, replaced by do's and don'ts and a rigid time schedule with no allowance for initiative. They just expect the inmates to do their time. Except for those who are a real and present danger to society (less than 20 percent), we will not break the back of a judicial logjam until we see that men and women need to be restored in relationships."

Yet in the manifest imperfection of prisons, lights shine. I saw people located in the darkest of concrete and steel bunkers radiate Christ's love. Where hopelessness reigns, expectation of life ahead simply defied my imagination.

Do you wonder if Jesus is alive? Has cynicism about God's work blinded your sight? Have religious self-promoters made you wonder if there are still true Christians serving with love? Take a trip with Ron Nikkel. In the darkness, light shines its best.

TODAY'S READING

Trust in the LORD and do good; dwell in the land and enjoy safe pasture. Take delight in the LORD, and he will give you the desires of your heart. Commit your way to the LORD; trust in him and he will do this: He will make your righteous reward shine like the dawn, your vindication like the noonday sun.

Psalm 37:3–6

ITEMS FOR PRAYER

- Countless ministries light the globe, offering love and caring service for millions, going into places and meeting people of all descriptions. These volunteers are recruited and trained by leaders. Think of those you know who serve in your country and elsewhere.
- Each generation needs its own set of leaders. As Chuck Colson chose Ron to build a global network of prison ministries, this next generation needs our prayer and support to launch and sustain what they lead.
- Decade by decade, new needs come to the surface, requiring those with vision and capacity to create. Let's keep our eyes open and hearts tender to these newly manifesting opportunities and the corresponding people who can lead and do the work.

PRAYER

Lord Jesus, in your literal coming to earth, the will of the Godhead was made evident and became what we could see and our hands could touch. Your life comes to us, and we in turn distribute and share with others. As I look around the world, I am grateful for leaders such as Chuck Colson who birthed the idea and Ron Nikkel who multiplied it for witness of the gospel and the benefit of those you came to save. Father, I know that your Spirit is active, giving vision to those whose hearts are tuned to you, and raising up those who can move it from an idea to reality. Help us, the church, to be an encouragement to those ideas and people. I praise you for the multifold ministries that bring your truth and forgiving love to those whose hearts are made open to receive. In your name that is above all others. Amen.

52

MEXICAN PRISONS

Not What I Expected on the Inside

In today's devotional, while we focus on Mexico, we look specifically at a world we most often forget: prisons and their inmates. Worldwide, there are 25 million people in various kinds of prisons, some rough and crowded and some modestly comfortable.

Once inside a prison, in most of the majority world, you feel the constraint of too many people in too small a space. It doesn't take long to see that the system has one driving interest: to exact a penalty, thus a penal institution. Dignity is stripped away and identity is replaced with a number. Hope is a rare commodity. Drugs cloud feelings, a coping mechanism to just get through the day. If one thinks ahead to the day of release, it seems so far away that surviving the day at hand becomes paramount. A little help from friends is always welcome.

In such places of desperation, the Spirit is alive and well. The most surprising flowers bloom out of cracked walls; fresh water bubbles up from broken cisterns. Caught in timeless constraint, judicial slowness, inability to pay legal costs, internally ruled by drug cartels, the men and women stay alive, and not surprisingly many are converted and determined to live faithfully for Christ.

> We need to think and pray for prisoners so that more of us will find Jesus' injunction compelling: *"For I was hungry and you gave me something to eat, I was thirsty and you gave me something to drink, I was a stranger and you invited me in, I needed clothes and you clothed me, I was sick and you looked after me, I was in prison and you came to visit me"* (Matthew 25:35–36).

Location: To the north is the United States, to the south and west the Pacific Ocean. To the southeast are Guatemala, Belize, and the Caribbean Sea, and to the east is the Gulf of Mexico.

Population: 113 million

Religion: Christian 98% (Roman Catholic 88%, Evangelical/Protestants 10%)

Dispatch
RECLUSORIO SUR PRISON, MEXICO CITY

It was one of those days I remember with acuity. I wanted to see life through the eyes of prisoners and observe this ministry, which began following the imprisonment of Richard Nixon's hatchet man, Charles Colson.

Reclusorio Sur Prison holds ten thousand men, where the minimum sentence is fifteen years. Sections of it are run by drug cartels, the underworld power of Mexico, linked into drug producing countries to the south. Sleeping space here is often just where you can find it—bathrooms and hall floors. We walked among the men without fear, many of them wanting a smile or a handshake.

As we made our way through a maze of outdoor corridors, we heard music and singing in a chapel built by Prison Fellowship International (PFI). The clean white building was constructed by inmates and paid for by PFI. Before we went in, I saw several men trying to persuade the guards to let them into the service, but only those who attended weekly Bible training were allowed in, and this morning for good reason, as I was soon to learn.

We were seated with the 120 inmates garbed in tan, their official color. At the front were twenty-five women in red PFI golf shirts, singing, playing instruments, and leading the men in worship.

I admitted to some skepticism: *Attractive women ministering to male inmates? Hardly the equation for unfettered spirituality,*

I thought. The singing progressed, and then two women, like a tag team, led in teaching the Lord's Prayer. They were dynamic, and the men sat at attention, listening for almost fifty minutes.

Next was a liturgical mass with the singers continuing to lead in highly spirited songs. While the music played, some left their seats for the side, where a priest was taking confessions. They would kneel, many sobbing.

After mass, the men stood and turned to face the back of the chapel. There, twenty-six volunteers passed out lunch—buns with a spicy beef and beverages, followed by a wonderfully rich chocolate cake.

But I wasn't ready for what happened next. The volunteers began passing out bags. As each took his bag, his hand was stamped to show he had received his. It was all carefully orchestrated, and I could see them following a learned pattern. When they had received their bags, they would move to another section of the chapel. What I didn't understand was their sense of excitement. When I moved to see what they had been given and the reason for such exuberant joy, I saw that each bag held two rolls of toilet paper and some toiletries. They were like excited teenagers at Christmas, and I still couldn't figure out their enormous joy.

I soon learned. In prison, the inmates have to buy their own toilet paper. Some have no family, no money, and no one to visit them and provide either such amenities or cash. This was better than Christmas.

I saw volunteers ministering to the men—careful, wise, and discreet. Grateful I had stuffed some tissue in my pocket that morning, I watched this ministry of love and healing—as moving and real a ministry as I've ever seen anywhere. My emotions were on a roller coaster as I saw kingdom life lived out in such pure and unadulterated ways.

Going to those forgotten and deemed unworthy in the name, love, and authority of Jesus gave these men what nothing else could. I left the prison that day with a new heart of understanding.

Today's Reading

When the Son of Man comes in his glory, and all the angels with him, he will sit on his glorious throne. All the nations will be

271

gathered before him, and he will separate the people one from another as a shepherd separates the sheep from the goats. He will put the sheep on his right and the goats on his left.

Then the King will say to those on his right, "Come, you who are blessed by my Father; take your inheritance, the kingdom prepared for you since the creation of the world. For I was hungry and you gave me something to eat, I was thirsty and you gave me something to drink, I was a stranger and you invited me in, I needed clothes and you clothed me, I was sick and you looked after me, I was in prison and you came to visit me."

Then the righteous will answer him, "Lord, when did we see you hungry and feed you, or thirsty and give you something to drink? When did we see you a stranger and invite you in, or needing clothes and clothe you? When did we see you sick or in prison and go to visit you?"

The King will reply, "Truly I tell you, whatever you did for one of the least of these brothers and sisters of mine, you did for me."

Matthew 25:31–40

ITEMS FOR PRAYER

- Ministries such as PFI are crucial in recruiting and training volunteers to become friends of those in prison. Pray for PFI and other such ministries, and for their leaders as they find selfless ways of bringing Jesus into prisons.

- Critical to entry are prison officials. Pray that in places where there is resistance for Christians to enter and minister, the growing credibility and effectiveness of such ministry will open doors for Christ's love.

- Find prisoners you can pray for by name. Learn about their needs. Ask PFI and others for specific people you can pray for. Pray as well for their global ministries, so in need of our support.

PRAYER

Jesus, you mentioned prisons as specific places for us to visit, for you knew that prisoners are some of the first we forget, stored away by society, out of sight, out of mind. And you

272

want us not to forget. Today set loose in my heart a recording that helps me not to forget those, many of whom are forgotten about over time, even by their families and friends. We lift to you Prison Fellowship and other ministries faithfully making their way through frisking guards into places most would rather avoid. Bring joy and blessing to those who visit, which they in turn transmit to those who need your love and joy. And please, Lord, help me not to forget. Amen.

ACKNOWLEDGMENTS

Mark and Janet Sweeney guided the writing of this book—prodding, encouraging, and advising. Carole Streeter helped with the organization, bringing clarity and precision to the chapters.

Friends, most often leaders of Evangelical Alliances in the countries I visited, introduced me to their countries, people, churches, and ministries.

Early on I asked a number of colleagues to sample chapters in their devotional life and let me know what was helpful, what was not, and what I should add. This was an enormous gift and helped me see how the book could become a source of encouragement in your life of prayer.

I found the book *Operation World* (InterVarsity Press) to be of enormous help, and suggest that you have it in your home library.

At Bethany House Publishers, Andy McGuire had the vision to make *An Insider's Guide to Praying for the World* a reality, and Jeff Braun and Nancy Renich edited the text with exquisite skill.

For all who had a part in the making of this book, I send my deepest thanks. Please know how appreciative I am.

PRAYER JOURNAL

A notepad is my faithful companion. I've long discarded the notion that what comes to mind I'll later recall. So noting ideas, thoughts, and concerns before I pray makes all the difference to my time of prayer.

The following pages are provided as a starting place for your prayer notes. Jot down your thoughts as you read each chapter and later as you reflect on the situations our brothers and sisters face around the world.

Country/Ministry: _____

Items of Interest

_____

_____

_____

Prayer Notes

_____

_____

_____

_____

Country/Ministry: _____

Items of Interest

_____

_____

_____

Prayer Notes

_____

_____

_____

_____

Country/Ministry: _____

Items of Interest

_____

_____

_____

Prayer Notes

_____

_____

_____

_____

Country/Ministry: _____

Items of Interest

_____

_____

_____

Prayer Notes

_____

_____

_____

_____

Country/Ministry: _____

Items of Interest

_____

_____

_____

Prayer Notes

_____

_____

_____

_____

Country/Ministry: _____

Items of Interest

_____

_____

_____

Prayer Notes

_____

_____

_____

_____

Country/Ministry: _____

Items of Interest

_____

_____

_____

Prayer Notes

_____

_____

_____

_____

Country/Ministry: _____

Items of Interest

_____

_____

_____

Prayer Notes

_____

_____

_____

_____

Country/Ministry: _____

Items of Interest

_____

_____

_____

Prayer Notes

_____

_____

_____

_____

Country/Ministry: _____

Items of Interest

_____

_____

_____

Prayer Notes

_____

_____

_____

_____

Country/Ministry: _____

Items of Interest

_____

_____

_____

Prayer Notes

_____

_____

_____

_____

Country/Ministry: _____

Items of Interest

_____

_____

_____

Prayer Notes

_____

_____

_____

_____

Country/Ministry: _____

Items of Interest

_____

_____

_____

Prayer Notes

_____

_____

_____

_____

Country/Ministry: _____

Items of Interest

_____

_____

_____

Prayer Notes

_____

_____

_____

_____

Country/Ministry: _____

Items of Interest

_____
_____
_____

Prayer Notes

_____
_____
_____
_____

Country/Ministry: _____

Items of Interest

_____
_____
_____

Prayer Notes

_____
_____
_____
_____

Country/Ministry: _____

Items of Interest

_____

_____

_____

Prayer Notes

_____

_____

_____

_____

Country/Ministry: _____

Items of Interest

_____

_____

_____

Prayer Notes

_____

_____

_____

_____

Brian C. Stiller is Global Ambassador of the World Evangelical Alliance, which serves 600 million evangelical Christians. He travels extensively, visiting churches, holding pastors' and leaders' conferences, assisting in peace negotiations, linking Evangelicals to the wider Christian community, and meeting with government officials. Brian lives with his wife in Newmarket, Ontario, Canada. Learn more at www.brianstiller.com.